Geoff Nicholson is
Street Sleeper, The Kn
Our Holidays and *Hu*   ...is jour-
nalism has appeared in *Time Out*, the *Guardian*
and *Street Machine*.

BIG NOISES

Rock guitar in the 1990s

GEOFF NICHOLSON

** Q**
QUARTET BOOKS

First published by Quartet Books Limited 1991
A member of the Namara Group
27/29 Goodge Street
London W1P 1FD

British Library Cataloguing in Publication Data

Nicholson, Geoff
  Big noises.
  I. Music. Guitar players, Popular
  I. Title
  781.63

ISBN 0 7043 01458

Phototypeset by Intype, London
Printed and bound in Great Britain by
Dotesios Ltd, Trowbridge, Wiltshire

For Steve Kenny,
connoisseur and creator of big noises

ACKNOWLEDGEMENTS

The following people have been kind enough to lend me records, recommend guitarists, discuss my half-baked ideas with me, not run away when I said, 'Hey listen to this . . .' and generally complete my education: Hugh Paton, Steve Kenny, Neil Whyte, Jake Fuller, Julian Kay, Gary Alexander, Richard Cook, Neil Reeve, Sue Jackson, Pip Cotterill, Joanna Moriarty, Jeremy Beale, Nick Sayers, Andrew Budd, Andrew Prescott, Mick Peace, Sandy Graham, Tom Pitt, Martin Shankleman, Simon Li and my mum.

Tessa Nicholson did photo research for this book and she would like to thank the following for the use of photographic stills: Lipsey Meade, EG Records, Epic, Polydor, MCA, Virgin, Arista, Island, RCA, Demon, Atlantic, Columbia, WEA, Food for Thought, Phonogram, the David Geffen Company, the *Guitarist* and the *Wire*.

Life's but a walking shadow, a poor player,
That struts and frets his hour upon the stage,
And then is heard no more . . .

CONTENTS

INTRODUCTION – A CASE-HISTORY

Establishing aerial shot, exterior, day. The camera pans across a city skyline, tall glass buildings, sunshine, bright blue sky. No music. The camera picks out and zooms in on one particular window in one of the tallest buildings.

Cut to interior, a psychiatrist's office – oak panelling, leather couch, antique desk, the works. THE DOCTOR, played by Dennis Hopper, cast interestingly against type, wears pinstripes, half-moon glasses, a grey goatee – the very stuff of cliché and stereotype. On the couch lies THE PATIENT. He is also, amazingly, the author of this book.

The doctor says: 'And so, Mr Nicholson, what will you be talking about today?'

The patient looks vacant. 'My childhood?' he suggests. 'My sex life? I dunno.'

The doctor, who has been here before, presses him, 'But what do you *really* want to talk about?'

The patient shrugs, is a little ashamed. 'Well, you know me, doc. I want to talk guitars, guitarists, guitar music.'

'Ah yes,' says the psychiatrist knowingly.

'But if you really insist,' the patient continues, 'we don't have to talk guitars. We can talk about my relationship with my mother, if you'd prefer.'

'Well yes,' says the doctor, 'that might be a fruitful area.'

'Right,' says Nicholson, and a kind of manic gleam comes into his eyes. 'There's this classic Frank Zappa song called "My Guitar Wants to Kill Your Momma". Now there's a title that sums up the special appeal of and the fantasies surrounding the electric guitar. Guitars are dangerous instruments, although they can be sharp or blunt. They're weapons. They're wielded by axemen. Killer solos get played on them. It's hard to imagine a song called "My Trumpet Wants to Kill Your Momma", much less "my keyboard" or "my alto sax".'

'It's kind of interesting too, that when Frank Zappa's son Dweezil made his debut album he called it *My Guitar Wants To Kill Your Momma*. No generation gap between Frank and Dweezil, eh doc?'

The doctor writes the word 'Oedipal' on his notepad.

Nicholson continues, 'Guitars are boys' toys. OK, so some girls appreciate a tasty solo, and some even play, like Brix Smith, Lita Ford, The Great Kat (and there's a girl you might want to make an appointment with, doc), but you know that girls are only playing. Boys want to do it for real. Girls just want to have fun, but boys want their guitars to make your ears bleed, give the neighbours a heart attack, bring down Western Civilization, and show everybody what a big willy they've got.'

'Even,' the doctor adds brightly, 'if it's only a *surrogate* willy.'

'Hey, I can see you're getting into this! You see the electric guitar is basically a power tool. It induces feelings of power, not to say megalomania. You hook your guitar up to a bank of amps, turn everything up to eleven, and you know that by moving your plectrum a couple of millimetres you can cause permanent hearing loss in someone standing two hundred yards away.

'You see, the electric guitar has no connotations of high art. It has no place in the concert hall. Mozart and Brahms didn't write for it. That means that people like me don't get overawed the way they might with a cello or a harpsichord. Sure, some guitarists have a classical training, but it's not necessary and half the time it seems to be a positive disadvantage.

'The electric guitar is subversive; even in the way it looks. OK, so some guitars are all polished wood and gold knobs and look like a piece of furniture or something, but they're not real rock and roll guitars. Real guitars are flashy and shiny and streamlined. They have a plastic look to them. They come in primary colours. They have more in common with a fifties Buick than with a Stradivarius.

'And like cars, guitars are both phallic and feminine. Yes, they're big and long and you can wave them around between your legs, but they're also curvaceous and prone to being given girls' names like Lucille. That sound kind of significant, huh doc?'

'Well, yes,' says the doctor ruminatively, 'but it seems to me it would be very good for your mental health if you could sort out whether the guitar is your girlfriend or your penis.'

'I can see that. But, you know, it's the *sound* that's really subversive. The electric guitar can make rude, ugly, disturbing, anti-social noises, like nothing else on earth. But the thing is, they're *human* noises. For all the boxes and pedals and processors you can attach to them, guitars somehow manage to sound organic, alive, real. OK, you can mess around with a Synthaxe or something and make some utterly fake, synthesized noise if you insist, but you have to try really hard to knock the humanity out of an electric guitar.

'And OK, some of those jazz dudes have spent a lot of time trying to get their guitars to sound restrained and tasteful. But let's face it, they don't count. Who wants to be restrained and tasteful? John Coltrane didn't. Miles Davis doesn't. So why do these jazz-guitar wimps want to take all the balls out of their instrument?'

'Beats me,' says the doctor.

'The kind of music guitarists make is qualitatively different from the kind of music, say, pianists make. "Candle In The Wind" isn't a song that a guitarist would have written, and a pianist would never have come up with the riff to "Sunshine Of Your Love". Riffs sound silly on a piano. A piano player wouldn't have invented thrash metal. The physical playing characteristics of the electric guitar determine the kind of music guitarists make. They make "Louie Louie", "You Really Got Me", "Jumpin' Jack Flash", "Roll Over Beethoven". I could go on.'

'It's your time,' says the doctor. 'You're the one paying for this session.'

'I can appreciate a good bit of smokey saxophone, or some nice piano chords, or even a drum solo, but nothing hits the spot like a great piece of guitar playing does. But what *is* a great piece of guitar playing?

'Ask a fool, "What is red?" and he'll say, "A colour." So you ask him, "What's a colour?" and he'll say, "A sensation of light induced on the eye by electromagnetic waves of a certain frequency." Then you ask him what's an electromagnetic wave, and so it goes on.

'But ask a wise man, "What is red?" and he'll answer, "A strawberry is red."

'Now, Matthew Arnold has a lot to say about this.'

'Matthew Arnold the guitar player?'

'No, Matthew Arnold the literary critic. He believed in "touchstones". So if anyone asked him what great literature was he wouldn't start theorizing or defining it, he'd simply say, "*Hamlet* is great literature." Likewise if you asked him, "What is a great writer?" he'd say, "Shakespeare is a great writer."

'Then he'd have said that if you're watching a play and you detect something Shakespearean about it, if it has some of the same qualities as *Hamlet*, the chances are that it might be a great piece of literature.

'This works just fine with guitar players too. Ask me, "What's great guitar playing?" and I reply, " 'Voodoo Chile (Slight Return)' is great guitar playing." Ask me, "What's a great guitar player?" and I'll say, "Hendrix is a great guitar player." If you're listening to a piece of guitar music and you detect something Hendrix-like about it, if it has some of the same qualities as "Voodoo Chile (Slight Return)" the chances are that it might be a great piece of guitar playing.

'First however, we need to realize what it is that's so great about Hendrix in the first place. Is it his abilities as an innovator with a wonderful technique and the capacity to electrify an audience? Or is it the fact that he used a lot of fuzz and played the guitar with his teeth? (Robin Trower and Steve Lukather are still working that one out.)

'These days Jeff Healey is talked about as playing "like Hendrix" but that seems crazy to me. Healey is an arch conservative. Hendrix was a radical. Lee Ranaldo and Thurston Moore of Sonic Youth seem to capture the adventurousness, the edginess, that sense of risk, that there is in the best of Hendrix, though they don't "sound like" him. I think Hendrix would have found Jeff Healey a bit of a bore. I think he'd have wanted to jam with Sonic Youth.

'But there is one sure way of spotting great guitar playing, and that's by the physical effect it has on you. If you're sitting comfortably in your chair one minute and you put on a guitar record and the next minute you're on your feet, experiencing chills and fever, there's a lump in your throat, tears in your eyes and you have an irresistible urge to play air guitar, then this too is an indication that something pretty good's going on in the guitar department.

'You see, the thing is, you don't need to be a genius to play great guitar music. Even the humblest guitar player will, once in a while, produce a terrific guitar solo or rhythm part. Has any guitarist ever come up with a better guitar riff than non-guitarist David Bowie's "Rebel Rebel"?

'There are some great guitar bands that don't contain a great guitarist, like the Velvet Underground. There are bands that contain a great guitarist without being a guitar band, like Pink Floyd. One of the joys of rock music is that it's quite possible to walk into a pub or bar where there's some band you've never heard of, where there's an indifferent audience, a lousy PA, and there'll be some little guy standing at the back of the stage who's performing absolute miracles on guitar.

'There are at least as many guitar players in the world as there are bands. Very few are great guitarists but every now and again one of them does something great. The truly great guitarists are the ones who do it more than every now and again.

'However, the very best guitar players are never *only* guitar players. A lot of them sing, they all compose, and what they do above all, even if in collaboration with others, is create an overall sound, an artistic vision, an aesthetic.

'Guitar playing isn't a sport. There are no championships, no league tables or knock-out competitions. Hendrix isn't regarded as the all-time great because he beat all-comers in some sort of guitar Olympics. He was, and remains, the best because he created a body of work that was coherent, articulate and whole. But there's a tendency to see him as some sort of cloud of free-floating genius. With the Experience he sounded like a genius, but listen to him playing with Curtis Knight or

Lonnie Youngblood and tell me how much of a genius he sounds. Equally, listen to Andy Summers. He sounded like a really hot guitarist when he was with the Police, but as a solo performer he sounds distinctly small potatoes.

'What this comes down to is the fact that guitar playing needs a context. You can't just crank up the volume and say, right, this is my solo and ten minutes later get back to the song. Or at least you can, but like Alvin Lee at Woodstock with "Goin' Home" you're going to look pretty silly. You still awake, doc?'

The doctor's mind has been wandering. He has been thinking about anal retentiveness, denial, repression, the super-ego, group therapy, lunch.

'I know what you're going to say,' says Nicholson solemnly. 'You're going to say, what's the role of technique in all this?'

The doctor nods sagely.

'Technique is a minefield, doc. In one sense, technique is quantifiable. Someone who knows and can play all the chords, all the licks, all the scales, has more technique than someone who doesn't and can't.

'It's probably a truism to say that guitarists today are doing things their predecessors would never have dreamed of. There are whole armies of superfast, supercompetent, guitarists out there who make guitar playing of, say, the 1970s sound as antique as the tango.

'But there's an argument that says rock music is a naïve form and that advanced technique is irrelevant. Technique is merely having the ability to play what you want to play, having the means to express what you want to express. This argument would say that Neil Young, for instance, is a "better" guitarist than Yngwie Malmsteen. If technique is a means to an expressive end, then Young certainly appears to have all the technique he needs to accomplish what he wants. Malmsteen has dexterity, skill, virtuosity, by the truckload, is "technically" amazing, yet doesn't seem to know what to do with it.

'But you know, times do change. Vogues in guitar playing come and go. At first the wah wah pedal is a brilliant innovation, then everybody uses one so it becomes old hat. Then years later the Stone Roses use lots of wah wah on "Fools Gold" by which time it's become a post-modernist reference.

One year jazz-rock looks like the way forward, next year it's being spat on from a great height. Twin lead guitars begin by sounding fresh and different, then they end up sounding like some boring old Eagles album.

'Hey, I can remember when a rock guitarist who played barre chords and used the little finger of his left hand was considered technically breathtaking. Today there's a whole generation of guitarists who don't think they're really playing at all unless they're doing two-handed tapping up and down the fretboard at a million notes a minute.

'But these, you might argue, are just changes in fashion. The essence of guitar playing doesn't come from the hardware, not even from the flying fingers, but from somewhere considerably more private and mysterious.'

The doctor perks up. This seems to be his territory, dark corners of the psyche, the hidden well-spring of creativity. 'Ah ha, so now we're getting to the roots of the problem.'

'Roots?' says Nicholson. 'Oh yeah, this thing goes way, way back. Scholars differ as to who was the first ever electric guitarist. Some would like to think it was Charlie Christian, but he was "taught" electric guitar by Eddie Durham who played guitar and trombone for Count Basie. Both of them were jazzmen, of course. They needed amplification simply in order to be heard above the noise of a big jazz band.

'But although the first electric guitars provided volume they didn't provide sustain. They still couldn't hold a note, so jazz guitarists had to play a lot of notes to be heard. (Old habits die hard.) The first electric guitars were trying to sound like an acoustic only louder, but those of us who love the electric guitar love it precisely because it doesn't sound like an acoustic. We love the use of reverb and echo, whammy bar and feedback and . . . '

The patient has grown visibly excited. The doctor tries to calm him down.

'I'm sorry, doctor, it just gets me like that sometimes. Always has.'

'Always?'

'Well, maybe not always always. I mean, it might be nice to be able to say that I grew up at my mother's knee listening to Scotty Moore and Chet Atkins and Wes Montgomery, but hell

I had a deprived childhood. Like most people of my generation the first guitarist I was ever aware of was Bert Weedon. Bert was about as good as it got back there in the fifties. Bert was an OK guy. Everybody I've ever met owned a copy of *Play In A Day*, but somehow I always knew he wasn't the real thing.

'I gradually became aware of Duane Eddy and Hank Marvin. They were OK, but Eddy's twang was always a bit pedestrian, and Hank with the suits and the specs and the synchronized strutting on stage, well, it wasn't rock and roll, you know?

'There had already been rock and roll. There had been Carl Perkins and Buddy Holly and Eddie Cochran. There had been Chuck Berry and Bo Diddley. They were certainly all guitar players; but in those days *every* pop star had a guitar slung round his neck, didn't matter if it was Elvis or Billy Fury or Tommy Steele. It was a prop. It didn't matter whether they could play it or not.

'Of course, there were some guys around who really could play guitar. I could have been listening to B.B. or Albert or Freddie King, to Muddy Waters or Buddy Guy. But because I was ignorant, I wasn't. Fortunately some people in England *were* listening to those guys and, via the Stones, the Yardbirds, John Mayall, some of that raw blues excitement finally got channelled into the white English teenage imagination. It was a shock to the system. But that was all still to come.

'The Merseysound and its imitators were guitar based too. It didn't matter who they were; Gerry and the Pacemakers, the Hollies, the Searchers, they all made great guitar noises. However much the Beatles got swamped by George Martin's strings and things, they still had great and varied guitar sounds. I remember getting very excited indeed by the fuzzed guitar on the Spencer Davis Group's "Somebody Help Me".

'The late sixties was, of course, the prime time for the guitar hero. It was the time both of blues revival and of psychedelia. Even at the time some of us felt a bit uneasy about that. Yes, we could relate to Eric Clapton, this young white guy with the frizzed-out hair and the flower-power trousers, but why was he playing like some old black guy who wore a suit and a tie? Later we had to work that out for ourselves. Then there was Hendrix and, you know, that was sort of *it*.

'If Bert Weedon was my first glass of shandy Hendrix was

twenty-five-year-old malt whisky. Hank Marvin was a mild shock to the system, Hendrix was a whole lightning storm flashing across the night sky. But hey, you must have heard all this from some of your other patients.'

'Alas,' says the doctor, 'it is not an entirely unfamiliar syndrome.'

'And anyway, I talk about Hendrix at some length in my book. But you see, as well as the real giants like Hendrix and Clapton, Beck and Page, the era threw up a whole gang of minor English guitar heroes for whom I still have an enormous affection; people like John Cann, Stan Webb, Tony McPhee. I loved 'em all.

'And in America there was Zappa and Garcia and John Cipollina, none of whom I had quite the same affection for, but hey, it was a mighty time for guitar players.

'Then suddenly, very suddenly, it was all over. Hendrix was dead. Clapton was out of it. Page was living in Aleister Crowley's old pad, and suddenly admiring guitar heroes was a very unhip thing to do. We were all ready for something else, and what we got was punk.

'Punk claimed to be nihilistic and anti-musical but when I hear "Anarchy In The UK" or "God Save The Queen" I hear some very fine guitar playing. OK, it's not a ten-minute guitar solo, it's not virtuoso, but it's not incompetent either.

'The Sex Pistols weren't the only guitar-based punk band, there was the Clash, Stiff Little Fingers, the Damned. The guitarists in those bands knew what they were doing, and if you liked the sound of an overcranked electric guitar there were still plenty of guitar thrills to be had.

'Then there were all those bands who could see that being associated with punk, or at least new wave, wasn't going to do their careers any harm. The Police, AC/DC, Dire Straits, all contained potential guitar heroes. Jimmy Page is reported to have visited the Roxy, that bastion of punk, but, being a millionaire rock star, he took his minders with him. Given the way that most people felt about Led Zeppelin in 1977 this was probably quite wise.

'It has always seemed to me that punk and heavy metal had a lot more in common than either camp was prepared to admit, but in 1977, if you'd wanted to find a guitar hero you'd have had to look to heavy metal. Ritchie Blackmore still had Rainbow. Tony Iommi was still running a version of Black Sabbath. Ted Nugent was proclaiming that if it was too loud you were too old. Not that many were listening.

'Then in 1978 up steps Eddie Van Halen and a whole new era of rock guitar begins. By 1984 the band Van Halen had sold several million records and Eddie, with his amazing speed and technical virtuosity, was picking up awards for being the world's best guitarist on a regular basis, and still nobody in England was even aware of his existence. The English idea of a good guitarist was Johnny Marr, precisely because he didn't do the kind of things that guitar heroes did.

'But the eighties weren't bad years for guitar playing. Clapton seemed to get his fire back. Adrian Belew was around. Zappa released ten sides of extraordinary guitar solos. Neil Young developed a late, guitar-laden, style. New bands like REM, Green On Red, even the Stone Roses, weren't afraid to spank the plank. Heavy metal produced stars like Randy Rhoads, Marty Friedman and, of course, Steve Vai.

'And the future . . . well, I'm not dumb enough to make predictions, but hey, it would be really nice if England could produce one or two interesting guitarists. I don't demand genius, I certainly don't demand heroism, I'd be quite happy to settle for interesting.

'And I'd watch what's going on in Japan. At the moment they seem to be producing some weary heavy-metal clones like Loudness and Vow Wow. But, you know, there was a time when they couldn't make a decent car in Japan either.'

Nicholson looks out of the window. The sky is clouding over. Time is running out. His session is nearly over and he still has things to say. Maybe it's finally time to talk about his book.

'I don't know, doc,' he says, 'I don't know if it's a form of exorcism, a way out of this obsession, or whether it's just a chance to wallow in it. What do you think?'

The doctor shrugs expensively. 'You tell me.'

'Well, look, it contains thirty-six "appreciations", I think that's the right word, of thirty-seven guitarists. They've been selected on the basis of historical significance, technical expertise, artistic merit and blind prejudice. I wouldn't claim that they're the world's best thirty-seven guitarists, though they're definitely not the worst thirty-seven. Yes, the book's kind of personal, but it's not my thirty-seven favourite guitarists either.

'There are about ten guitarists who would have to be in any book of guitar players – Hendrix, Clapton, Page, Beck, Garcia, Cooder, Zappa, Keith Richards, Neil Young and B.B. King. They're the greats, the ones there's no point arguing about. I mean, you can debate whether or not Nils Lofgren is a great guitar player, but with B.B. King there's no argument. There comes a point where you don't judge the guitarists, but where you're judged by your response to them. If you think Eric Clapton is a ham-fisted loser, you're wrong, it's as simple as that.

'Beyond that group there are players without whom rock guitar wouldn't be the same. This doesn't make them geniuses, but it means you have to deal with them. This would include Van Halen, Blackmore, Chuck Berry, Malmsteen.

'Some get in because they're very good and have been very good for quite a long time, that's guys like Albert Collins, Gary Moore, Carlos Santana, John McLaughlin.

'Some are serious, interesting players who are too quirky ever to achieve mass popularity but who are, nevertheless, creating wonderful guitar music – players like Derek Bailey, Allan Holdsworth, Adrian Belew, Marc Ribot.

'There are those who get in on the grounds of being distinctive; they're contenders but nobody could pretend they're geniuses. Fripp, Knopfler, Angus Young, The Edge, Jeff Healey, Brian May.

'Then, despite my refusal to make any sort of prediction, there are those who look like the future of the electric guitar: Vai, Satriani, Frisell, Reid, Cray, Thurston Moore and Lee Ranaldo.

'Only two get in just because I like 'em, and that's Howe Gelb and Henry Kaiser, and after a beer or two I'd be happy to discuss their greatness with anyone who wants to argue about it.

'But hey, doc, you don't need me to tell you that categories are arbitrary, and I know that guitar fans love to argue about who's an innovator and who isn't, and who's a killer axeman and who's a stiff, so, yes, I'm ready for some good old healthy debate here, and for letters from people who think I don't know what I'm talking about.'

'But you're certain you *do* know what you're talking about?'

'Hey, it's not like I think I'm God or anything. I'm an enthusiast before I'm a critic. I'm a fan, not some kind of *expert*. When you write a book like this, you're bound to sound like some kind of arrogant s.o.b. who has all the answers, but I know I'm fallible. It's OK for people to disagree with me, and if they disagree with me strongly enough they can go and write their *own* book about guitar players. Hell, it's still a free country . . .

'But, you know, the biggest problem I had in all this was describing the sound of the electric guitar. Guitars sound like . . . well, guitars; but that doesn't help you much when it comes to distinguishing between Angus Young and John McLaughlin. People compare guitar sounds to buzz-saws and explosions and rockets and bombs, but I don't know that that helps very much.

'I found myself using words like stinging, screeching, seething, snarling, wailing, roaring, wild, dirty, manic, sick, abrasive, aggressive, violent, demented, to describe guitar sounds. I used words like, bite and edge and attack and noise and grunge. And you know what? These were all words of approval!'

'Now this is interesting,' says the doctor. 'And did you find yourself using words ike mellow or gentle or laid back?'

'Well occasionally, but really only as a kind of deadly insult.'

'I see,' says the doctor weightily.

'What do you see?'

'I see the root of your problem. You might as well face it, you're addicted to skronk.'

'Skronk?'*

'Yes,' the doctor continues, 'it means . . . '

'*I* know what it means, I'm just a little surprised that *you* do.'

---

* Lester Bangs writes: 'Christgau calls it "skronk". I have always opted for the more obvious "horrible noise".'

'Well, psychiatry is full of surprises.'

'Do you think, do you think there's any hope for me, doctor?'

'You know, Mr Nicholson, the concept of cure is very outmoded . . . '

The alarm chirps in the doctor's wristwatch and abruptly announces the end of the session. The patient gets groggily to his feet and begins straightening his clothes.

'So,' he says, 'the same time next week, I suppose.'

'Certainly. Make an appointment with my secretary on the way out. Oh, and another thing . . . '

'What is it doc?'

'Next time, do you think you could bring your Bill Frisell records with you?'

Freeze frame. The titles roll and savage music begins to play. It is a medley of those two Naked City favourites, 'Jazz Snob Eat Shit' and 'Perfume Of A Critic's Burning Flesh'.

THE END

Photograph courtesy of Jak Kilby

DEREK BAILEY

Born 1932, Sheffield

On the surface Derek Bailey might appear to be to rock music what Slash is to clean living and good table manners, i.e. not much. And it's true that Bailey has yet to make his MTV debut.

Bailey is part of, indeed a figurehead for, that movement that is variously known as free music or free jazz. Above all he is an improviser, arguably *the* improviser. John Scofield, B.B. King and Jerry Garcia would consider themselves to be improvisers too but what they do doesn't seem to have much in common with what Bailey does.

In the early part of his career he used to play with conventional jazz and dance bands, and had been a professional musician for ten years before he discovered his real calling, via Tony Oxley, the Spontaneous Music Ensemble and the London Jazz Composers Orchestra in the sixties.

Today he plays with large and small improvising groups, often under the banner of his own Company, with collaborators like Anthony Braxton, Han Bennink, Paul Rutherford, Evan Parker and Barry Guy. But he also plays solo guitar, and personally I've always enjoyed him best on his own.

Bailey is a complete original and sounds like nobody else, although one or two avant-gardists have been known to imitate some of his sounds. These sounds tend to be a series of clicks, twangs, pops, harmonics, volume-pedal swells, controlled, gentle feedback, scrapings and scurryings up and down the strings, plus noises made with parts of the guitar other than the strings. There is little recognizable in the way of conventional chord patterns or melodies, although he certainly doesn't appear to be without technique, and a lot of what he does is obviously difficult to play.

There used to be some kind of debate along the lines: Derek Bailey – genius or charlatan? These have mercifully ceased. At the very least a charlatan is someone who deceives the public, and the vast majority of the public remains blissfully unaware of Bailey's existence. The question remains: What exactly is Bailey up to?

He offers us one or two oblique clues. In a 1988 interview with Mark Dery, the interviewer says, 'You seem to use a lot of [Wes] Montgomery-like unisons and octave doublings. Also you seem to be coming from a Django-like sensibility, working from chord shapes.' To which Bailey replies, 'I'd say you're being very perceptive there.' Personally, I don't find this very helpful.

Bailey, it seems to me, is essentially an ascetic. He knows that it isn't so very difficult to make a pleasing sound on a guitar, whether it's a minor seventh strummed on an acoustic, or a power chord played on an electric. But these are simple pleasures. Bailey wants to deny himself any such easy options. He has decided to make life difficult both for himself and his listeners. His austerity is admirable if not always likeable.

In one obvious way Bailey is extending the range of sounds that a guitar can make; and such things as prepared guitar, unusual plectrum techniques, stereo manipulations, bending strings behind the bridge, have all been useful to him at various times, even if he abandoned some of them later. They are not sounds that most guitarists make, but most guitarists don't want to. One could imagine a guitarist who would use all these techniques in addition to all the more orthodox ones, but Bailey uses them *instead*. He starts where others leave off and he stays there. However, he doesn't seem to be interested in extending the expressive possibilities of the guitar and his innovations remain formal, not emotional.

There are some problems in understanding exactly what improvisation means in this context. Clearly Bailey's music is not rehearsed note for note, and I'm sure he never plays exactly the same thing twice. There are elements of risk and adventure in his playing; on the other hand, it's hardly unpredictable.

You know he's *not* going to strum a minor seventh or an electric power chord. Bailey always sounds like Bailey and he never 'improvises' himself into a rendition of 'Light My Fire'.

In live performance he uses more attack, more sheer volume than you might expect from listening to his records. The downside of his live performances is that in the spirit of freedom he'll play with just about anyone. In my experience this seems to mean there's always some damned woman on stage with him who thinks she can scat sing.

The biggest attraction of seeing live, improvised music is that you know you're seeing and hearing a one-off event. The music is created out of nothing and is then gone forever. Tomorrow's audience won't be hearing what you've just heard. The role of records in this can be a problem. The record is inevitably reduced to the status of souvenir. Nevertheless, souvenirs are often worth having.

With the Spontaneous Music Ensemble, Bailey seldom did much up-front soloing, but sections of 'Oliv I' from the album *Spontaneous Music Ensemble* show him playing with great restraint and sensitivity to the other musicians.

'83, An Update On 38' from the solo album *Notes* shows that even if Bailey rejects many of the expected satisfactions of music, he still retains a clear notion of development and shape.

The album *In Whose Tradition?* makes a fair introduction to Bailey's music. One side contains solo improvisations recorded at home, in public or in studios in the early seventies. Side two contains 'domestic pieces', including the remarkable 'The Last Post' in which he takes the listener on a sound tour of his kitchen, describing his new flat, talking about politics and the weather, and all the time playing a guitar solo. It also contains the voices of Margaret Thatcher and Edward Heath that are on the radio at the time. It's as radical a piece as anyone could want and it's actually very funny.

So, no, Bailey isn't any sort of a rock guitarist but he's influenced guitarists as diverse as Henry Kaiser, Marc Ribot, Bill Frisell, even Johnny Marr, although the influence may be at the level of integrity and commitment as much as at the level of the way their guitar playing actually sounds. But he sits rather uneasily in the jazz world too. If anything, he may come to be seen as the creator of some sort of modern, avant-

garde classical music; and that's not going to get him on MTV
either.

DEREK BAILEY: SELECTED DISCOGRAPHY

Solo: *Improvisation* (1975)
   New Sights Old Sounds (1978)
   Aida (1980)
   Notes (1985)
   In Whose Tradition? (1988)
With Spontaneous Music Ensemble: *Spontaneous Music Ensem-
   ble* (1969)
   85 Minutes Part One (1987)
   85 Minutes Part Two (1987)
With Anthony Braxton: *Royal Volume 1* (1974)
   Duo (1974)
   Moment Precieux (1986)
With Dave Holland: *Improvisations For Guitar And Cello* (1971)
With Tony Coe: *Time* (1979)
With John Zorn and George Lewis: *Yankees* (1982)
With Christine Jeffrey: *A View From Six Windows* (1982)
With Evan Parker: *Compatibles* (1986)

Photograph courtesy of Epic Records

JEFF BECK

Born 24 June, 1944, Surrey

Here's a dirty trick you can play on a Jeff Beck fan: ask him to tell you the name of a good Jeff Beck album. There's endless amusement to be had watching him squirm and mutter about 'brilliant moments' and 'flawed masterpieces'. The fact is, even the best Jeff Beck albums are as much padding as substance. Everybody agrees he's a great guitarist, but isn't a great guitarist one who creates great music?

Ask a common or garden rock fan to name some music that Jeff Beck's associated with and he'll come up with 'Hi Ho Silver Lining' and maybe 'Shapes Of Things' and when you really press him he might remember 'Love Is Blue', though that's something Beck would probably rather forget. It's not a lot for a career that's been going for about twenty-five years.

My *Illustrated NME Encyclopedia of Rock*, the 1977 edition, tells me that 'Beck established himself as one of the UK's all-time great hero axemen during a two-year stint with the Yardbirds from whom he split in 1966'. I can't help asking what Beck's been doing since 1966 to sustain his 'all-time great' status.

The Yardbirds was, of course, a hotbed of English guitarists; and compared with the market standards of the time, compared with Bert Weedon or Hank Marvin, Beck looked truly remarkable. Guitarists always rate 'Jeff's Boogie' from the album *Over Under Sideways Down* as a fantastic piece of guitar playing. They'll tell you how it was ahead of its time. They'll talk about all the unique licks and tricks it contains. What they won't talk about is feeling. Has Jeff Beck's guitar playing ever really moved anybody? Answers on a postcard please.

Beck is flashy, he is inventive and he can certainly be very exciting. He makes some thrilling noises. But his bands have never had a distinctive sound and he has never had what amounts to an artistic vision. Guitarists who are far less accomplished in their playing than Beck often sound more effective, and certainly sound more recognizable. Beck's playing has somehow never found its context.

Take, for example, *Cosa Nostra Beck-Ola*, his 1969 album. There are long r & b versions of 'All Shook Up' and 'Jailhouse Rock', a piano instrumental by Nicky Hopkins, and on the second side we're treated to two extended jams, 'The Hangman's Knee' and the truly awful 'Rice Pudding'. On this latter you can almost hear the musicians saying to each other, 'if we can only keep playing this crud for another five minutes we'll have filled the side.' Even in 1969 this was no way to make a decent record. Sure there's some nice guitar playing here and there but so there should be. What is really lacking is any sort of guiding intelligence or sensibility.

Two years later on *Rough And Ready*, an album that is certainly rough though you could argue about its readiness, the most interesting track is 'Max's Tune', a gentle eight-minute piano and guitar piece, played with Max Middleton. But again you feel that it's eight minutes long because they needed an eight-minute track to fill out the side, not because they needed all that time to explore the musical ideas in the piece.

With the exception of Rod Stewart, Beck was never able to find a good vocalist to work with. Neither was he very lucky in his choice of collaborators, though that is probably an area where musicians make their own luck. Nor was Beck ever much of a writer of music. Moving into jazz/rock did away with the need for a vocalist, but he still needed material and he still needed other people to play with.

So in 1976 he was to be found playing with Jan Hammer and Narada Michael Walden on the album *Wired*. The sound is pretty much that of the Mahavishnu Orchestra but minus McLaughlin, Goodman or Ponty (i.e. like *Hamlet* without the prince). Most of the music is written by Walden and anybody who has suffered through the Mahavishnu album *Inner Worlds* will be all too aware of Walden's creative gifts. (It's when he starts giving thanks to God for the fish in the sea that I really want to reach for my revolver.) Beck's at his best on Hammer's 'Blue Wind', where he does some Mahavishnu-style duelling with Hammer, and on Mingus's 'Goodbye Pork Pie Hat', where he plays with great looseness and inventiveness. The music has a welcome air of sophistication that earlier Beck albums never had.

In 1984 we find Beck in the Honeydrippers along with Page and Plant doing cover versions of the songs of their youth. The record (you couldn't really call it an album, it only has five songs) is as much a send up as it is an affectionate tribute. Somehow the music has quotation marks around it, and even though 'Sea Of Love' was a hit single, I don't think many people bought it for the quality of the guitar playing. And even given that the record is extremely short, 'Rockin' at Midnight', despite some neat guitar bursts, has filler written all over it.

Guitar Shop (1989) is generally reckoned to be Beck's best album for years. There are some horrors like 'Two Rivers', all gooey synths and a moody, trebly guitar solo that sounds like Focus on a bad day, but there's some fine guitar playing.

The title track is a raucous, muscular guitar workout, driven by a drum noise, from Terry Bozzio, that sounds as though it's about to smash its way out of your speakers. 'Big Block' is simple, brash, bluesy and gives Beck the chance to let rip. 'Stand On It' is very straight-ahead rock, and Beck dazzles with the range of exciting guitar tones he can produce. But exciting guitar tones do not a great album make. Sure it's better than having a lot of rotten guitar sounds, but they need to be harnessed and directed to some purpose. On *Guitar Shop* they seem to be an end in themselves.

Beck has sold a lot of records over the years. He isn't wondering where his next meal is coming from. In fact, knowing what we do about Beck, the chances are he's probably far more interested in where his next '32 Ford is coming from. And maybe that's the problem. Maybe Beck just isn't hungry enough.

OK, so the B.B. Kings and the Eric Claptons of this world aren't exactly starving to death either, and yet in their different ways both those guys seem hungry to play. They're eager to get out there, to perform, to invent, to deliver to an audience. I just don't sense that eagerness in Jeff Beck.

By any ordinary standards Beck is a fabulous guitarist. In fact, he's so good that you start to judge him by higher than ordinary standards, and that's when he doesn't quite make it. I suppose this is simply to say that he isn't quite a genius, that he isn't a Hendrix, but then, let's face it, who is?

JEFF BECK: SELECTED DISCOGRAPHY

Solo: *Truth* (1968)
  Beck-Ola (1969)
  Rough And Ready (1971)
  Beck Bogert Appice (1973)
  Wired (1976)
  There And Back (1976)
  Flash (1985)
  Guitar Shop (1989)
With the Honeydrippers: *The Honeydrippers Volume One* (1984)
With the Jan Hammer Group: *Live* (1977)

Photograph by Denis O'Regan
Courtesy of Idols

ADRIAN BELEW

Born 1949, Covington, Kentucky

'Big Electric Cat', the first song on the first side of Belew's first solo album, is awash with an amazing number of his trademark noises. These include very long sustain and over-the-top tremelo, loads of squeal and seething fuzz and guitar that sounds as though it's being played backwards. Sometimes it actually *is* being played backwards, i.e. played normally then recorded and reversed, but at other times he gets the same sort of noise playing 'forwards'.

Belew has the desire to make his guitar sound like anything but a guitar. Sometimes he wants it to sound like keyboards, or a sax or bagpipes, but more often he wants it to sound like chimes or a train whistle or a rhino or a whale or an elephant (on Laurie Anderson's 'Talk Normal').

His sound is fluid, elastic, bendy, yet at the same time strident and astringent. He seems to have no desire to impress with speed, preferring the odd squall of feedback or sheet of wavering sound, although he's a strong rhythmic player too. He embraces technology, going for guitar synths and for incredibly elaborate banks of state-of-the-art effects on stage.

But all this makes him sound as though he might fit into a New York garage noise band, and that would be wrong, because Adrian Belew is a sophisticate. If you're looking for someone with a hip c.v. Belew is your man. He's played with Laurie Anderson, Talking Heads and Frank Zappa, and with Bowie and King Crimson. And although the hipness of the last two comes and goes over the years, Belew had the knack of playing with them when they were at their hippest.

Although his work might be loosely described as avant-garde he remains essentially mainstream, which is perhaps to say that he is the mainstream's idea of avant-garde and the avant-garde's idea of mainstream.

This means that on his own albums he's very concerned with songs, proper songs with words and choruses, not just excuses for guitar workouts. It also means that when, for example, Bowie wants someone to add wild guitar noise to an album he thinks of Belew before he thinks of Fred Frith or Davey Williams.

What Belew shares with Anderson, Zappa and David Byrne is a quirky sense of humour and a taste for irony. Now, you don't need me to tell you that humour and irony are the two things rock performers don't need for success, in fact it's a major disadvantage to have them. But if you have them you're stuck with them. So there's Belew doing silly dances and Bob Dylan impersonations live with Zappa; there he is wearing a bag over his face and sombrero on his head for the movie *Home Of The Brave*. And he can write a song like 'Oh Daddy' in which he confronts the fact that he hasn't lived up to his seven-year-old daughter's idea of what a guitar hero ought to be.

But, of course, Belew isn't a guitar hero, and you assume he doesn't want to be (although 'internal evidence' in 'Oh Daddy' suggests that he could probably live with it). Rather, he is a consummate sideman. When he's screaming away on Talking Heads' 'The Great Curve' he sounds like a real star. Unfortunately when he stands centre stage he looks like a sideman.

This is probably seen at its worst on *Desire Caught By The Tail*, described on the cover as 'instrumental music for guitar and percussion composed and performed by Adrian Belew'. I had great hopes for this album. It sounded like a perfect opportunity for him to shut up and play his guitar, and sure enough there's no shortage of guitar on the album, but there's a distinct lack of focus. This time he favours a guitar sound like Middle Eastern pipes. The result sounds like music for a performance by an alternative mime troupe, and when did you last enjoy a performance by an alternative mime troupe? It's genuinely experimental. Belew is trying to do new things with the sound of his guitar, but in the end it's doodling, an experiment that's failed.

On *Mr Music Head*, by contrast, he seems reluctant to take a solo. Mostly he plays for texture and fills, and the occasional opening burst like on 'Bird in a Box'. It's good stuff but I could do with more of it. And when he does take a solo of sorts, like on 'Motor Bungalow', it lasts twenty seconds when it might be even better if it lasted a minute. OK, so I'm biased, I'm a fan of guitar noise, so I *would* say that, but I think most people who enjoy Adrian Belew are fans of guitar noise too.

I have written in the Robert Fripp section about the joys of King Crimson with Adrian Belew. Although King Crimson remains very much Fripp's band, they wouldn't have sounded that way without Belew. On 'Frame By Frame', for example, the music starts with one of those familiar fast, complex, relentless Fripp guitar lines, but it is completely transformed as Belew plays lovely, rubbery chords on top which lurch in and out of tune as he (I guess) tugs the twang bar. With Belew you can never be sure. Sometimes he just wiggles the guitar neck so that it moves in relation to the body and produces tremelo that way.

There's evidence that maybe Belew recognizes he's happiest as part of a band. With the Bears he is much more than a sideman yet he doesn't have to carry the whole weight of the band. The Bears are a guitar outfit featuring melodic songs and harmony vocals, with strong whiffs of the Beatles and the Byrds, yet when the time comes for Belew to turn out a solo, as on 'Not Worlds Apart' (a song that sounds every inch a hit single to me), not only is the solo wholly him, it also really fits the song and it is that interestingly little bit different from the 'typical' Belew solo. Of course, that doesn't mean it couldn't be longer.

My favourite Belew album, perhaps the archetypal Belew album, remains *Twang Bar King*. You can imagine certain guitarists (Ritchie Blackmore?) taking a title like that seriously. Belew obviously sees the absurdity of being a twang bar king and writes a consciously frivolous song with that title, which he then embellishes with seriously brilliant twang bar abuse. This album as a whole has excitement, experimentation, intelligence, technique and wit. Some of us are prepared to settle for that.

ADRIAN BELEW: SELECTED DISCOGRAPHY

Solo: *Lone Rhino* (1982)
  Twang Bar King (1983)
  Mr Music Head (1989)
  Desire Caught By The Tail (1986)
  Young Lions (1990)
With Talking Heads: *Remain In Light* (1980)
  The Name of This Band Is Talking Heads (1982)
With Laurie Anderson: *Mr Heartbreak* (1983)
  Home of the Brave (1986)
With King Crimson: *Discipline* (1981)
  Beat (1982)
  Three Of A Perfect Pair (1983)
With David Bowie: *Stage* (1978)
With the Bears: *Rise and Shine* (1988)
With Frank Zappa: *Sheik Yerbouti* (1979)

Photograph by Bob Gruen
Courtesy of Star File/Pictorial Press

CHUCK BERRY

Born 18 October 1926, San José, California

I had some doubts about whether Chuck Berry should be included in this book. The first doubt was caused by the fact that he is so much more than just a guitarist and to talk about him simply in those terms might be to miss what he's really about. The second doubt was that, influential though Berry undoubtedly is, I wasn't sure he could still be said to 'cut it' in today's world.

The first doubt was overcome by telling myself that although Berry's singing and songwriting are as important to his success as his guitar playing, he *is* a guitar player and his guitar is essential to his sound, his performing and his songwriting. If Berry had been a pianist he'd never have written 'Johnny B. Goode'. That is a guitarist's song, not only in its subject matter, but in the way it's constructed and the way it sounds.

The other doubt, about Berry somehow no longer being relevant, lingered for a while. And then one day I was listening to a record by Pat Metheny and wondering did I really want to write about him for this book and suddenly as I listened, gentle boredom giving way to bad-tempered irritation, I was struck by a blinding revelation: *I would rather listen to Chuck Berry than to Pat Metheny.*

How come? Because Chuck Berry speaks to me more in a four-bar introduction than Pat Metheny does in forty minutes of improvisation. Put them on stage together (the mind boggles at the prospect of the Berry-Metheny Band but let's go with it) and of course Berry's guitar playing is going to look positively

Neanderthal by comparison with Metheny's, but I don't have the slightest doubt that Berry would be more fun, more entertaining, more simply able to *do the business*. (Nothing personal you understand, Pat.) So I decided, yes, Chuck Berry can still cut it.

There would still have been rock and roll even if there had never been Chuck Berry, but you have to wonder whether there would still have been rock and roll guitar playing. There certainly wouldn't have been Keith Richards.

In his book *Crosstown Traffic*, Charles Shaar Murray describes Berry's fingers as 'impossibly long and spidery' (p. 120). Has he ever seen Chuck Berry's fingers? Long and spidery they are not. They're big all right, but they're about as spidery as half a pound of sausages. And I don't think it's being too ingenious to say this is largely responsible for why he plays the way he does.

His fingers don't tease out long, fluid patterns of notes up and down the fretboard. They grab the strings hard and firm, in bunches, in little clusters of half-chord shapes, and if his plectrum hand happens to hit a wrong string now and again, such are the 'Chuck Berry chords' that it will go pretty much unnoticed.

That chunky rhythm sound and those 'Chuck Berry licks' have become the basic currency of rock and roll guitar and even if Berry hardly invented them out of nothing, he made them inerradicably his own. Even though most of his songs stick close to blues chord progressions, and 'Wee Wee Hours' is as authentic a blues song as you could want, it's impossible to think of Berry as a blues player. He is coming from a different, more upbeat, more vaudevillian tradition. He is far more of a Louis Jordan than a Robert Johnson.

Again, Chuck Berry was not the first 'mover' among guitarists, but the duck walk and the splits are as familiar and as much a part of his vocabulary as licks. Certainly duck walks and splits are gimmicks. They're not 'music'. But they're the very stuff out of which rock guitar playing is made. Wouldn't John Scofield be more listenable if he did the splits once in a while?

There have always been contradictions at the heart of Berry's music. His songs were teenage anthems but he was by no means a teenager even when he first wrote them. The songs celebrate the rawness of rock and roll and yet they are witty, sophisticated, well-crafted, not raw at all. Berry would never have written a song like the Stones' 'Satisfaction'. He would have found the lyrics a bit simple-minded, not clever enough.

Plus you can hear every word he says. How un-rock and roll can you get?

But the essential contradiction remains that his performances from the earliest days have been inspired by the urge to make a fast buck and not to be ripped off by promoters rather than by any love of his art.

He is legendary for turning up for gigs ten minutes after he's due to go on stage, playing (but never rehearsing) with bands provided by promoters, and never playing a note more than he has to. This ought to be no way to make good music, yet Berry somehow carries it off. He is conscious of his own legend and manages to convey good humour and remain likeable despite a no doubt well-deserved curmudgeonly reputation.

And, of course, rehearsals aren't strictly necessary when every band in the land knows your complete repertoire by heart, even knows that you play some of the songs in pretty weird keys too. And this, I suspect, is Berry's real genius. He has created a body of great music that 'anybody' can play. This is not true of Beethoven, nor for that matter of Steve Vai.

Berry is also author of a wonderful, unghosted autobiography written in no known language. In it he says:

> I was not and will never be one who can come to accept the honour or gratitude that is forwarded from those who see in me that which is only an image they conceive. In other words my conception of me is: I am only what I am and not what one may believe me to be from the image he sees in my work . . . I've long thought that people who reach out beyond their grasp to praise or condemn something that is not worthy of either are knowledgeable of neither.

I'll remember that.

CHUCK BERRY: SELECTED DISCOGRAPHY

Chuck Berry is essentially a singles artist. He has been recording and rerecording and record companies have been packaging and repacking a lot of the same songs since 1955. This being the case, here's a list of his singles with their original release dates.

'Maybelline' (1955)
'Thirty Days' (1955)
'Roll Over Beethoven' (1956)
'Too Much Monkey Business' (1956)
'School Days' (1957)
'Rock And Roll Music' (1957)
'Sweet Little Sixteen' (1958)
'Johnny B. Goode' (1958)
'No Particular Place To Go' (1964)
'You Never Can Tell' (1964)
'My Ding A Ling' (1972)

Photograph courtesy of RCA

RITCHIE BLACKMORE

Born 14 April 1945, Weston-Super-Mare

There are three good reasons why you might respect and admire Ritchie Blackmore. First, he has come up with more attention-grabbing guitar riffs than any other player I can think of. Secondly, his use of twang bar was always adventurous and way ahead of its time. Thirdly, with Deep Purple he was one of the forefathers of heavy metal. Some would say this last wasn't something to command respect and admiration, but put these three together and they certainly make him a big noise.

I have to admit I've never been a great admirer of Blackmore, and I'm not entirely sure why, but I think it has something to do with student discos. Back in '71 or thereabouts at the end of the Union disco they'd always put on 'Black Night' and all the engineering students and the nurses, the ones who normally hated 'progressive' or 'heavy' music, would all get up on the dance floor, go crazy and think they were being really modern. Those of us who had any sort of vested interest in heavy music knew there was something wrong here. Surely you weren't supposed to be able to dance to heavy music. Nobody ever danced to the Groundhogs, not even to 'Sunshine of Your Love'. Damn it, heavy bands weren't even supposed to release singles, and yet here were Deep Purple having top-ten hits and packing the dance floor.

I think this may be another way of saying that Deep Purple were always terminally unhip. They were po-faced without being credible. Beck, Clapton and Page were serious musicians. Blackmore was the also ran. The others were aspiring to art. He was in showbiz.

Blackmore had been in showbiz from the beginning. When Clapton was learning how to play like a Chicago bluesman, Blackmore was already on stage with Screaming Lord Sutch, dressed only in a Tarzan-style leotard while Sutch rose from a coffin and attacked him. Later, in the Three Musketeers, he would have staged sword fights and play 'Flight of The Bumble Bee' very, very fast. And that's sort of the story of his life.

Deep Purple were never quite right. They were musicianly in the sense that they were competent players and they liked to take a good long solo, but they weren't musicianly if you compared them with the Mahavishnu Orchestra or even Colosseum. There was something missing.

But they did have those riffs. There were two kinds. There were those giddy-up type riffs like 'Black Night' and 'Fireball', and then there were the doomy, ponderous riffs like 'Smoke On The Water' or 'Child In Time'. If these seem a bit obvious and old hat today that's chiefly because Blackmore so completely exhausted the possibilities of that form. After him the deluge. Once you've played the definitive guitar riff what else do you do? Blackmore has never worked this out. Chunks of Rainbow sound as though he's ripping off himself.

The live album *Made In Japan* shows all Blackmore's and Deep Purple's good and bad points. There are some terrible longeurs (and these were terrible longeurs even in 1972 when it was released) but there is still some listenable guitar playing that's stood the test of time. The solo on 'Child In Time' still sounds flashy and exciting, although if you were being hard you'd have to say that it's a lot of flashy and exciting bits stuck together rather than an integrated whole.

For my money his short non-solo on the single 'Fireball', which is just a burst of highly controlled, fuzzy feedback noise, is probably his finest moment. It has the great virtue of being short, and Blackmore is one of those guitarists who need reining in rather than letting slip. I'm also fond of 'Speed King' where Blackmore and Jon Lord exchange untypical, jazzy licks. This of course has very little to do with the shape or sound of the rest of the song, but that is another Deep Purple trait.

The gossip always was that the members of Deep Purple

hated each other with a hard and gem-like flame. But all ego aside Blackmore supposedly left the band because they were getting funky and weren't heavy enough for him. And so he founded Rainbow and began the fairly rapid drift into fairyland and self-parody.

'Since You've Been Gone', 'All Night Long' and 'I Surrender' sound like a reasonable update of Deep Purple, and 'Since You've Been Gone' even has a good riff, though it was written by Russ Ballard, not Blackmore. But then there's 'Sixteenth-century Greensleeves' with maidens in towers and crossbows in the firelight. Or 'Babylon' with nonsense lyrics about nocturnal arrangements with Satan. By now Blackmore seemed to be tagging along with one of the least interesting strands of heavy metal. He'd become a follower, not a leader.

In all this shambles it must be hard to hold your head up and play good guitar. Given some of the material, it must be hard to keep a straight face some of the time. There's some quite interesting guitar on 'Stargazer' if you can get past all the swords and sorcery, but who can? This is not music for adults.

In 1983 Deep Purple reformed with a more or less classic line-up and I'm sure they'll make a good living as long as they can endure the slog of touring and playing hits from the seventies. People will want to see Deep Purple in the way they want to see Vera Lynn, as a piece of living history.

Blackmore's problem as a guitarist is that a lot of players have caught up with and overtaken him. Heavy metal has increasingly become a proving ground for red-hot guitarists with astounding technique and not much soul. Blackmore looks and sounds like an anachronism.

It would be nice to be able to say that nobody does it better, but in fact quite a few people do. If you're the kind of person who likes Ritchie Blackmore these days you're probably the kind of person who likes Yngwie Malmsteen a lot more. But, of course, Malmsteen and a thousand other guitarists wouldn't be playing what they're playing if it weren't for Blackmore. This is a large legacy though not an entirely unmixed blessing.

RITCHIE BLACKMORE: SELECTED DISCOGRAPHY

With Deep Purple: *Shades Of Deep Purple* (1968)
  Book Of Taliesyn (1969)
  Deep Purple (1969)
  In Concert (1970)
  In Rock (1970)
  Fireball (1971)
  Machine Head (1972)
  Made In Japan (1972)
  Burn (1974)
  Stormbringer (1974)
  Perfect Strangers (1984)
  House Of Blue Light (1987)
With Rainbow: *Ritchie Blackmore's Rainbow* (1975)
  Rainbow Rising (1976)
  Long Live Rock 'n' Roll (1978)
  Down To Earth (1979)
  Difficult To Cure (1981)
  Bent Out Of Shape (1983)
  Finyl Vinyl (1986)

Photograph courtesy of Duck Records Reprise

ERIC CLAPTON

Born 30 March 1945, Ripley, Surrey

If Eric Clapton had died in 1970 he would now be safely regarded as the second best rock guitarist who ever lived. However, he survived, not without alarms, for another twenty years, and that makes judgements about him far more tentative and problematic.

Listening to his recordings with John Mayall's Bluesbreakers, one is struck by how complete, how fully formed Clapton's talent was at that early stage. He had left the Yardbirds because they were too 'pop', and working with Mayall was a way of establishing the purity of his blues credentials.

The problem I've always had with John Mayall's Bluesbreakers is John Mayall. Presumably the guy does have some genuine feeling for the blues (after all, he's dedicated most of his life to it), but he doesn't *sound* as though he does. Clapton's playing on 'Have You Heard' is a formidable piece of sustained and contained aggression. There's feeling there, and it's as good an impersonation of Albert King as anybody could want, but you wish John Mayall wasn't fouling it up with his crappy vocals.

From there to Cream, and a pretty good singer in Jack Bruce. It's almost impossible to overestimate the influence of Cream on rock music. So much of what we now take for granted starts with them, and yet they were genuinely radical. They championed the use of volume as a physical presence, they 'invented' extended rock improvisation, and they insisted on the album rather than the single as pop music's essential form.

On *Fresh Cream* they were a blues band. On *Disraeli Gears* they seemed to be adherents of drug-influenced psychedelia. By the time of *Wheels of Fire* they were state-of-the-art experimentalists. Shrewd listeners, however, will note that Clapton was playing much the same thing throughout. It was fashionable to think of Cream as three competing virtuosi, but they weren't. Bruce might just possibly claim that status. But Ginger Baker? And Clapton was what he always was, a blues guitarist.

The version of 'Crossroads' from *Wheels Of Fire* is probably the highpoint of Clapton's playing, four minutes or so of flatout, no nonsense electric blues guitar. But the record is transformed by the thunderous, extraordinary counterpoint provided by Bruce's bass. It is not your average blues bass line and it makes Clapton's solo sound all the more remarkable for that reason.

Cream imploded because it's simply impossible for a threepiece group to create two hours of improvised music for vast audiences across America every night of the week. But by then Clapton's status as guitar hero was impregnable. Now he could be God if he wanted to, but, of course, he didn't. From then on, like David Frost, he rose without trace. He said he wanted to avoid the spotlight.

In retrospect, Blind Faith seems chiefly to have been an elaborate way of stabbing Jack Bruce in the back. Clapton and Baker brought in Steve Winwood, hired Rick Grech to replace Bruce, and produced some very ordinary music.

Other dire career moves followed. Clapton joined Delaney and Bonnie and Friends, but with friends like those . . . He formed Derek and the Dominos and they managed to pull one good song and one good cover version out of the bag: 'Layla' and 'Little Wing'. Today it is possible to buy a three CD set called the *Layla Sessions* featuring jams and out-takes from the making of that album. This seems not so much to be asserting Clapton's God-like status as his suitability as a PhD subject.

Then things got really rough: drug addiction, alcoholism, stealing his best friend's wife, making the truly dire *No Reason To Cry*, then *Backless* (also known as '*Spineless*'). On these albums he doesn't merely seem to want to avoid the spotlight, he seems to want to avoid playing altogether.

Nevertheless, the hits did (sort of) keep coming, with songs like 'I Shot The Sheriff', 'Knockin' On Heaven's Door', 'Wonderful Tonight' and the ludicrously titled 'I've Got A Rock 'n' Roll Heart'. Let's face it, he hasn't.

Over the years Clapton has worked on his singing, with considerable success and has done some very effective film music. He wrote the score for *The Hit*, for *Homeboy* and most effectively for the BBC's *Edge of Darkness*. The latter in particular shows how exciting a guitarist Clapton is when he strays from the confines of laidback rhythm and blues.

Throughout his career he has continued to be a stage performer. Once you accept that he was never really an innovator there seems no real objection to him working through a fairly predictable live set that might include 'White Room', 'Crosscut Saw', and inevitably 'Wonderful Tonight'. The blues has always been about interpretation rather than innovation.

There is an idea that the blues are a transparent vessel. The basics of the blues are so simple that 'anyone' can play them. The catch is that if you have the soul of an estate agent, the blues will reveal this.

Clapton is no estate agent and yet when playing live he is likely to veer from quite startling originality to banal cliché within the same solo, sometimes within the same lick. This doesn't suggest lack of technique so much as failure of instinct.

There are two other points worth mentioning about Clapton. First, when he was being God back in the Cream days, he would be playing a storm of raucous, liberating noise and stand on stage looking totally impassive. Now that his guitar playing is more restrained, more orderly, Clapton has become one of rock music's great face-pullers. It's as though he's signalling to the audience about how much feeling is going into his playing, just in case they hadn't noticed.

Secondly, somewhere in the seventies Clapton stopped playing Gibsons in favour of Fender Strats. Now, as Hendrix demonstrates, Strats are perfectly capable of making a big sound, but as a rule they are chosen for their inherent 'thinness' of tone. (Neil Young uses Gibson Les Pauls, Robert Cray uses Strats.) And I think that was an aesthetic choice by Clapton. Whereas with Cream the guitar was the whole sound, Clapton's guitar has increasingly become one element in a band sound that usually has a rather inert organ tone at its centre.

With 'Crossroads' the guitar playing *is* the song. With 'I Shot The Sheriff' or 'Wonderful Tonight' the guitar is an optional extra.

The received opinion is that with the albums *August* and *Journeyman* Clapton has returned to form. Having Robert Cray as a sideman does no harm. Today he can sell out the Royal Albert Hall for twenty odd consecutive nights. And hell, who is anybody to knock Eric Clapton? He may not be God but he's not a bum. Sometimes I ask myself, if he isn't the world's best white, blues guitarist then who is? But then I ask myself what's the big deal about being the world's best white, blues guitarist?

There is a recurrent image of Clapton today as a man in an Armani suit, playing rock standards to large, uncritical yuppie audiences. Sometimes he does it for charity in which case he tends to be standing shoulder to shoulder with Knopfler and Phil Collins. The CD generation certainly knows him as a great guitarist, but who else do they know?

ERIC CLAPTON: SELECTED DISCOGRAPHY

With Cream: *Fresh Cream* (1966)
  Disraeli Gears (1967)
  Wheels Of Fire (1968)
  Goodbye (1969)
  Live Cream (1970)
  Live Cream Vol. II (1972)
Solo: *Eric Clapton* (1970)
  Eric Clapton's Rainbow Concert (1973)
  461 Ocean Boulevard (1974)
  EC Was Here (1975)
  Slowhand (1977)
  Backless (1978)
  Money and Cigarettes (1983)
  August (1987)
  Journeyman (1989)
With Derek and the Dominos: *Layla* (1970)
With the Yardbirds: *Five Live Yardbirds* (1964)

Film Score: *Edge of Darkness* (1985)
With Blind Faith: *Blind Faith* (1969)
With John Mayall: *Blues Breakers – John Mayall with Eric Clapton*
(1965)

Photograph by John Wooler
Courtesy of Virgin Records

ALBERT COLLINS

Born 1932, Leona, Texas

If you demanded to know why Buddy Guy, Albert King, Son Seals, Clarence 'Gatemouth' Brown, Johnny Copeland, Otis Rush, or any number of other older, black blues guitarists aren't included in this book, I couldn't really give you a convincing answer. I wouldn't deny that they're good and although I might make out a case that they're blues rather than rock guitarists, I'd understand if that didn't seem a satisfactory reply. However, if you said, 'How come these guys aren't included when Albert Collins is?' I'd have what I consider a cast-iron answer. I'd simply say, 'They haven't had a major work written for them by John Zorn.' Of which more later.

Collins' guitar playing has a number of eccentricities, and eccentricities are always helpful in fixing a musician in the public mind. He begins by tuning his guitar to a minor chord. He then puts a capo round the seventh, or sometimes tenth, fret, and he then plays with his bare fingers and thumb, plucking or snapping the strings without the use of picks or a plectrum. He wears his guitar strap slung across his right shoulder, school-satchel fashion, and uses a hundred-foot guitar lead that enables him, when playing live, to wander into the audience, into the bar, or even into the car park.

He is known as the Master of the Telecaster or, more usually, the Iceman, and his guitar tone is invariably described as 'ice cold'. I think this comes about chiefly because his first hit single, back in 1958, was called 'The Freeze' and subsequently all his song and album titles have punned on the words cold, ice, freeze, frost, etc., etc. This again is a good trademark but must have become a little tedious over the years. It's as though Hendrix, having had a hit with 'Purple Haze' had been forced to have the word purple in all his subsequent titles. Yes, you might describe Collins' guitar sound as cold, but you might just as well describe it as stinging or twangy or explosive. But whatever you call it it's exciting, raw and very distinctive. Collins doesn't play long fluid runs, although he can be very fast. He goes in for popping, snarling, stuttering clusters of notes, usually played over an organ-based shuffle or boogie. He sometimes employs long sustain and there's certainly no emotional coldness about his playing.

To say that Collins has had a checkered career isn't saying half of it. He was taught to play guitar by his cousin Lightnin' Hopkins, who recommended him to use the open tuning. In the 1960s he toured with Clarence 'Gatemouth' Brown and was guitarist for Little Richard, occupying the guitar slot left vacant by Jimi Hendrix. Throughout this period he was making instrumental singles for small, local Texas labels, but until 1968 he still wasn't making a full-time living from music and had a day job as a truck driver. Bob Hite of Canned Heat eventually 'discovered' him and took him to California where he arranged a record deal. It was only now that Collins started to sing regularly. Until then he'd been almost exclusively a guitar player. Collins got work and made records but, even so, the late sixties' vogue was for Chicago blues and Collins was a Texan, and he never became as well known as he might have.

The seventies were comparatively lean years for Collins. He had no band of his own and when he played he had to make do with local pick-up bands. He was fortunate with some of these and was backed by the likes of Jimmy Vaughan and Robert Cray. Nevertheless, he made no records between 1972 and 1978 when he was signed up by Alligator Records. Albert Collins' star has been ascending pretty much ever since. He has steadily been recording and touring and doing sessions with Cray and Johnny Copeland, Jack Bruce and, of course, John Zorn. He played at Live Aid with George Thorogood (a mixed blessing some would say) and has even appeared in an American TV commercial with Bruce Willis.

Collins' early instrumentals, which can be heard on the collection *The Cool Sound of Albert Collins*, are undoubtedly blues numbers but they're not the 'I woke up this morning' kind of blues. They sound more like Booker T and the MGs than like Howlin' Wolf. Considering their age the guitar is amazingly modern sounding, very electric and searing. Even today that kind of organ shuffle is still what he does best and you can hear Collins playing and refining that style throughout his career, whether it's an update of 'Frosty' on the album *Frozen Alive* from 1981 or whether it's 'Mr Collins, Mr Collins' from his 1991 album *Iceman*. But over the years he has played all manner of blues cover versions, be it 'Caldonia', 'Too Tired' or 'Blues You Can't Lose'. These, however, never seem to me to be a hundred per cent convincing. It's as though in order to survive in the seventies he had to remake himself more in the image of the 'traditional bluesman', which is a shame because Collins is more interesting than that, as his outing with John Zorn proves.

I don't know what moved Collins to play with John Zorn, whether it was economic necessity or a spirit of adventure, whether Zorn flattered him into it or whether Collins simply didn't know what he was letting himself in for. Whatever, he must have got the shock of his life when he found the second guitarist was Robert Quine, he of Richard Hell and the Voidoids.

The composition that Zorn created for and around Collins is 'Two Lane Highway' on the album *Spillane*. In Zorn's words, it's an eighteen-minute opportunity for Collins to 'wander across the Texas landscape'. Sometimes it's very much business as usual for Collins as the band, which contains John Patton and Ronald Shannon Jackson, plays some hot, organ-based blues, but at other times the landscape becomes far more abstract and features whining guitar noise from Quine, *film-noir*-style piano, bass and drum thrashings. The joy is that Collins is both strong enough and flexible enough to go with what's happening. His instincts see him through and although he must be playing in contexts that are at times both unfamiliar and uncomfortable, these unaccustomed settings concentrate rather than dilute the essential Collins talent. Zorn says the piece is his 'portrait of a great bluesman'. But it's also a rich and detailed self-portrait by Collins himself.

ALBERT COLLINS: SELECTED DISCOGRAPHY

Solo or as band leader: *Frosty* (1962)
  Love Can Be Found Anywhere Even In A Guitar (1968)
  Ice Pickin' (1978)
  Frostbite (1980)
  Frozen Alive! (1981)
  Don't Lose Your Cool (1983)
  Live In Japan (1984)
  The Cool Sound of Albert Collins (1985)
  Cold Snap (1986)
  Iceman (1991)
With Cray and Copeland: *Showdown* (1986)
With John Zorn: *Spillane* (1987)
With Jack Bruce: *A Question Of Time* (1990)
With Gary Moore: *Still Got The Blues* (1990)

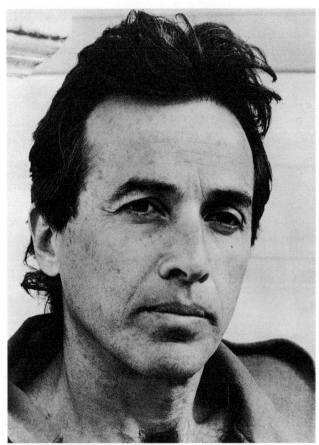

Photograph by Susan Titelman
Courtesy of Warner Bros.

RY COODER

Born 1947, Los Angeles

Why don't slide players become guitar heroes? Well, often they die before they get much of a chance, like Elmore James or Duane Allman. Sometimes they go crazy and join religious cults like Jeremy Spencer of Fleetwood Mac. Or they may just not have the right looks. They may be like David Lindley and in 1990 still be wearing the same red flares that they bought in the mid-sixties. Or they may be tattooed, anorexic albinos like Johnny Winter. But the only thing stopping Ry Cooder from being a guitar hero, apart from maybe his glass eye, is the fact that he doesn't want to be. And he doesn't want to be with a passion.

Some years ago when he was interviewed for the Radio One series *Guitar Greats* he said what a good man John Hiatt was to have in the band because his playing left plenty of room for Cooder. 'Most guitar players play too much you know,' Cooder said. 'That's an affliction of guitar players. They're always playing.' Spoken like a true anti-guitar hero.

Sometimes I wonder if he protests too much. It's one thing not to want to stand centre stage all night with all the spotlights on you and blast away like a maniac, but you don't have to go quite as far as Cooder sometimes does in order to prove that you're not Yngwie Malmsteen. Some of his rambles into Tex-Mex and Hawaiian music were so 'uncommercial' as to be downright perverse. And yet, despite his protests, he is still a contender whenever guitar players are discussed. And without being a megastar he has continued to make and sell records

and to fill concert halls when other, apparently far more assert-
ive and money-spinning acts have fallen by the wayside.

In the cruel world of popular music it might seem absurd to
account for Cooder's continuing success by pointing to his
musicianship, integrity, taste and dedication; but it seems to
work for him.

Cooder's music covers a lot of ground, embraces American
folk, country and western, Cajun, soul, rhythm and blues, as
well as jazz, although he says he hates his album of that name.
More than almost any other guitarist I can think of, Cooder
puts the sound of the band and the sound of the music before
the sound of his own guitar playing. Like Jerry Garcia, though
for very different reasons, his guitar has lots of space around
it. When he plays a solo it inhabits the song, and the song
remains primary. You can hear this on 'Crazy 'Bout An Auto-
mobile (Every Woman I Know)' as well as anywhere. The
guitar solo on the album version kind of glows in a little pool
of stillness, and it's interesting that the live version on the
twelve-inch single is much busier. On the single Cooder plays
more fully and is somehow closer to and more hemmed in by
his backing.

You could never say about a Cooder track, 'Great guitar
playing, shame about the song.' The best moments of Ry Cooder's music are when his voice, choice of material, the arrange-
ment and his guitar playing form a whole. You feel this
shouldn't be a particularly rare phenomenon but in researching
this book I've found it to be a less than common thing.

To some extent the songs on his early albums, songs like
'How Can A Poor Man Stand Such Times And Live?' and
'Vigilante Man' seem to be dominating Cooder. They're singing him, rather than him singing them; and I think that much
of his career has been a search for a style and a repertoire that
is entirely suited to him. Usually he does pretty well. If ever
there was a man born to sing 'He'll Have To Go' it was surely
Ry Cooder, and his rendering of 'All Over Now' makes it a
completely different song from the one the Rolling Stones
sang. And his skill at digging out songs that suit his talent
makes numbers like 'Crow Black Chicken' and 'I Can Tell By
The Way You Smell' real finds, not just archaeology. One sees
Cooder entirely at home on those springy, good-humoured yet

faintly ironic tracks like 'I'm Drinking Again' '634 5789' or 'Little Sister'. There's no shortage of guitar on these songs and yet they're in no sense guitar showcases. Even as he plays an instrumental like 'I Think It's Going To Work Out Fine' the guitar is articulating the song, not just showing off.

Above all else Cooder is an ensemble player and that is no doubt what made him attractive to Keith Richards when the Stones needed a guitarist. Obviously there is some bad blood between Cooder and the Stones and he refuses these days to talk about it. Apparently he was taken down to Redlands to meet Richards and invited to jam. The jam was recorded and some time later Cooder discovered he was playing on a Rolling Stones record and was duly outraged. Cooder and the Stones doesn't sound like a marriage made in heaven. Cooder was too straight. Jack Nitzsche says that when Cooder first walked into Richards' house, Richards was sitting on the floor, stoned, with three strobe lights flickering into his eyes. 'His glass eye nearly popped out,' says Nitzsche. But even if Cooder wasn't the right man for the Stones, he was the right sort of musician.

This kind of flexibility, this willingness to be part of a greater whole must have made him an ideal choice to write film music. He has produced scores for many films, including *The Long Riders*, *The Border*, *Johnny Handsome* and, triumphantly, *Paris, Texas*. The music for that film is some kind of high point both in film music and in Cooder's career. The music is yearning, haunting and has an eerie strangeness and seriousness that is at the heart of the film but is a side of Cooder seldom seen. Mind you, I still love his playing on Beefheart's *Safe As Milk*. The wild weirdness of the track 'Electricity' has some of that same quality.

There is always an eccentricity about Cooder's playing, often accompanied by a detached sense of irony. At its best, however, his playing – on *Paris, Texas*, on 'Electricity', on 'Sister Morphine' – is still certainly eccentric yet it doesn't have the detachment and is all the better for it. Even if Cooder is not the most emotional of players he is certainly not afraid to express emotion, and even though he seldom wears his heart on his sleeve, there is always plenty of heart in his playing.

RY COODER: SELECTED DISCOGRAPHY

Solo or as band leader: *Ry Cooder* (1970)
  Into The Purple Valley (1971)
  Boomer's Story (1972)
  Paradise And Lunch (1974)
  Chicken Skin Music (1976)
  Show Time (1977)
  Jazz (1978)
  Bop Till You Drop (1979)
  Borderline (1980)
  The Slide Area (1982)
  Why Don't You Try Me Tonight (1986)
  Get Rhythm (1987)
With Captain Beefheart: *Safe As Milk* (1967)
Film soundtracks: *The Long Riders* (1980)
  Southern Comfort (1981)
  The Border (1982)
  Paris, Texas (1985)
  Crossroads (1986)
  Johnny Handsome (1989)

Photograph courtesy of Demon Records

ROBERT CRAY

Born 1 August 1953, Columbus, Georgia

It's tempting sometimes to think that Robert Cray is the guitarist the world has been waiting for: a young, black guitar player with a profound respect and feeling for the blues, a modest man, articulate, thoughtful, accomplished, concerned with his craft, a contemporary figure but one who is connected with the origins of the blues.

However, it is rather a small segment of the world that has been waiting for him, and that segment, I suppose, is mostly white. The young black audience understandably is reluctant to hark back to days on the plantation. They're more likely to be impressed by Ice Cube than by B.B. King. Cray's music is as distant from rap as the music of any white musician.

One reason for this must surely be that as young, black guitarists go, he really isn't all that young. He was twenty-seven when his first record was released in 1980, an age at which some acts are embarking on their second comeback. In 1980 a blues record was not a fashion item and by that time Cray and his band had been on the road for a good six years – since 1974, again, not a good year to start playing the blues.

He chose an older tradition, but it *was* a choice. Cray didn't learn his blues down on the plantation any more than Jimmy Page did. Cray came from a comfortable American home and spent his spare time in the family den listening to records and practising his guitar. He heard Hendrix and Clapton long before he heard Buddy Guy or Albert Collins. But that doesn't matter. When he heard the blues he clearly knew that was his music.

But to think of Cray simply as a blues guitarist only catches part of his essence. He has obviously listened to a lot of soul music as well and it shows in his music. His voice, guitar and choice of material add up to a classy and seamless act.

His debut album *Who's Been Talkin'* is unusual when compared to later recordings in that Cray plays a lot of guitar on it. 'If You're Thinkin' What I'm Thinkin'' features a long, expansive solo that he would certainly deny himself these days.

Cray's guitar tone is deliberately 'pure', usually pure Strat, unmediated by effects or pedals. There is no fuzz or compression, not even any twang bar. It has a springy, snappy, rubbery tone, low on sustain, and can sometimes sound a little thin and weak. But this means that you listen through the guitar sound to the melody and to the player. There's a lot to be said for the joys of technology and the weird and wonderful sounds it can create, but there are occasions when you listen to Cray and all that stuff sounds like so much fussy decoration. When the real man comes through so eloquently using the simplest of means such effects are likely to seem redundant.

Cray's best songs tend to involve narratives or at least dramatized situations. In the archetypal Robert Cray song it's late at night, he's in his lonely motel room, a telephone rings unanswered, and his woman isn't there because she's run off with his best friend. It doesn't matter much whether these situations have been lived through or in some spurious sense 'come from the heart'. They are fully imagined, and Cray performs the songs the way a great actor might, and convinces you of their truthfulness by the skill of his performance. These are blues songs and to a large extent they deal in the standard currency and imagery of the blues, yet they depict the complexity and difficulty of life, and particularly of relationships, in a way that seldom becomes clichéed.

'Playin' In The Dirt' from the album *False Accusation* describes the dubious pleasures and inevitable pains of adultery with great economy and a complete lack of moralizing, and its yearning, equivocal guitar solo comes from the heart of the song. This is Cray's forte.

Cray's success has meant that he now gets to play with Eric Clapton or Tina Turner, and this is some evidence of his maturity and status. His music is, in the best sense, sophisticated, but there's more to sophistication than ditching a T-shirt in favour of a designer jacket. One fears that he might drift into middle-of-the-road territory. Would he still record a simple Willie Dixon song like 'Too Many Cooks'? There has been a tendency for him to become smoother as his work has progressed, and I don't know that that's entirely a good thing. 'Night Patrol' from *Don't Be Afraid Of The Dark* describes the horrors you might see on a nocturnal tour of a big city, and it's dangerously close to being an update of 'Streets Of London'. Nevertheless, 'Night Patrol' ends with a wonderful guitar solo on which Cray really lets himself go.

Personally, I enjoy my Robert Cray more when he's unencumbered by a horn section. The simple, direct sound of 'Smokin' Gun' from *Strong Persuader* seems to give him more room to stretch, certainly more room to play his guitar, than the neat, tight, horn arrangements of 'Nothin' But A Woman.'

But these are quibbles. Cray is a major artist and a remarkable guitar player. 'The Forecast Calls For Pain' from *Midnight Stroll* contains a guitar solo that really is loaded with pain. On 'I Can't Go Home' from *Don't Be Afraid Of The Dark* he plays a searing, articulate solo that speaks with uncomplicated eloquence about the miseries of being on the receiving end of infidelity and betrayal.

The blues takes time and Cray has taken his time, time to mature and develop. OK, so at thirty-seven he isn't young but he's young compared with John Lee Hooker. He's playing in a genre where there are no points scored for being a bright young thing. It is grown-up music, and although there are times when we don't necessarily want to be grown up, on the occasions that we do, Cray is the man.

ROBERT CRAY: SELECTED DISCOGRAPHY

Who's Been Talkin' (1980)
Bad Influence (1983)

False Accusation (1985)
Strong Persuader (1986)
Don't Be Afraid Of The Dark (1988)
Midnight Stroll (1990)
With Albert Collins & Johnny Copeland: *Showdown* (1985)
With Eric Clapton: *Journeyman* (1989)
With Tina Turner: *Tina Live In Europe* (1988)

Photograph by Jim Rakete
Courtesy of Régine Moylett Publicity

THE EDGE

Born 8 August 1961, Dublin

One story is that when U2 was formed in Dublin in the late 1970s, the various members not only didn't own and couldn't play any instruments, they hadn't even made up their minds which instruments they would play. If you were teenager David Evans looking for your first and only band and you couldn't play guitar at all you could do a lot worse than joining U2, even if it did mean that you were to be known thereafter as The Edge.

In other words The Edge's guitar playing created U2 while the process of being in U2 taught him all he knows about guitar. It is a formidable piece of on-the-job training.

The Edge is one of those non-technical, self-tutored guitarists who has turned his limitations to advantage. He does a lot with a little because a little is all he's got. But it's enough for his purposes. This means that he comes to the instrument without preconceptions. It means that he embraces effects, echo, unusual tunings, the E-bow, the 'infinite guitar'.

He is primarily a rhythm player and, like Keith Richards in quite a different way, he doesn't have very many rhythms. But the rhythms he uses, despite being processed and larded with echo, come over with spectacular clarity. This is evident on all U2's best songs, 'Pride', 'Sunday Bloody Sunday' and 'In God's Country' to name but three. They are guitar-driven, high-powered, anthemic.

When he does play lead guitar it still tends to be textural, employing slide or feedback or drone strings. He cites Neil

Young and Tom Verlaine as his influences, not the most technically accomplished of players but musicians who place a high
value on freshness of approach and feel.

His guitar makes a big sound. It fills up a lot of space. It is
the sound of big American stadia, not of cramped, smoky
clubs. The music is vast and epic. Of course this kind of music
can drift into the pompous and bombastic, and sure enough
that's precisely what U2's songs sometimes do.

Their first album, *Boy*, released in 1980, certainly sounds like
an early work and shows its new-wave origins very clearly.
But The Edge's guitar playing is remarkably mature, bright and
incisive. 'I Will Follow' comes complete with a hard, sparkling
rhythm, damped strings, harmonics, the lot. Later on, the
album 'Into The Heart' is full of great guitar sounds and texture
although none of it likely to satisfy technique freaks. And yet
The Edge is completely a guitarist. The kind of music he creates
couldn't come out of any other instrument. It is pure guitar
music. On 'Another Time' he lets rip with what is undoubtedly
a guitar solo. It's serviceable enough but you can tell he's not
going to make a name for himself as a player of guitar solos.

Apparently Bono lost his 'lyric book' just before U2 recorded
their album *October* – so on that album we have the slightly
bizarre phenomenon of The Edge playing a more orthodox
rhythm guitar while Bono's voice becomes a lead instrument.
His vocals become a kind of scat, repeating one phrase or
word over and over again, words like 'rejoice' or 'gloria' or
'Jerusalem'. For my money this doesn't work, because it gives
The Edge's guitar playing only a supporting role. Nevertheless,
there are many moments when his playing is as clangy and
thrilling as ever. Despite avoiding standard guitar pyrotechnics
there is nothing self-effacing or modest about his playing.
There's more than one way to show off.

U2 always had friends and fans in high places, but they
didn't 'go global' until their album *The Unforgettable Fire*. It was
produced by Daniel Lanois and Brian Eno, and the band had
to try long and hard to talk Eno into doing the job for them.
I'm not sure that this album is a straightforward bid for international rock stardom, nevertheless it got the job done. It's
probably significant that whereas Bono once sang about Bloody
Sunday, The Edge here plays an instrumental called '4th Of

July'. For all the string arrangements and keyboards and use of a Fairlight, and for all the generalization of the band's energies, The Edge's guitar playing on *The Unforgettable Fire* sounds just great.

The Joshua Tree remains the high point of what The Edge and U2 are all about. The four opening tracks, 'Where The Streets Have No Name', 'I Still Haven't Found What I'm Looking For', 'With Or Without You' and 'Bullet The Blue Sky', state completely what they are and what they do best, and here the guitar provides a lucid setting for Bono's vocals which soar and wander and yet remain under control. The guitar is alert and strikingly alive. The use of feedback on 'Bullet The Blue Sky' is particularly effective.

Perhaps that peak couldn't last. *Rattle And Hum* seems to me to be a perfect example of a band finding room to stretch themselves and then finding themselves stretched beyond their limits. Admittedly it's the soundtrack to a film, but so what? An album should work as an album, not as some sort of souvenir of an evening at the movies.

Nobody is better than U2 at doing what they do best, but there's evidence on *Rattle And Hum* that they don't know what they do best. What they don't do very well is cover versions. Nobody is ever likely to do a better version of 'Desire' than they are, but at any given moment there must be twenty-five bands in Dublin alone who could make a better fist of 'All Along The Watchtower' than they do. OK, so it was a free concert and they didn't have their own equipment, OK, so there are mitigating circumstances, but why inflict it on the record-buying public?

Again, what The Edge is good at is electronically processed rhythm, so here he is strumming his way through 'Van Diemen's Land' on acoustic guitar; a performance that you'd scorn in a local folk club.

And again, if you're a guitarist of limited gifts it really isn't very wise to put an extract of Hendrix's 'Star Spangled Banner' on your album.

But on *Rattle And Hum* we see the real drawback of a steady, relentless rhythm is that it gives Bono room to express himself; and express himself he does. He *talks* to his audience about apartheid (a bad thing), about Martin Luther King (a good thing, although obviously his death was a bad thing). This is bad enough but then he says on the live 'Silver And Gold', 'OK, Edge, play the blues.' There may be many words to describe what The Edge plays but it definitely isn't the blues. It would be nice to think this was a joke, but jokes are another thing U2 don't do very well.

THE EDGE: SELECTED DISCOGRAPHY

With U2: *Boy* (1980)
   October (1981)
   War (1983)
   The Unforgettable Fire (1984)
   Under A Blood Red Sky (1985)
   The Joshua Tree (1987)
   Rattle And Hum (1988)
Film soundtrack: *The Captive* (1986)

Photograph courtesy of Mel Yates

ROBERT FRIPP

Born May 1946, Dorset

Sometimes I wonder if Robert Fripp produces quite enough material for the number of records he releases. There are three extant versions of '21st Century Schizoid Man', two of 'Under Heavy Manners' and it's a pretty discriminating ear that can tell one bit of Frippertronics from another, or can be bothered to. Also Fripp is surely the only rock musician ever to have recorded a 'revised version' of an album. *God Save The King* by the League of Gentlemen is a 'revised version' of his solo work *God Save The Queen*.

Fripp's music at its best has an edgy, hyperactive quality that can be heard on, say, *Larks' Tongues in Aspic* as much as on *Beat* or on 'The Zero of the Signified'. At his worst Fripp looks like a ludicrous poseur.

After the cheerful, or otherwise, insanity of Giles, Giles and Fripp, he formed, in 1969, King Crimson, in many ways the ultimate art-rock band; loads of Mellotron, loads of pretentious lyrics, loads of solos for everyone.

What saved King Crimson from the worst excesses of art-rock was their willingness to go out there and have a good blast. For all the arty lyrics and swoony backing, when you get right down to it, '21st Century Schizoid Man' has a heavy riff that you could bang your head to.

Crimson went through endless personnel changes with Fripp as the only fixed point, and through half a dozen albums which were highly respected and enjoyable in their day but which now seem decidedly plodding and po-faced. An era

certainly seemed to have come to an end when the band split
in 1974 and released the posthumous *Red* and then the live
USA.

Like most early seventies bands King Crimson questioned
all those assumptions about pop songs having to concern
themselves with teenage love, having to have three verses, a
chorus and a bridge, and having to last two and a half minutes.
Alas they replaced this with pop songs that lasted seven and
a half minutes and were about nothing in particular. Whereas
most pop music has drifted back to the old format, Fripp, to
his credit, has carried on asking questions.

After the rigours of touring with a rock band the attractions
of ambient music are obvious enough. The notion that music
doesn't have to be extrovert or bombastic or overpowering is
a very appealing one. And so Fripp began to make music, both
alone and with Brian Eno, that could seep into the listener's
consciousness rather than hit him between the eyes. The
theory of this is easier to accept than the reality. I do believe
most people would still rather listen to *Islands* rather than *No
Pussyfooting*.

But Fripp's reputation was such that he could still get a gig
in the real world, and so, thanks to Eno, he recorded with
Talking Heads, and made a considerable contribution to the
sound of Bowie's *Scary Monsters* and *Heroes* albums.

On 'It's No Game' he sometimes roars in the background,
sometimes plays wild, repeated figures, has a guitar tone that
is always on the point of feedback, and he always seems to be
playing against rather than with the rest of the band, and yet
everything he does fits perfectly. And at the very end of the
song he plays a harsh little burst of guitar while Bowie screams,
'Shut up!'

Fripp is responsible for at least one unique guitar sound; a
high-pitched tone that is simultaneously buzzy and whiney,
of apparent infinite sustain, with dirty edges, that twirls and
swirls and turns back on itself in sonic spirals. It's heard at its
most archetypal on 'The Sailors Tale' from the album *Earthbound* or 'Asbury Park' from the album *USA*.

That sound, somewhat modified, is at the heart of the electronic experiments he refers to as Frippertronics. Using complex technology that enabled him to multitrack in a live situ-

ation and create a full sound without the need for other musicians, Fripp toured extensively as a high-tech one man band. This too can be read as a reaction against the ponderous, unwieldy business of rock touring.

But in 1981 he reformed King Crimson and it found its most creative flowering with Fripp, Bill Bruford, Tony Levin and Adrian Belew. Good as *Beat* and *Three Of A Perfect Pair* are, *Discipline* seems to me to be some kind of watershed for Fripp. Apart from their considerable musical talents, the other musicians brought with them a sense of humour, a thing Fripp is not exactly famous for. The music is still 'arty' but it has an alertness, a busyness, perhaps a neurotic quality that is a million miles away from the smug certainties of art-rock. It is an album heavy with guitars and yet it is equally far away from received ideas of how a band consisting of bass, drums and two guitars is supposed to sound.

Pieces, you hesitate to call them songs, like 'Elephant Talk' have a stirring, relentless intensity about them, and on this particular track Fripp plays a solo that is as close to a standard guitar break as he is likely to get (not all that close). The other stand-out track is 'Thela Hun Ginjeet' which crackles with the edgy excitement of New York streets and features superb ensemble playing with all manner of thrilling guitar noise. You might have thought Fripp and Belew were too similar in style to play together effectively and yet they are able to give each other room to thrive.

These days Fripp does a lot of teaching and writes a column for *Guitar Player* magazine which contains gems like: 'The inevitable and necessary reponse to release is return. Having gone nowhere we return to where we were.' Pretentious, *lui*? Nevertheless he has released a highly original and listenable album called *Robert Fripp And The League Of Crafty Guitarists Live!* which comes out of his classes in 'guitar craft' and must be unique in featuring a line-up of seventeen acoustic rhythmic guitarists. The sound is not unlike that of an acoustic Glenn Branca. Guitar is layered on top of guitar to form a sound that is rich and complex without any of the guitar playing being, in itself, virtuoso.

In the mid 1980s Fripp met and married Toyah Willcox. The first fruit of this liaison was a record called *The Lady Or The*

Tiger? on which the League of Crafty Guitarists provide accompaniment while Toyah reads stories: or so I'm told. There are some things a man cannot bring himself to do, not even in the interests of research, and sitting through fifty minutes or so of storytime with Toyah is one of them. They also formed the band Sunday All Over The World. On their first album, *Kneeling At The Shrine*, Toyah sometimes sings like Kate Bush, sometimes like Grace Jones, sometimes like Ethel Merman, while Fripp (sounding entirely like himself) puts some wonderful guitar sounds at the disposal of some fairly perfunctory songs. Some of us find Sundays a little depressing.

ROBERT FRIPP: SELECTED DISCOGRAPHY

With King Crimson: *In The Court Of The Crimson King* (1969)
  In The Wake of Poseidon (1970)
  Lizard (1971)
  Island (1972)
  Earthbound (1972)
  Larks' Tongues In Aspic (1973)
  Starless And Bible Black (1974)
  Red (1974)
  USA (1975)
  Discipline (1981)
  Beat (1982)
  Three Of A Perfect Pair (1983)
Solo: *Exposure* (1979)
  God Save The Queen/Under Heavy Manners (1980)
  Let The Power Fall (1981)
With Brian Eno: *No Pussyfooting* (1975)
  Evening Star (1976)
With the League of Gentlemen: *God Save The King* (1980)
With Andy Summers: *I Advanced Masked* (1982)
  Bewitched (1984)
With the League of Crafty Guitarists: *Robert Fripp And The League of Crafty Guitarists Live!* (1986)
Toyah and Fripp, featuring the League of Crafty Guitarists: *The Lady Or The Tiger?* (1987)

With Sunday All Over The World: *Kneeling at the Shrine* (1991)
With David Bowie: *Heroes* (1977)
  Scary Monsters (1980)

Photograph courtesy of Andrew Pothecary

BILL FRISELL

Born 1951, Baltimore

Some guitarists are born interesting. Some become interesting. Some have interestingness thrust upon them. Bill Frisell was definitely not born interesting. In fact, he's like some Woody Allen character who, rather late in his career, learned how to express his anger.

After attending Berklee College of Music, Frisell was considered, in the early 1980s, to be a suitable replacement for Pat Metheny in the Paul Motian Band. From there he became virtually the house guitarist with the New Age record label ECM. So far so laid back.

Today, among many other things, Frisell is to be found along with John Zorn and Fred Frith playing the most extreme sort of thrash jazz under the name of Naked City. This is real music from hell, a frenzied (though not humourless) assault on the ears and the mind; music to torture small animals by. And Frisell, all guitar weirdness and demented sonic attack, is completely at home.

To be fair, Frisell's current playing doesn't consist solely of sonic attack. It's characterized on the one hand by gentle, mellifluous, jazzy, chordal swells, but on the other by real go-for-the-throat guitar skronk. But he plays everything in between too.

His guitar tone is endlessly malleable. Sometimes it changes completely from one note to the next, sometimes it changes within the note itself. Or it may be moulded by guitar synths, or by judicious use of a volume pedal, or by his favourite bit of equipment, an Electro-Harmonix 16-Second-Delay Box, which allows a slice of guitar playing to be held, delayed, flanged, chorused, speeded up or slowed down and repeated backwards or forwards.

But what really produces these constantly changing sounds is not simply technology, but Frisell's desire to keep on the move, and the desire never to play the same thing twice. One finds in his playing an endless, teeming, inventiveness. The number of 'ideas per minute' he gets through is staggering.

So a typical recent Frisell piece might contain umpteen different kinds of guitar texture, from warm, fusion sounds, via six- and twelve-string acoustics, banjo and ukelele through to really evil, dirty, snarling fuzz. And when he goes for a nasty, raucous solo he really *goes* for it. He has that thrilling capacity to let go, to go all the way, and yet, however far he goes, he has at least set off from somewhere recognizable.

No, it certainly wasn't always like this. Parts of his early solo work do sound New Age-ish, something like 'The Beach' from his first album *In Line* made in 1983, which is one long wash of 'atmospheric' guitar sound. Admittedly it has a few unusual squawks and noises laid over the top, but in the end it just isn't all that interesting.

Frisell admits to being unhappy with that album. By the time of the album *Look Out For Hope*, made five years later, he is still mostly concerned with texture and atmosphere, but New Age it ain't. And he's starting to play some fast, growling, abrasive guitar, like on the track 'Remedios The Beauty'.

If you really want to hear how far and how fast he's come it's worth listening to two versions he's recorded of 'When We Go'. The first version appears on *Rambler* and is a light, lilting, jazzy number with cheerful trumpet and tuba. The second version is on the Power Tools album *Strange Meeting*, by which time it's become a strange, haunting, angular, edgy piece. But this doesn't seem to indicate a simple change in approach, rather it signals a radical change in sensibility. Essentially, Bill Frisell has stopped being *mellow*.

You could blame this on experience, or you could blame a few years in New York. But personally I blame John Zorn and I think we should be eternally grateful to him.

John Zorn, saxophonist, composer and organizer, is perhaps

the most notorious figure to have emerged from the New York downtown jazz community of the 1980s. He is the king of the limited-attention-span generation. His music channel-hops every thirty seconds or so (actually it sometimes hops less often than this, but in practice it feels as though it changes *more* often). It's as though the slate is being constantly wiped clean, and both listeners and players have constantly to reorientate themselves. It is a process of endlessly starting from scratch. This would be as much of a shock to a John Coltrane as to a Carlos Santana. Serious musicians have constantly demanded space to explore their ideas. With Zorn there is never room to stretch out. Sometimes players have only seconds to make their statement and then the chance has gone. However, it does concentrate the mind wonderfully. As Frisell obviously discovered.

On Zorn's *Spillane*, Frisell produces little splashes of blues or country picking or hot jazz or *Paris, Texas*-style slide as required. There are those who think *Spillane* is a high point in western art, and they'd get no argument from me.

So when Frisell came to record his album *Before We Were Born* he got Zorn to 'arrange' a piece called 'Hard Plains Drifter', putting Frisell and his band through a serious session of jump-cuts, switching rapidly between hard rock, soft jazz, cowboy music, psychedelic blues, spacey noise. What unites the music and prevents it from being a string of separate pastiches, is that each segment is always slightly askew, never quite a straight imitation, but deliberately distorted through Zorn and Frisell's off-the-wall outlook. If you were going to complain about 'Hard Plains Drifter' you'd say that it sounds like a John Zorn piece rather than a Bill Frisell piece, but with a musician as strong as Zorn this is probably inevitable.

Of course, all this requires a great deal of versatility from the musician. Most major guitarists choose not to be versatile. You wouldn't expect Hendrix to do a bit of country picking. You wouldn't want Allan Holdsworth to come out on stage and play some good ol' uncomplicated rock and roll. Most guitarists want to be a giant in one field. Zorn forces his collaborators to wander all over the farm.

If anything, Frisell's album *Is That You?* suffers from an excess of versatility. It is as though he consciously wants the record to be a summing up of his career to date, encompassing all the many styles he's played in. This doesn't quite work. It feels as though he's displaying not his versatility, but a multiple personality. The more or less 'straight' rendition of 'Chain of Fools' sticks out like a sore thumb, and 'The Days Of Wine And Roses' is left stranded somewhere between Frisell's opposing desires to be faithful to the original and yet to be radical in his playing.

But it has its moments when this multiplicity of guitar sound and style works beautifully. 'No Man's Land' starts with spaghetti-westernish guitar arpeggios over which acidic guitar attacks sweep from time to time. Or on 'Yuba City', quirky, Eastern-sounding percussion provides a backdrop for a solo that begins with controlled feedback and then goes on to skewed, stinging rock-based guitar.

Strange Meeting however, remains my favourite Bill Frisell album. It is attributed to Power Tools, a trio consisting of Melvin Gibbs on bass and Ronald Shannon Jackson on drums, but one inevitably thinks of it as Frisell's record.

Some of his playing is extremely soft and subtle but long stretches consist of savage angry guitar noise. Yet Frisell's playing here is anything but schizophrenic. He establishes that both styles are part of the same continuum, part of the same artistic vision, and he doesn't switch from one style to the other, he makes them part of the same style.

This is displayed throughout the album, but perhaps most dramatically on 'Wolf In Sheep's Clothing'. And there are times when he says to hell with being soft and subtle and just goes for sonic mayhem like on 'The President's Nap'.

More, much more, please.

BILL FRISELL: SELECTED DISCOGRAPHY

Solo: *In Line* (1983)
   Rambler (1984)
   Lookout For Hope (1988)
   Before We Were Born (1988)
   Is That You? (1990)

With John Zorn: *The Big Gundown* (1986)
   Spillane (1987)
   Cobra (1991)
With Bass Desires: *Bass Desires* (1986)
   Second Sight (1987)
With Paul Motian: *Psalm* (1982)
   It Should've Happened A Long Time Ago (1985)
With Vernon Reid: *Smash and Scatteration* (1985)
With Naked City: *Naked City* (1989)
   Torture Garden (1991)

Photograph courtesy of Arista Records

JERRY GARCIA

Born 1942, San Francisco

If ever a band was not 'built to last' it was surely the Grateful
Dead. They never sold many records (and didn't care about
it), they were heavy drug users, they spent a lot of time on
the road (an inevitably loss-making activity according to
received rock wisdom), they had keyboard players who tended
to die with their boots on, and they had a guitar player, Jerry
Garcia, who had always looked fat and old and who eventually
fell into a diabetic coma. Well, OK . . . maybe rock is meant
to be ephemeral. But the big reason you wouldn't have
expected them to survive is that they were so much a part of
one particular point in history, that of late sixties Haight Ash-
bury psychedelia. You wouldn't have given them odds on
surviving beyond 1972, never mind 1991. In other words they
were a bunch of boring old hippies. And what was worse they
seemed to be proud of it.

But they *have* survived, albeit with plenty of grey hairs and
a certain amount of memory loss. In the late eighties they even
had their first American top-ten hit. Garcia and the Dead aren't
quite museum pieces but they carry a truckload of history with
them.

So what exactly is invoked when you hear a Grateful Dead
song, a Jerry Garcia guitar solo? You inevitably think of acid
tests, Ken Kesey, amazing light shows, love-ins, be-ins, groovy
chicks dancing in the nude, gigs at the foot of the Sphinx with
the Pyramids as a backdrop, attempts to perform at Ayers Rock
or in front of the Great Wall of China, concerts that last for

five hours. You know about the self-sufficient army of Dead-
heads who follow the band around the world. You know that
the band's sound system can always be guaranteed to be the
world's best. You know that the Dead positively encourage
bootleggings, setting aside whole areas of the auditorium for
people who want to record their concerts. The Dead are a
community band. There is this enormous myth of a generation
in revolution, of people being brought together and changed,
of egos being merged.

And then you listen to 'Casey Jones' and you think, hey,
wait a minute, is that really what this whole thing is about? Is
that all there is? The music doesn't seem to be anywhere near
big or substantial enough to justify the myth.

Of course, any Deadhead, indeed any member of the band,
would tell you that the records aren't the point, that they're
only pale reminders of the idea that is the Grateful Dead.
But even at concerts the uncommitted are likely to feel like
wallflowers at a party where they don't know anybody. With
the Grateful Dead there's no neutral ground. You're either on
or off the bus.

At the very centre of all this mythology it's Jerry Garcia's
job to play guitar, not an easy act. Prior to being in the Dead,
Garcia had formed Mother McCree's Uptown Jug Champions
and the eventual success of the Dead enabled him to play some
distinctly uncommercial music either with his own acoustic
band or with *ad hoc* bands called things like Old And In The
Way. In retrospect it seems that Garcia's roots in American
folk and country may have saved him from becoming the
anachronism that he would have turned into had he been just
a psychedelic guitarist. But when Garcia was getting famous
there wasn't much of a market for jug bands, whereas psychedelic guitarists were welcome just about everywhere.

'Dark Star' was, and to a great extent remains, Garcia's finest
moment. The version on the 1970 *Live Dead* has suffered with
the passage of time, but it's still clearly an attempt to create a
major work. It is large, expansive and free form. It is spacey
in at least two senses, and Garcia's guitar playing consists of
thin, delicate lines, a kind of tracery or filigree. The last thing
he's attempting to do is sound like a power trio, like a Clapton
or a Hendrix. He leaves plenty of room. Those who don't like

this sort of thing are going to say that it's slack, rambling and doesn't go anywhere. But let's face it, this is not music to get critical about; it's music to get stoned to.

Those who love 'Dark Star', like Henry Kaiser for instance, say that what's wonderful about it is that, and I quote, 'The Dead don't just improvise *within* a form, they improvise *with* the form.' In other words, 'Dark Star' could be anything they ever wanted it to be. This sounds utterly admirable, but again it's more interesting as an idea than as an actual piece of music.

Today the band can sound frighteningly middle of the road. The 1988 album *Built To Last* has them fretting wimpishly about the fate of the planet, but the Dead have always had wimpish tendencies. Is there any wimpier album than *American Beauty*, also recorded in 1970? And *American Beauty* doesn't even have any stand-out guitar playing to liven it up. At least *Built To Last* contains 'Victim or the Crime' which has a wonderful long, rising, twisting guitar solo from Garcia.

But what are the great Dead tracks? Where is the killer guitar playing? 'King Solomon's Marbles'? 'Feel Like A Stranger'? 'Mississippi Half-Step Uptown Toodeloo?' Well no, not really.

Garcia does seem to be technically excellent. He doesn't play any bum notes, his solos fit the songs, and if you want someone to play modal, improvised guitar who else is there? He's intelligent, subtle and intricate. He's a formidable ensemble player, he's a virtuoso who doesn't hog the centre of the stage, and he's a fine example of a musician who can play a *lot* of guitar without swamping the music or the rest of the band. All these sound like considerable virtues. So why does it have to be so dull?

Maybe the problem isn't so much dullness as mellowness; a commodity devised and perfected in California these last several decades. Now, mellowness isn't always to be despised. When it comes to instant coffee or acid trips, mellowness is just fine and dandy. When it comes to guitar playing it's a dead loss. Mellowness means Pat Metheny, Vini Reilly, George Benson. It was not for this that we bought our Gibson Les Pauls and Marshall stacks, surely. Hey Jerry, how about some excitement, some risk, some bite, some edge?

There are those who say what's good about the Grateful Dead and Garcia is that they convey a wonderful sense of power in reserve. I just keep wanting to know why it always has to be *kept* in reserve.

JERRY GARCIA: SELECTED DISCOGRAPHY

With the Grateful Dead: *Grateful Dead* (1967)
  Anthem Of The Sun (1968)
  Aoxomoxoa (1969)
  Live Dead (1970)
  Workingman's Dead (1970)
  American Beauty (1970)
  The Grateful Dead (1971)
  Europe (1972)
  Wake Of The Flood (1973)
  Live From the Mars Hotel (1974)
  Blues For Allah (1975)
  Steal Your Face (1976)
  Terrapin Station (1977)
  Shakedown Street (1978)
  Go To Heaven (1980)
  Reckoning (1981)
  Dead Set (1981)
  In The Dark (1987)
  Built To Last (1989)
  Without A Net (1990)
Solo: *Garcia* (1972)
  Compliments Of Garcia (1974)
  Reflections (1976)

Howe Gelb fourth from left
Photograph courtesy of Demon Records

HOWE GELB

Born 1958, Pennsylvania

You probably haven't heard Howe Gelb play, possibly you haven't even heard of him or his band Giant Sand, and he sure as shoot doesn't appear to be on the way to international superstardom; but he really is good.

There are all sorts of reasons for admiring guitarists and not the least of my reasons for admiring Howe Gelb is that he writes great cover notes (a dying art). I like the way he tells you how much his guitars cost: a red-sparkle EKO bought for sixty dollars and a Harmony bought for seventy-five. I like the way he tells you that his recordings are made on tape that's already been used once. I like it when he admits that he's forgotten how to play some of the guitar parts on his albums. And I entirely understand his craving to have female backing singers and how he's never managed to organize it, but I love the fact that he says, 'Oh well, I hear them anyway.'

I realize this makes him sound a bit of a hayseed, but he isn't. He writes highly intelligent songs about the Berlin Wall, about children's bones found in the desert, about trickle-down systems. He is influenced by country music, but in a twisted, convoluted sort of way. Occasionally he plays what appears in itself to be an unironic country and western tune like 'Loving Cup', but in the context of the rest of his work it still ends up sounding ironic.

Country music influences never do that much for a guitarist. I mean, everybody goes on about how wonderful Albert Lee is but who actually wants to listen to that stuff? Fortunately Howe Gelb sounds nothing like Albert Lee.

A more important influence for Gelb than the country is the desert. You can take the man out of the desert, but you can't take the desert out of the man, or out of his guitar playing. Gelb is a desert rat from Arizona and there is plenty of desert in his playing: a harshness, a wildness, a sense of desolation. You can hear the influence of those other two desert rats, Zappa and Beefheart, and an occasional Dylanish strain, and of Neil Young, especially in his 'Tonight's the Night' mode.

Gelb has become looser and more wayward, more himself, as the years have gone by. The best of his early work was based around fairly straightforward songs, such as the moody, introspective 'Black Venetian Blind' which has two lean, stinging guitar solos, one in the middle and another at the end. The 'sampler' album *Giant Sandwich* contains part of an earlier, much faster version of the same song of which Gelb writes, 'If you tune the high E string way loose and yank it just so . . . it talks at ya.'

'Hard Man To Get To Know' contains one of those twangy, country rock riffs that sticks in the mind forever. 'Thin Line Man', a long complex song, ends with an extended solo that starts out low and melancholy but becomes increasingly high pitched and wild. But most of this stuff you would not be too surprised to find on a 'conventional' rock album. However, with *Long Stem Rant* Gelb throws convention and caution to the wind.

The album was recorded in three days in an unairconditioned red barn in Rimrock, Arizona; and essentially the band is a duo, Gelb, plus drummer John Convertino. There are songs on the album, some subtle and thoughtful like 'Paved Road To Berlin', some straight-ahead rockers like 'Get To Leave'. But the best parts are what Gelb describes as 'miracle minutes', to which he gives titles like 'Smash Jazz', 'Anthem' and 'Drum And Guitar', which are so wild and loose and sound like, well, some guy sitting in an unairconditioned barn in the desert getting frazzled and letting rip.

On the later album *Swerve*, Gelb has an apparently more orthodox band line-up and more 'real' songs than miracle minutes, and by the standards of *Long Stem Rant* he is quite restrained in his guitar playing; but it still isn't exactly Top Forty material.

Where Gelb comes from it always seems to be three in the morning, and he's been out in the desert too long, and he's not slept for days, he's feeling simultaneously wired and wasted, his voice is cracking; so he picks up his guitar and lets it all come out. Sometimes he wants to rock, to play scorching solos, even play some wah wah, as on 'Can't Find Love'; and sometimes he wants to play weird 'tone poems' full of scat singing and cocktail piano; and other times he just wants to slump over his guitar and mumble and strum.

On 'Angels At Night' the vocals sound weary to the point of passing out. The song lumbers along, sometimes the backing is incredibly thin with just a single electric guitar, sometimes there's a full band with electric organ. At one point a voice babbles, 'I'm a professional. I'm not no improviser, not no scat musician,' and as the song builds to its passionate, heavy finale, Gelb plays a crazy, fuzzed solo that seems to be in no particular key, certainly not the key the rest of the band are playing in, and finally he pitches the song into complete disarray and it ends.

If this kind of thing sounds interesting to you then you'll like Gelb a lot, if not, not. His work is deliberately messy, deliberately sloppy and unfinished. The brilliant, accomplished guitar playing is thrown in casually, carelessly. Partly, I think, he does this to stick two fingers up at 'the rock establishment', but also because he realizes that if you're trying to make music for our times then you'd better make something a bit messed up.

HOWE GELB: SELECTED DISCOGRAPHY

With Giant Sand: *Valley Of Rain* (1985)
  Ballad Of A Thin Line Man (1986)
  Storm (1988)
  The Love Songs (1988)
  Giant Sandwich (1989)
  Long Stem Rant (1989)
  Swerve (1990)

Photograph courtesy of Arista Records

JEFF HEALEY

Born 1966, Canada

The story is that when Jeff Healey was first looking for a recording contract some company executive offered the opinion that he needed a gimmick. Some would think that being a blind Canadian who played sitting down, his guitar in his lap, holding down the strings as though he was playing a keyboard and making a fearsome noise somewhere between Clapton and Hendrix, might be gimmick enough for anybody. And yet, and it pains me to agree with anything a record company executive says, I think the guy might have had a point.

For all the oddness of Healey's technique the sounds he produces are fairly orthodox, indeed his music seems to hark back to a much earlier time. 'I Can't Get My Hands on You' would have sounded quite 'progressive' had it been written in 1968, but Healey wrote it a couple of years ago. In the world of rock he is a conservative.

He says he holds his guitar in his lap because it's more comfortable that way, not because he has any theories about it giving him greater reach or increased vibrato, although of course it does. And he doesn't just bend or pull the strings, he really snatches them with his fist. But I know this from having seen him play, not from hearing him.

But he doesn't sit all the time. Sometimes he gets up and shambles awkwardly around the stage (awkward because he has to hold his guitar, he doesn't use a strap) then plays the guitar with his teeth or behind his head (ho hum).

As his first album, *See The Light* was both his calling card and his chance to prove his credentials. This, I suppose, is why it contains two twelve-bar instrumentals. Even though one of them was the Freddie King classic 'Hideaway' this was still a pretty weird thing to find on an album made in 1988. It asserts that Healey is a 'serious' blues player. You know it's serious because it's not much fun to listen to. Far more impressive was his brash, no nonsense, grab you by the ear attack on 'Confidence Man' and 'See The Light'.

Throughout the album he plays stinging, scorching, abrasive lines and fills. At his best he gets the job done briskly and with a kind of furious efficiency. This guy isn't going to hang around. The problem is, his playing remains stinging, scorching and abrasive regardless of what song he's playing. The aggression of his solo on 'My Little Girl' just doesn't fit the song. He's fast and he has fire but too often he's playing too many notes for the music's good.

On the evidence of *See The Light* Healey sounded like a hot guitarist in a luke-warm band. (The inner sleeve told us that Tom Stephen gave up a 'promising position' as an urban planner to drum with Healey.) Healey's voice was so-so, his material a bit thin.

We were told that he was something of a student of blues history, yet his playing sounded like someone who'd spent a lot of time listening to Eric Clapton rather than Freddie King, much less to Robert Johnson. What's more, he played as though he'd never even heard Eddie Van Halen or Adrian Belew, and any self-respecting twenty-two-year-old guitarist ought to have listened long and hard to those two and taken at least some of it on board.

When I saw that the second album, *Hell To Pay*, contained collaborations with Mark Knopfler and George Harrison I feared the worst. Call me an old stick in the mud, but I don't think the world needs another version of 'While My Guitar Gently Weeps'. And if you force one on me I'll take the comically 'deconstructed' version by Marc Ribot thanks very much. It's a dumb song and where it's intelligible at all it's smug and complacent. Healey pulls off a very ordinary cover version but it does have a nice guitar solo. And the Knopfler song 'I Think I Love You Too Much' just goes on and on with endless rounds of wheedling guitar from Healey and Knopfler. Although they play 'together' on the track, Knopfler recorded his part in London while Healey remained well across the other side of the Atlantic.

But then suddenly, there seemed to be real evidence of an individual voice coming through. On 'Something To Hold On To' his playing seems to be subtler and more eloquent than anything on the first album. His singing is much improved and so is his songwriting; at times he sounds a little like Elvis Costello, though if the Attractions had ever had a lead guitarist like Healey they'd have been a different proposition completely.

Hell To Pay is much less of a blues album than *See The Light*. This is a step in the right direction. There's no reason why he shouldn't play the blues. Being young and white aren't in themselves disqualifications. But somehow when he plays the blues he sounds like a boy, while Robert Cray, for instance, sounds like a man.

Healey has a lot of career in front of him. He should do what he does best. Let's hope he doesn't get saddled with the reputation as 'that blind Canadian who plays the blues sitting down and sometimes behind his head'. That isn't the kind of gimmick he needs.

JEFF HEALEY: SELECTED DISCOGRAPHY

See The Light (1988)
Hell To Pay (1990)

Photograph by Tony Gale
Courtesy of Pictorial Press

JIMI HENDRIX

Born 27 November 1942, Seattle
Died 18 September 1970, London

Jimi Hendrix is the only dead guitarist to be featured in this book and there do seem to be certain absurdities in including him in a book about rock guitar playing in the nineties. Not only did he not make it to the nineties, he barely made it to the seventies. However, he's included because his importance and influence are as great today as they ever were. No guitar player and certainly no book about guitar players can ignore him and what he did. Our problem is in seeing exactly what it was that he did.

He should not be regarded as the all-time great electric guitarist simply because he played loudest, or had the hottest moves or the weirdest clothes, but because he created music, indeed a whole aesthetic that spoke and still speaks to people.

Hendrix was and remains a giant because he made gigantic music. That music had scale, size, grandeur. It contained anger and technique in vast equal quantities. Neither anger nor technique are in themselves uncommon in rock music but nowhere else do they balance and reinforce each other the way they do in Hendrix's playing. His music is violent, indeed apocalyptic, but he is articulating that violence rather than being a victim of it. His rage is colossal and it takes a colossus to control it. The rage is at the disposal of his art. He uses it and expresses it. This is not, historically, what pop music does. It is not what Abba did, but nor for that matter is it what 'serious' rock musicians like Elton John do either. It is more the kind of thing that Picasso was doing in *Guernica* and in that sense Hendrix changed forever what popular music might be capable of.

Hendrix's guitar playing is alive with the sounds of pain, wrath, torment. He is wrestling with something huge and difficult to control, and in live performance he seems to have lost the battle quite often, but when he won he won magnificently.

He wrote some great songs and had the capacity to transform other people's songs and make them his own. Even Dylan adopted his 'reading' of 'All Along The Watchtower'. 'Wild Thing' became sexy and raw and dangerous when Hendrix performed it, whereas it had sounded like a comic song when performed by the Troggs. 'Hey Joe' sounds like a magnificent song when Hendrix performs it, but it sounds pretty insubstantial in the hands of anyone else.

But Hendrix was human. He needed a context in which he could thrive. Say what you like about The Experience but they *were* a band. There was a coherence about Hendrix, Mitchell and Redding that there never was about Hendrix, Mitchell and Cox or about the Band of Gypsys. For all that Noel Redding seems to have been a numbskull without the slightest idea of what he was involved with, he was the right man for the job at the time. He gave Hendrix room to express his anger and violence while Mitchell egged him on.

A couple of young white guys with long hair and psychedelic clothes was precisely what Hendrix needed for success. If Hendrix thought that was some sort of ugly compromise, if he really wanted an all-black band, he kept quiet until he was in a strong enough position to do something about it. After all he had played in black bands with Little Richard and the Isley Brothers and that had hardly brought him untold fame and fortune.

I remain unconvinced by accusations that Hendrix was an Uncle Tom, a white man's black man, or that he was some sort of clown for the white folks. Black musicians, from Louis Armstrong to Anthony Braxton, are constantly being accused of betraying their blackness. My memory is that Hendrix was anything but a tame Negro. I think he genuinely scared the hell out of a lot of white folks. Some liked being scared, they found it exciting or sexy, but far more felt threatened.

Partly it was his image, his clothes and his hair, but his image was a perfect correlative for his music. He was judged to be dangerous, indecent, a wild man; and inevitably there was a whole culture's racial, sexual and political fears going into that judgement, but the people who were scared by the vehemence and power of Hendrix's music were obviously listening to it quite intelligently, a good deal more intelligently than a lot of fans who simply hear him today as a guitar hero. Dead heroes are always much easier to deal with than living ones.

How about the burning of the guitar? Sometimes I think this was a serious, indeed the ultimate, attempt to 'extend the vocabulary of the guitar'. In Hendrix's music there is always the sound of explosions, crashes, bombs, machine guns; so here he is at Monterey taking those ideas to their ultimate conclusion, making his guitar squeal and howl with pain before setting it on fire. It is a piece of rock theatre. The act invokes ritual sacrifice, book-burnings, self-immolation, the napalming of Vietnamese villages. Sometimes I think it really does that.

Keep in mind also that in his act at Monterey Hendrix had already driven home fairly hard the idea of the guitar as a phallus. What kind of guy sets fire to his phallus, beats it against the floor of the stage, smashes it to pieces against his amp? A guy with a certain amount of self-hatred and some highly self-destructive urges.

It is a thrillingly dangerous and insane thing to do. Look at the face of that girl in the film, the one with the long hair and the big eyes. She's watching Hendrix and she's not having a one-hundred-per-cent-undiluted good time. She looks scared. What the hell is this crazy bastard likely to do next? This is profoundly what rock music is about. In one act he seems to have fused together all the danger, excitement, edginess of a whole generation. That takes some doing.

That's what I sometimes think. Other times I think he was just being silly. As silly as Pete Townsend or Keith Moon. And that, of course, is another explanation for the burning. At Monterey, The Who didn't want to follow Hendrix and Hendrix didn't want to follow The Who. Hendrix lost. He had to go on stage after The Who's smoke bombs and instrument smashing. He had to find some way of following that, and being a consummate showman, he did. That's all it was, showbiz.

At Monterey, Hendrix announces he's going to make this important 'sacrifice' of something he really cares about. He wants the audience to know they're about to see something really special. According to Redding's autobiography Hendrix was burning guitars long before he got to Monterey. Somehow the significance of the action is lost if it's something that can be seen twice nightly at the Wolverhampton Gaumont.

What would have become of Hendrix had he lived? That's an impossible question to answer, but it's worth trying.

We know that at the time of his death he was bored with his own music. He was bored with having to go on stage, play his hits, play the guitar with his teeth, etc., etc. Watching the film of his Isle of Wight gig there is certainly evidence that his music is becoming more free-form, more exploratory than we're used to with Hendrix. Solos come where you least expect them, songs lurch in and out of focus. But I don't know if this means Hendrix was moving in some new direction or whether he was so pissed off, so bad-tempered, so unhappy with the gig, that he thought it didn't matter much *what* he did.

There was talk of him working with Miles Davis but I can't imagine him ever fitting into a Miles Davis line-up. You could argue that Hendrix 'improvised' on stage, but Hendrix's version of improvisation was for him to do whatever the hell he liked while the rest of the band tried to keep up. This might be OK if you just have a drummer and a bass player and you're playing the blues, but you can't seriously imagine the members of a Miles Davis band (say, Billy Cobham, Keith Jarrett, Jack DeJohnette) putting up with that kind of nonsense, much less Davis himself.

Possibly Hendrix might have turned into an Eric Clapton, a survivor who came back from the brink and found a way of rediscovering and retaining his enthusiasm and appetite for creating music. But he might just as easily have turned into Peter Green. He might, of course, have turned into some sort of mature rock musician of a type we've never seen and in its absence can't even imagine. But I don't know . . .

I am left with the inescapable feeling that the body of work Hendrix left behind is curiously complete. You couldn't have said that before *Electric Ladyland* but afterwards you could. Hendrix was always reckless, with his use of drugs certainly, with money, with other people's time and efforts, and also with his own talent. Today when we hear his best performances there is a sense of risk, a creative tension that comes from knowing that here's a genius who is about to, who was always likely to, piss it all away.

Hendrix's early death may seem like a waste, but Hendrix himself was intensely wasteful. It may seem tragic but it also seems inevitable. There are, however, worse things than an early death, ask Peter Green.

JIMI HENDRIX: SELECTED DISCOGRAPHY

Are You Experienced (1967)
Axis – Bold As Love (1967)
Smash Hits (1968)
Electric Ladyland (1968)
Band of Gypsys (1970)
Cry of Love (1971)
Rainbow Bridge (1971)
Isle Of Wight (1971)
In The West (1972)

Photograph by Glen Laferman
Courtesy of Intima Records

ALLAN HOLDSWORTH

Born 1948, Bradford

Just as Steve Vai looks like most people's idea of a guitar hero, so Allan Holdsworth looks like most people's idea of a good plumber. Allan Holdsworth has an image problem in that he doesn't have an image. He's just an ordinary-looking guy who wears jeans, trainers and a worried expression, and happens to play extraordinary guitar. The story is that he's an unhappy character who gets depressed because he doubts his ability and thinks nobody likes his music. His ability is not in doubt, but it's true that he's never found a large following, especially not in England.

Holdsworth is a guitarist's guitarist; in other words the public doesn't know or care about him but other guitar players think he's great. Now, this is a peculiar concept at the best of times. Try to imagine a plumber's plumber who never had a satisfied customer but was thought to be a wizard by his fellow plumbers. The analogy can't be pushed too far. Of course, the customer isn't always right, but one way or another a guitarist needs satisfied customers as much as a plumber does, he needs to find his audience.

Holdsworth's output is not overwhelmingly diverse yet it's comparatively hard to define. He says he doesn't consider himself to be a jazz player yet his music can only just be called rock. In fact, his strength is that his guitar playing is remarkably free from cliché, remarkably unlike anyone else's. But this only adds to the problems. It isn't easy selling a product that is hard to define and unlike anything else on the shelves.

Holdsworth's guitar playing can be blindingly fast, is always fluent, positively liquid. He is helped by a huge reach, a very light plectrum technique and a distinctive sound which has a mellow, violin-like tone. He was, and to a lesser extent still is, an enthusiastic user of the Synthaxe, of which more later.

His first major band was John Hiseman's Tempest as far back as 1972, but it was with Soft Machine that he drew real interest. I remember Soft Machine playing in Newcastle at about this time. In retrospect it appears Karl Jenkins was about to hi-jack the band, Robert Wyatt was long gone and a disaffected Mike Ratledge spent the first twenty minutes or so twiddling with some hand-held noise box that created serious pain in the ears. Then suddenly he stopped and Holdsworth played fast, fluid, elegant solos for the rest of the set. It was a long way from 'Esther's Nosejob' but it was great. 'Hazard Profile' from the album *Bundles* shows Holdsworth in this phase and is extremely fresh and bracing. It's often forgotten, but Soft Machine could move like a train when they wanted to, and I'm not sure that Holdsworth has ever found a better setting for his guitar playing, although the music is some way from what we now consider 'his' sound.

From Soft Machine it wasn't such a big step to Gong, and Holdsworth appears doing sterling service on *Gazeuse!* – and by then, say on 'Night Illusion', he is starting to sound like himself. His solos constantly reject the obvious notes and the obvious patterns, and it seems to me that even then he was embarking on the task of extending the emotional range of the guitar. By rejecting both the polite twiddlings of jazz and the predictable impolitenesses of rock he is pushing at the boundaries of what the electric guitar is capable of expressing.

One recurring difficulty he has had in this enterprise is finding some role for a vocalist. You might say there's *no* role for a vocalist but Holdsworth seems to want one. So on the mini-album *Road Games* we have Jack Bruce, no mean singer, struggling manfully with some cripplingly unsingable melody lines on 'Was There?', though I'll admit that Holdsworth plays some terrifically varied guitar on that song. In fact, the only place where Holdsworth seems to be even half successful with a vocalist is towards the end of 'White Line' from the album *Allan Holdsworth, i.o.u.* where the vocals (by Paul Williams) are free from unnecessary complexity and difficulty for its own sake; and the words, music and guitar come together admirably, if briefly.

Road Games carries an inscription that reads, 'There is no synthesiser or keyboards on this record.' If only things had stayed that way. Some of us have always been baffled by the attractions of the Synthaxe, and Holdsworth has done little to lift that bafflement. To my ears it has a cheap, wheedling, heartless sort of tone. It can sound like keyboards but like rather poor keyboards. It can sound like a violin, but Holdsworth can get that tone without a Synthaxe. It doesn't, and here's the all-important thing, sound like a guitar. OK, so there's nothing holy about the guitar *per se*, but it's a lot holier than the brittle fakery of a Synthaxe. Apparently these things require a great deal of precision to play; the pulling and bending of strings, the blurring of notes isn't on, and to that extent it might seem that Holdsworth was born to play one, but it's done him no favours.

Anyone wanting to savour the true awfulness of Holdsworth and his Synthaxe could do no better (or worse) than to listen to *With A Heart In My Song*, an album made with keyboardist Gordon Beck. You know the kind of music they play on aeroplanes to sedate you before take-off . . . ? It has all the heart of Lucrezia Borgia. The track 'So, So, Calypso' is the sort of toothaching musical jollity that makes you want to throw yourself off high buildings.

On the cover of the album *Secrets* Holdsworth is quoted as saying, 'When I hear criticism for choosing the Synthaxe as my instrument it makes me feel as though those people aren't relating to the music or the notes, they're relating to something physical. They're hearing with their eyes.' But this is crazy. One objects to the Synthaxe not because of 'the music or the notes' but because of the dismal noise it makes. It doesn't make an eloquent sound, just as a thumb piano doesn't make as eloquent a sound as a Bechstein. I don't understand why Holdsworth can't hear that.

Fortunately he doesn't play it all the time nowadays. He plays Synthaxe on only three tracks of *Secrets*. I don't want to fall into the trap of saying everything he plays on guitar is great and everything he plays on Synthaxe is terrible but on 'City Nights' or 'Joshua', for example, there's a passion, a roughness, a simple humanity, to the guitar playing that shows up the Synthaxe as the toy it is.

ALLAN HOLDSWORTH: SELECTED DISCOGRAPHY

Solo or as band leader: *Velvet Darkness* (1976)
  i.o.u. (1982)
  Road Games (1983)
  Metal Fatigue (1985)
  Atavachron (1986)
  Sand (1987)
  Secrets (1989)
With Tempest: *John Hiseman's Tempest* (1974)
With Tony Williams: *New Life Time*
  Believe It
  Million Dollar Legs
With Bill Bruford: *Feels Good To Me* (1978)
  One Of A Kind (1979)
With UK: *Danger Money* (1978)
With Soft Machine: *Bundles* (1975)
With Gong: *Gazeuse!* (1977)
With Gordon Beck: *Sunbird* (1979)
  The Things You See (1980)
  With A Heart In My Song (1988)

Photograph courtesy of Reckless Records

HENRY KAISER

Born 1952, Oakland, California

There can't be many musicians who have taken up the electric guitar on the strength of hearing Derek Bailey, but Henry Kaiser is one of them. He started playing in 1972 and was a late starter as guitarists go. What's even more surprising is that having been inspired by Bailey, he should find himself, eighteen years later, fronting his own band and playing killer, off-the-wall rock solos on cover versions of Neil Young's 'The Loner' or Hendrix's 'Are You Experienced?'

This takes some explaining. The word eclectic might have been invented to describe Kaiser. He appears to thrive on diversity and hard work. In any given year he plays on eight or nine albums. These might include a solo guitar project, an album of traditional Korean music, a Synclavier duet with the Russian keyboard player Sergey Kuryokhin, an album with Fred Frith, various tribute albums to the Stones, the Shadows or Nick Drake. There might also be sessions with such outfits as Crazy Backwards Alphabet, Invite the Spirit, French-Frith-Kaiser-Thompson, as well as with the Henry Kaiser Band. He can be found playing solo concerts, free jazz, blues, rock, Hawaiian music, or collaborating with the likes of Herbie Hancock, Terry Riley, Bob Weir and Bill Laswell. And just in case this isn't enough, he has a day job teaching underwater scientific research at Berkeley.

This kind of variety and prolificness of output can make him sound uncommitted or a dilettante, but that isn't the case. There is no sense of his talents being spread too thin or being diluted. On the other hand, it means that he isn't as instantly recognizable as some guitarists who are only famous for doing one thing. But let's face it, the guy obviously likes to play guitar and make records and you can't say that about every guitar player. And although Kaiser has a jazz background of sorts, he is refreshingly rockist when he chooses to be.

In interview (he is a fiercely articulate interviewee), he says his guitar playing is influenced by experimental film, information theory and what he has to eat. But he has clearly spent a fair amount of time listening to Jerry Garcia, Hendrix, Albert Collins, the various guitarists in Beefheart's Magic Band, and indeed to hundreds of other players.

He is something of a guitar scholar and used to write highly intelligent columns in *Guitar Player* magazine. He also has a reputation as an innovator with electronic equipment, and his music is full of strange, unique and exciting sounds.

It would be hard to cover the whole vast range of Kaiser's recordings, and frankly I haven't tracked down items from his back catalogue such as *Teen-Aged Sex Therapist/Party* nor *The World and Raw People* though it's not for want of trying. Instead here are a few ‚'snapshots' of Kaiser at various points in his career.

His first recording was on *Eugene Chadbourne Volume 3: Guitar Trios* where he does indeed sound like a man who's been inspired by Derek Bailey. Kaiser plays electric and acoustic guitar and 'plastic horns', while Chadbourne plays prepared six- and twelve-string guitars, unamplified electric 'toys', 'siren' and (again) 'plastic horns'. Yes, it's that sort of album. Owen Maerks makes up the trio.

In 1979 on *Protocol* he plays improvised duets, with Toshinoro Kondo (trumpet and alto horn) and Andrea Centazzo (percussion and 'cheap electronics'). This stuff is about as unlistenable as Kaiser ever gets. The more listenable side, with Centazzo, sounds like two men having a fight in a recording studio and occasionally brushing against a guitar and knocking over a set of drums. Certainly Kaiser became a much more interesting player once he freed himself from free music.

Two albums he made with Fred Frith show his staggering rate of development. *With Friends Like These* made in 1979 is all groans and crackles, twangs, guitar swells and feedback. There

are some lovely, unusual noises here and there and a lot of it
is very subtle and shows a terrific interaction between the two
players, but I don't believe anybody ever *enjoyed* that album.

By 1983, the album *Who Needs Enemies?* is full of rhythm and
light, with blues picking, bits of searing distorted guitar, a
touch of Talking Heads, a hint of gamelan. Some of it you
could almost hum. It's still experimental and it isn't easy listening (thank God) but it's not an endurance test either. The
longer pieces like 'The Golden Eighties' and 'Roy Rogers' are
especially enjoyable.

But if sheer no nonsense guitar playing is what you're after,
then *Marrying For Money* (1986) is the one. There are guest
guitarists on the album but essentially it's a free improvised
showcase for Kaiser's guitar heroics. All his many and various
influences pour out on to the record, shades of Beefheart,
searing acid guitar, massive amounts of sustain and whammy
bar abuse, cosmic, mutant blues, free jazz from hell, warped
bleetings from outer space. There is real adventure, freedom
and excitement there. It's magnificent and for my money this
is the best record Kaiser's made. It's certainly the best *guitar*
record he's made.

Latterly Kaiser began to make cover versions of pop classics
with the Henry Kaiser Band, a group that 'plays at psychedelic
dance parties'. Some of these are consciously provocative or
outrageous. He 'dares' to do a version of 'Dark Star'. On the
other hand the band plays 'Anyone Who Had A Heart' or
'Ode To Billy Joe' which you would think were less than ideal
vehicles for experimental guitar playing. But no.

At first the idea of playing a killer guitar solo in 'Ode To
Billy Joe' sounds like a joke or a send up, but it isn't that.
Kaiser's solo is indeed wild, weird, wonderful and unexpected
but it's a solo that derives its power and meaning precisely
from the fact that it's played as part of 'Ode To Billy Joe'. The
solo is neither extraneous nor detachable.

Cover versions, however, are a pretty good tactic for getting
people to listen to strange guitar noise. An experimental guitarist can blast your eardrums with strangeness for forty-five
minutes or, like Kaiser, he can play a well-known pop tune
with five minutes of strangeness in it. The latter sounds like a
better way of getting through to people who don't want to

listen to forty-five minutes of strangeness. Which is to say that I imagine Henry Kaiser pulls in bigger audiences than Derek Bailey.

However, with a typical reluctance to be categorized, after *Hope You Like Our New Direction* (1991), which contains covers of 'Rock On' and 'Japan in a Dishpan', Kaiser has decided to stop doing cover versions. 'Oddly enough,' he writes, 'even though I have recorded eighty or ninety different record albums (which were ninety-five per cent original material) people seemed to be starting to type me as some kind of cover artist. So enough of that.'

Ah shucks, Henry, just when we starting to feel comfortable . . .

HENRY KAISER: SELECTED DISCOGRAPHY

Solo: *Protocol* (1979)
    Marrying For Money (1986)
    Devil In The Drain (1987)
    Those Who Know History Are Doomed To Repeat It (1988)
    Heart's Desire (1990)
    Hope You Like Our New Direction (1991)
With Eugene Chadbourne: *Volume 3: Guitar Trios* (1977)
With Fred Frith: *With Friends Like These* (1979)
    Who Needs Enemies? (1983)
With French-Frith-Kaiser-Thompson: *Live, Love, Larf & Loaf* (1987)
    Invisible Means (1990)
With Bailey et al: *The Science Set* (1981)

Photograph courtesy of MCA Records

B.B. KING

Born 16 February 1925, Itta Bena, Mississippi

There is a standard biographical myth about old, black, blues players. This states that they are born into mean, vicious poverty, discover the blues as a means of expression and escape, make a record or two, get ripped off by white record companies, die young and then years later get hailed as geniuses by the white world. Like all myths and many clichés there is some truth in it. This outline pretty much describes the life of Robert Johnson. But it fails to take into account B.B. King.

B.B., real name Riley, gets referred to these days as the elder statesman of the blues or, God help us, as an ambassador for the blues. Surely the blues is not such a distant country that it needs ambassadors, and aren't elder statesmen worthy old guys who play a ceremonial rather than an active role in the world? But inaccurate though these words may be, they are intended as compliments and are, I guess, designed to confirm B.B. King's heavyweight status and his essential dignity. Now, dignity is not always required in rock music (ask Iggy Pop), and it's certainly more likely to concern those like King who've made it out of the plantation rather than those like Brian Jones or Joe Strummer who've barely made it out of suburbia. King seems happy enough to accept respectability.

But above all else, B.B. King is not a diplomat or politician nor some living symbol of the blues, primarily he's a *trouper*. He goes out and sings and plays, and records, and he has an enormous respect for his audience. He has as much integrity as Miles Davis but you wouldn't find him playing with his back to the audience.

For King a gig's a gig. He'll play to black audiences or white audiences. He'll play at rock venues, at jazz festivals. He'll play in Russia. You name it. He'll play with black or white musicians, old lags or young hot shots. He'll play with Albert King or Joe Walsh, U2 or even Bart Simpson. (Though I'm not sure he'd go so far as to put himself in the hands of John Zorn the way Albert Collins did.)

One of the reasons he's so well known must simply be that he's played so much. At one time he was playing over 300 dates a year, and given that he's been playing the blues for over forty years that adds up to a lot of dates. It also adds up to a staggering number of guitar solos. how many times has he played 'Three O'Clock Blues'? Six thousand? Seven thousand? How does he manage to retain his enthusiasm? How does he prevent his guitar playing becoming merely perfunctory? How does he stop himself turning into Chuck Berry? These questions are unanswerable except by saying that his genius is precisely his ability to do just that.

What I assume this must mean is that when B.B. King comes to play one of his songs, be it 'Help The Poor' or 'Sweet Sixteen' or 'You Upset Me Baby' he can't be concerned with trying to play the definitive guitar solo for that song, since if he plays the definitive version tonight, by definition he won't be able to do the same thing tomorrow night. So each solo becomes one of many many thousands of solos that might be played in that song, and each solo must leave room for all those possible others.

Of course, one factor that must affect all this is that if he wasn't playing this particular twelve-bar blues he'd be playing some other twelve-bar blues. It's not as if he's going to stop playing 'Three O'Clock Blues' in favour of 'Court of the Crimson King'. Arguably it's the form, not the song or the player, that has the freshness.

In 'Lucille' where he tells the history of his guitar he says he thinks his guitar only wants to play the blues, but that's just fine by him. The blues is all he wants his guitar to play. And yet King is hardly a purist. In fact his career seems to have perfected the very fine balancing act between moving with the times and staying close to his roots. He is thought of as a classic not as a relic.

One's access to King and to his recordings has varied and will no doubt continue to vary with time. As I write, the English record shops are well stocked with all kinds of quality B.B. King albums. (In 1985 he made his fiftieth 'official' album.) It wasn't always like that. I can well remember a time when if you could find B.B. King at all you had to make do with some dubious *Best Of . . .* or *Greatest Hits . . .* album of no known pedigree.

And yet there is a certain charm to these undated, uncredited, anonymous collections. Undoubtedly the spirit of B.B. King is present. You put on one of these records. There's a badly recorded backing band with lots of horns. You know it might have been recorded anywhere between 1955 and 1980. You don't know who any of the musicians are. Sometimes you can't be absolutely sure whether it's recorded live or in the studio. But then the voice and especially the guitar of B.B. King cuts through all this vagueness and uncertainty, and it's wonderful. It's tempting to say his playing has a timeless quality and yet it seems to come out of the history of the blues rather than out of any high-fidelity state-of-the-art present. I prefer to hear my B.B. King a little muffled, a little dated.

His guitar tone changes somewhat from year to year and from record to record. Sometimes it can sound thin and reedy, other times it will sound rather harsh and distorted. I've always thought this had more to do with the accidents of the particular recording session than with King's desire to make changes. He is a player who relies on the notes to speak for themselves. He needs to be heard but beyond that the actual tone can vary and he wouldn't worry too much.

He talks about his guitar 'singing' and it's almost inevitable that we think of it as a voice. The fact that he never sings and plays at the same time means that the guitar lines often 'answer' his vocal lines. And certainly his guitar playing tends to be a melody line which sings over the backing in the way a singer does. It's never part of the rhythm section, never part of the music's basic sound.

It's hard to say what influence B.B. King has had on today's guitarists. Undoubtedly most of them respect him but I don't know how many, except the pastiche blues players, are influenced by him. And I certainly don't think many of them would want to emulate him. The idea of Steve Vai or Thurston Moore aged sixty and still wielding their axes is beyond human imagining.

There is a wonderful bit of stagecraft that I've seen King do at the end of his set. While the band plays some closing chords he holds out his plectrum as though to give it to a member of the audience as if it was some holy relic. Eventually someone takes it, at which point King reaches into his pocket and we see he has twenty or thirty others to give away. It's as though he's saying there's nothing special about that one relic. For him there'll always be another plectrum, another guitar solo, another version of 'The Thrill Is Gone'. Fortunately the thrill never is.

B.B. KING: SELECTED DISCOGRAPHY

Live At The Regale (1965)
His Best – The Electric B.B. King (1968)
Live at Cook County Jail (1971)
L.A. Midnight (1972)
The Best of B.B. King (1973)
Midnight Believer (1978)
Love Me Tender (1982)
Six Silver Strings (1985)

Photograph courtesy of Damage Management Ltd.

MARK KNOPFLER

Born 12 August 1949, London

In that tangle of social, political and technological upheaval that we refer to as 'the Sixties' rock music became, briefly, central to Anglo-American culture, particularly to the culture of the young. Pop music was no longer just entertainment, it was serious and important. We had all always known about the power of cheap music but in the sixties a Jimi Hendrix solo, a Beatles song, a Doors performance seemed suddenly to be the best way of discoursing about what was going on; about love, sex, violence, spirituality, Vietnam. Rock music had the power to address, encapsulate and change the world. Or so it appeared.

Perhaps it was always naïve to believe this, perhaps it was 'only rock and roll' the whole time, but few could have guessed that the subversive energies of rock would so quickly become so stable and so marketable. Of course, people will always write songs that have some social or political relevance, but throughout the seventies and eighties rock became more and more impotent and irrelevant. In 1969 it was crucial to our experience. Today it is background music, noises off, a sound-track.

Yet despite music's increasingly peripheral existence the flow both of musical hardware and software keeps on coming. Everybody 'needs' a good sound system these days, in their home, in their car, in their pocket in the form of the Walkman. This has nothing to do with a mass love of music. It has to do with the need for constant, undemanding aural stimulation. It

doesn't matter much what's played, so long as *something* is.
But people do have to buy fodder for their sound systems,
they have to make choices, and so they choose something
inoffensive, like Phil Collins or Fleetwood Mac or Chris Rea
or, indeed, Dire Straits. Dire Straits, I'm suggesting, make
records for people who don't actually like music very much.

Look, I can remember when people thought Dire Straits
were hip. I can remember when people thought they were
new wave. They weren't punks, of course, they didn't wear
bondage trousers and have 'no future' tattooed across their
foreheads, but they were young (ish), they were new, Mark
Knopfler had hair and looked sulky, and they made a sound
that was unlike the pop mainstream.

Now they are the mainstream, loved by millions, hated by
other millions, and either way, terminally unhip. But even
those who heartily despise Dire Straits and all their works have
a grudging respect for Knopfler's guitar playing.

There is a Platonic model of a Dire Straits song. It starts out
as a mid-tempo, soft-rock song, slightly portentous, slightly
Dylanish, with Knopfler putting in some bright, brisk guitar
fills. He sings a verse or two, then the band slows way down,
goes quiet, the keyboard player puts down some rippling,
grandiose classical-sounding chords and Knopfler plays a
moody, reflective, brilliant solo. This goes on for some time
until everything speeds up again and he plays a last galloping
set of guitar runs before it all ends.

I know I go on about guitar playing needing a context and
needing to grow out of the music, but many of us would
be quite happy to ditch the songs, the Dylanish words, the
grandiose piano chords, if we could somehow keep Knopfler's
guitar playing. Nobody wants to hear 'Tunnel of Love' or
'Romeo and Juliet' one more time, it's only the self-renewing
freshness of the guitar solos that make it all tolerable.

Dire Straits supposedly play Adult Oriented Rock, but often
it isn't rock at all. Sometimes it's silly pop tunes like 'Twisting
By The Pool' or 'Walk Of Life', sometimes it's a soft ballad
like 'Portobello Belle', sometimes it's a mawkish saga like
'Telegraph Road'. In concert these songs are given the steroid
treatment, pumped up, inflated, made muscle-bound. That

Knopfler can find something relevant to play in this context is not only endearing but amazing.

Some bands seem greater than the sum of their parts, but Dire Straits seem to be less than Mark Knopfler. He is more diverse, interesting and intelligent than his band, though it's completely his band and nobody else's. They're his songs, his guitar solos. The band is absolutely nothing without Knopfler yet Knopfler would still be something without the band.

Knopfler always sounds like himself; that light, thin, ringing tone; and it doesn't seem to matter much whether he's playing a Schechter Strat or a National Steel or a Steinberger, he's always unmistakeable. The sound is natural and clear, though in fact quite a lot of artifice goes into producing that naturalness. And, of course, he plucks the guitar strings with his fingers rather than with a plectrum, doesn't utilize distortion, can't hide behind noise. People tend to use words like tasteful, subtle, restrained, to describe his playing. I think this is only partly true. He isn't flashy the way Van Halen is flashy but he's not a shy little flower either. When he plays guitar he holds centre stage. The spotlight, the attention, the applause, is all for him. And he probably deserves it.

Dire Straits have sold I don't know how many millions of records by now and maybe one would be more tolerant of them if they were strugglers like the Sultans of Swing. That song sums up completely the joys of amateurism in music played for its own sake. That, of course, isn't what Dire Straits are up to, but that song remains one of their finest moments, not least because it completely defines Knopfler's guitar style. What else can you say in their favour? Well, there are a couple of great chords in the otherwise embarrassing 'Private Investigations' and 'Money For Nothing' contains a great guitar riff and a nice piece of characterization, though I'm never quite sure where Knopfler stands in relation to the character he's created in that song.

Knopfler doesn't need anyone's approval to feel good about himself. He's constantly in demand to shed some of his magic on other people's music. He's played with Dylan, Bryan Ferry, Kate and Anna McGarrigle, J.J. Cale. He's produced for acts as different as Tina Turner and Aztec Camera. Not all these collaborations appear strictly mercenary. And he writes film music and is very much the man you'd want in your all-star band for your next big charity gig. His playing, although distinctive, is pliable.

The album *Neck and Neck* made with Chet Atkins is, perhaps curiously, very satisfying. Knopfler shows a relaxed good humour that Dire Straits never gave much room for. On 'There'll Be Some Changes Made' he trades licks with Atkins and sounds as though he's been a country picker all his life. And on 'Tahitian Skies' the guitar playing is lilting and wistful without becoming sugary. This is, in almost every sense, good guitar playing, though it remains safe and unchallenging. You wouldn't mistake it for a Sonic Youth album.

Ultimately one can only object to Knopfler by wishing he was somebody else, somebody more adventurous, and one knows that's absurd. It would be nice if he took a few more risks and asked a few more questions. But he is a man of his times and, having earned however many million bucks it is, he might well say, 'Why should I?' The answer is, 'Because that's what truly great guitarists do.'

MARK KNOPFLER: SELECTED DISCOGRAPHY

With Dire Straits: *Dire Straits* (1978)
  Communiqué (1979)
  Making Movies (1980)
  Love Over Gold (1982)
  Alchemy (1984)
  Brothers In Arms (1985)
Film scores: *Local Hero* (1983)
  Cal (1984)
With Chet Atkins: *Neck and Neck* (1990)

Photograph courtesy of CBS Records

JOHN MCLAUGHLIN

Born 1942, Kirk Sendall, near Doncaster

There is a story that in his early druggy days when playing with the Graham Bond Organisation, John McLaughlin once fell off the stage in mid-solo. As he hit the ground he landed on his guitar and it let out a strange, complex chord. Fortunately Jack Bruce was in the band and he jotted down the notes in the chord for use in some future composition.

John McLaughlin is not a man popularly associated with drugginess. Rather we tend to associate him with very fast guitar playing and with spiritual aspirations. It is to his infinite credit that his music manages to combine both these elements, indeed makes them one and the same thing. When you hear McLaughlin playing faster and faster, reaching higher and higher on the fretboard, this is the sound of a man attempting to transcend, attempting to soar spiritually. It is rather different from what most guitarists do when they try to play very fast.

Too often McLaughlin seems to have thought spirituality involved dressing all in white, embracing things Indian and giving his music titles like 'Wings of Karma'. Nevertheless, any aesthetic that contains the idea that music is about something other than elaborate technique and ego gratification is very welcome, in whatever form.

Much of McLaughlin's very best work has been done with Miles Davis, not the most spiritual of guys you might think, on albums from *In A Silent Way* to *You're Under Arrest*. There's a wonderful guitar solo on 'Go Ahead John' on the album *Big Fun* (and big fun isn't a thing you'd expect from Davis *or*

McLaughlin) which has been electronically treated so that it sounds as though it's being played through a transistor radio which has a speaker that keeps cutting out. It's one of those rare occasions when McLaughlin plays sound rather than notes. And there's some exquisite snarling, bad-tempered guitar on the medley 'Gemini, Double Image' on *Live Evil*.

McLaughlin came to Davis's attention after playing with Tony Williams' Lifetime. I remember seeing Lifetime at the Sheffield City Hall round about 1970, and being part of a more or less stunned and uncomprehending audience. I guess we had probably expected something a little like Cream – after all, Jack Bruce was in the band. Instead the band came on and launched into a ten-minute opening number of quite terrifying sound and fury, very loud, played very fast and utterly alien. And when they finished that first piece there was silence and somebody said, 'What the fuck was that?' and one or two people clapped and then they were off again.

Well, times change, what seemed wild and alien in 1970 doesn't seem so wild today, and albums never captured the excitement and strangeness of Lifetime, and Tony Williams would insist on singing all over the place and ruining things. But on pieces like 'Vuelta Abajo' the whole band, and McLaughlin in particular just lets rip, and there have been many times in McLaughlin's career when you'd wish he would let rip a little more.

Personally I'm very fond of McLaughlin's work on *Escalator Over The Hill* where he plays in a quartet with Jack Bruce, Paul Motian and Carla Bley. On tracks like 'Rawalpindi Blues' he plays very fidgety, fuzzed, Eastern sounding repeated lines and riffs. The setting offers an ideal balance between structure and freedom which helps him to play at his best.

It was always easy to mock the Mahavishnu Orchestra for being show-offs, for being pretentious, for being founders of the much abused 'fusion'. But I think the Mahavishnu Orchestra are still listenable because of the high quality of the musicianship, because the music has a genuine stature and ambition, and because nobody before or since has sounded like that. And the sound they make is a very exciting one. On the album *Between Nothingness And Eternity*, which was recorded live in Central Park, they sound like a surprisingly raw, gutsy, hard-edged rock band and not at all the spiritual, jazz/rock poseurs that history tends to remember them as.

Somewhere along the line McLaughlin seems more or less to have abandoned his electric guitar. It's not clear whether he simply went off it or whether, more plausibly, he saw that the world had enough electric guitar players and that as a jazz-influenced acoustic guitarist he would be a bigger fish in a much smaller pond.

Consequently he seems to spend a lot of time perched on top of a stool playing with the likes of Larry Coryell, Al DiMeola and Paco DeLucia. Some would question the essential entertainment value of this stuff but it certainly has its fans. I was always more impressed by his acoustic work with Shakti. Pieces such as 'Face To Face' seem to me to fuse Western and Eastern music wholly successfully.

McLaughlin's note selection and his approach to the instrument remain consistent, and certainly unmistakable, whether he's playing electric or acoustic. However, when, for example, he's playing duets with the pianist Katia Labèque and his fingers swirl up to the strings' highest register and he's reduced to playing what amounts to a series of very fast clicks, you know that if he was playing an electric the sound would be screeching and soaring, and I for one sometimes think that might be preferable.

John McLaughlin Trio Live At The Royal Festival Hall shows him in excellent form. If speed is a metaphor for spiritual aspiration, then improvisation is an equally good metaphor for self-exploration, and this album is, in the best sense, exploratory. The music has a searching, restless quality, pushing ahead, unpredictable. 'Florianopolis' shows this splendidly.

However you rate John McLaughlin, you have to respect him for following his own star. The guy has integrity. You couldn't imagine him writing the theme music for *Miami Vice* the way one Mahavishnu Orchestra alumnus has. And if McLaughlin's individuality means there will be some years when he's very unfashionable, there's unlikely to be a time when he's not a contender.

JOHN MCLAUGHLIN: SELECTED DISCOGRAPHY

Solo: *Extrapolation* (1969)
  Devotion (1972)
  Electric Guitarist (1978)
With Lifetime: *Turn It Over* (1970)
With Miles Davis: *Bitches' Brew* (1969)
  In A Silent Way (1969)
  Jack Johnson (1971)
  Live Evil (1972)
  Big Fun (1974)
  You're Under Arrest (1985)
  Aura (1989)
With Mahavishnu Orchestra: *Inner Mounting Flame* (1972)
  Birds Of Fire (1973)
  Between Nothingness And Eternity (1973)
  Apocalypse (1974)
  Inner Worlds (1976)
With Jack Bruce: *Things We Like* (1970)
With Shakti: *Shakti* (1976)
  Natural Elements (1977)
With Al DiMeola and Paco DeLucia: *Passion, Grace And Fire* (1983)
With the Jazz Composers Orchestra: *Escalator Over The Hill* (1971)
John McLaughlin Trio: *Live At The Royal Festival Hall* (1989)

Photograph courtesy of Polydor

YNGWIE J. MALMSTEEN

Born 1963, Stockholm

What exactly goes on in Sweden? What are the social, economic and cultural forces that create on the one hand Abba and on the other Yngwie J. Malmsteen? How is it that the Swedish foursome had this instinctive flair for and understanding of Anglo-American pop music, while Yngwie J. doesn't seem to have a clue?

In 1984 Mike Varney of Shrapnel Records took Malmsteen away from his native Sweden and delivered him to America to make a solo album and then to form Alcatrazz. Interviews conducted with him at the time show him to be a confident but essentially likeable twenty year old; gifted, but not entirely certain in which direction he might be heading. Within a few years he had become some loud-mouthed egomaniac entirely convinced that his every musical utterance was of God-like grandeur. OK so there may be some Cassius Clay style 'I am the greatest' element about this, just a way of whipping up the crowd, but I'm not so sure. I suspect he really does believe he's Godlike and in this, as in much else, he's mistaken.

The most important thing to know about Malmsteen, argu-ably the only thing to know about Malmsteen, is that he plays his guitar fast, very, very fast, probably as fast as anyone does or ever has played. This in itself is fine. There is some excitement to be had in watching and hearing a guitarist play at an astonishing speed, the same kind of excitement as watching a dancer jump very high. There is a thrill in watching someone perform a feat that is technically very difficult. But simply being able to play guitar very fast doesn't make you a great guitarist any more than simply being able to jump very high makes you a great dancer (it might just make you a great high-jumper). Malmsteen has all the 'technique' that anyone could possibly want, yet he doesn't seem to have the faintest idea of what to do with it.

He plays classically-based licks on a highly overdriven Strat. This has been dismissed as Bach-rock and via a whole heap of imitators has become very familiar. But what on earth are these imitators imitating except fabulous dexterity?

Malmsteen, of course, plays heavy metal, but even then he doesn't seem to have a particularly thorough understanding of the form. His writing abilities don't amount to much and his choice of other people's material has been unexciting. There are those, like Megadeth, who are at least wringing some vestige of originality out of heavy metal, but Malmsteen doesn't seem to want to do that. He just wants to play very, very fast.

He would tell you that his influences are Paganini, Beethoven, Blackmore and Hendrix. These aren't such a bad bunch of people to be influenced by, but what it means in practice is that he runs round the stage playing manically (like Paganini) then plays the *duh duh duh DUH!* bit from Beethoven's fifth, then some riffs (like Blackmore) and then he goes into a version of 'Spanish Castle Magic'. Not only is this a misunderstanding of what 'influences' are about, it seems to be a misunderstanding of what music is about.

Malmsteen's playing is not what anyone, except him, would call varied. When you've heard some of it you've pretty much heard it all. But you can hear the quintessential Malmsteen on the album *Trial By Fire*. It's recorded live in Leningrad and the cover shows Malmsteen burning his guitar (now why didn't *I* think of that). On the second side he plays a piece called 'Spasebo Blues' which must surely be the best ever recorded example of how not to play the blues. It crams the absolute maximum number of notes and the absolute minimum of feeling into its minute and a half. Then (oh no) he starts playing 'Air On A G-string', which rapidly becomes 'Für Elise' and then we're back with loads of wailing guitar and a million notes a minute.

In live performance he doesn't so much play 'solos' as play one continuous lead-guitar break. Occasionally the rest of the band may drop out so that he's playing alone, but the notion of shaping or building a solo seems pretty alien to him, and the quantity of notes is relentless and more or less constant. To say that this lacks light and shade is probably to miss the point.

His stage act does, however, contain one truly amazing noise. He kneels down at the front of the stage and rubs his guitar along the foldback speakers (so far so predictable) but then he twiddles some kind of device that he has down there and this noise starts: a sound like half a dozen jet fighters taking off inside the hall, and it builds and builds until it sounds as though the jets are taking off inside your head. It is a genuine mindblower (and ear-damager) but it lasts a very short time in the general run of things.

Malmsteen does indeed do amazing things on guitar. *You* try playing like that. It's not easy, in fact at times it seems scarcely believable. And undoubtedly he plays with no shortage of fire and zest. His playing isn't terrible and yet his music is. It never seems to have crossed his mind that the 'best' playing isn't necessarily the loudest and the fastest. His skill is enormous, and yet he is a prime, perhaps an ultimate example of someone whose talent is utterly devoid of a critical sense.

Perhaps finally Malmsteen ought to be taken as some kind of terrible warning. He ought to warn us a) that speed kills (although Alvin Lee already told us that) and b) that intelligence is as useful to a guitar player as it is to anyone else. Wit, lightness, style and taste are handy too, but intelligence is a start. Malmsteen has none of the above. Malmsteen, it seems to me, is the world's worst major guitarist, and a living example of just how good you can be without being any good at all.

YNGWIE J. MALMSTEEN: SELECTED DISCOGRAPHY

Solo or as band leader: *Steeler* (1983)
  Rising Force (1984)
  Odyssey (1988)
  Trial By Fire (1989)
  Eclipse (1990)
With Alcatrazz: *No Parole From Rock 'n' Roll* (1983)
  Live Sentence (1984)

Photograph by Simon Fowler
Courtesy of Parlophone

BRIAN MAY

Born 19 July 1947, Hampton, Middlesex

Queen are one of those bands that reduce writers to quoting statistics. In 1979 (1979 mind you) they were in *The Guinness Book of Records* for earning salaries of three-quarters of a million pounds each. In São Paulo, Brazil, they performed in front of a crowd of 131,000 people, the biggest ever paying audience at a rock concert. The record company Hollywood has just bought the US rights to Queen's back catalogue for a rumoured ten million dollars. They're one of the most successful groups ever in terms of ticket and record sales. The international public loves them, but not the critics. If you needed a good press in order to be successful then Queen would still be rehearsing in a church hall. But Queen have never received or looked for approval, and to that extent they find themselves today almost beyond criticism.

And Brian May is the guitarist in this phenomenally successful band; yet his guitar playing isn't much responsible for that success. Fans of Queen love the self-parody, the campness, the grandiloquence, the operatic qualities of the band. They're not there for the guitar break, which is a shame because May is the lead instrumentalist (in live performance more than on record) and because he's actually pretty good.

Statistics don't help to describe Brian May, but a certain number of 'amazing facts' do. He still plays his first guitar, a guitar he built himself with his Dad's help, out of an old wooden fireplace, with buttons used as pearl markers and a knitting needle for a tremelo arm. He uses a coin instead of a plectrum. On stage he uses old Vox AC 30s, banks of them, as many as nine at a time, and there was a time when he had teams of roadies scouring the country for spares. He has also, most amazing of all, kept the same haircut for the best part of twenty years.

Queen came into being on the fag-end of glam rock. You feel that Freddy Mercury would have been glam regardless of the musical fashions of the time, whereas May always looked highly uncomfortable (not to say highly silly) in his silvery capes, and tunics with bell-bottomed sleeves. By the time of *Greatest Hits* he can be seen on the album cover wearing a suit and tie and looking far more at home.

Brian May's greatest skill is that his solos are always gloriously appropriate to the songs in which they appear. Imagine Freddy Mercury turns up one day with a new song, called 'Bicycle Race', and tells you, his lead guitarist, that he wants a guitar solo for it; I mean, how many guitarists would come up with something even slightly relevant? It's not the sort of song most rock guitarists are used to dealing with. But May manages to come up with a solo that fits perfectly. Likewise, many years later on 'I'm Going Slightly Mad' from the album *Innuendo* he plays a great solo that sounds, well . . . slightly mad. What more could anyone ask for? Nevertheless, despite their undeniable appropriateness, would anyone, apart from guitar addicts, miss them if they weren't there?

His playing has certainly needed to be versatile over the years. It has had to encompass the rockabilly of 'Crazy Little Thing Called Love' at one end, and the football chants of 'We Will Rock You' at the other. This latter has a lovely guitar overlay at the end. Yet there is a distinctive Brian May tone and I don't think it's being too fanciful to say it contains important similarities to Freddie Mercury's voice. The guitar tone is thick yet strident, piercing, on the grand scale, heavy, powerful yet sometimes lacking character. Just like Mercury's singing. It can be a bit over the top, too lush, too clever for its own good. It can somehow appear to be in inverted commas. But this makes him a perfect foil and partner for Mercury. He is profoundly the right man for the job. When Jimi Hendrix plays 'Star Spangled Banner' it is startling, thrilling and dangerous. When Brian May plays 'God Save The Queen' it's a kitsch joke. But that isn't exactly a criticism. May obviously intends it as a kitsch joke, that's the kind of guitar playing that fits with the rest of Queen's music, and he succeeds entirely in doing what he sets out to do.

Of course, May isn't only a soloist. On 'We Are The Champions' his soaring, ascending guitar makes the song build and build. There is a wonderful, luminous guitar sound that gives life to 'A Kind Of Magic'. In more recent times the thick, chewy, Latin-style solo on 'Rain Must Fall' from the album *The Miracle* is a great, uplifting piece of music.

But there are times when May's guitar playing can seem surplus to requirements. His solo on 'Play The Game' is like a thick, sweet sauce poured on top of a dessert that's already plenty sweet enough. While on 'Sweet Lady' from *A Night At The Opera* he is allowed a real guitar work out but sounds decidedly short of ideas.

I guess 'Bohemian Rhapsody' is still the song that sums up Queen for most people. There is in fact no shortage of guitar playing on that song, but that's not what anybody remembers about 'Bohemian Rhapsody'. You remember the layer upon layer of harmony vocals, the moody, rippling piano, and above all Mercury's engagingly ludicrous performance. I wonder how Brian May feels about that. I wonder if he even realizes.

BRIAN MAY: SELECTED DISCOGRAPHY

With Queen: *Queen* (1973)
Queen II (1974)
Sheer Heart Attack (1974)
A Night At The Opera (1975)
A Day At The Races (1976)
News Of The World (1977)
Jazz (1978)
Live Killers (1979)
The Game (1980)
Flash Gordon (1980)
Hot Space (1982)
The Works (1984)

A Kind Of Magic (1986)
Live Magic (1986)
The Miracle (1989)
Innuendo (1991)
With Eddie Van Halen: *Star Fleet Project* (1983)

Photograph by George Bodnar
Courtesy of Virgin Records

GARY MOORE

Born 1953, Belfast

Gary Moore is one of those guitarists that half the world thinks is wildly underrated and the other half thinks is wildly over-rated. I find I move from one camp to the other depending on who I'm talking to. To those who don't rate him I wax lyrical about his refreshing lack of complication and pretention, about his directness. To those who say he's one of the greats I find myself protesting that his playing is a bit dull and feeble-minded.

This is to say that his virtues and his faults are essentially the same. He is a traditionalist. He plays good old-fashioned hard rock, skilfully but without any frills. He gets good guitar sounds but they're never surprising or out of control. He never makes any totally duff music and he never takes any big risks. Depending on your point of view all the above may be a good or a bad thing. He's younger than Bill Frisell or Adrian Belew but he sounds as though he belongs to a much older school.

This has a lot to do with the fact that he started so young. He was only sixteen when he joined Skid Row in 1970, and over the years he's made a lot of albums. He's played jazz rock with Colosseum, had a love/hate on/off relationship with Thin Lizzy, formed G-force, had various versions of the Gary Moore Band, had a top-ten hit with 'Parisienne Walkways', had a dozen or more albums under his own name, and most recently won wide exposure and acclaim for *Still Got The Blues*, an album of blues songs where he's joined by Albert King and Albert Collins. The guy is obviously no mug. He can play. Yet somehow he's always lacked that little bit of magic or glamour that makes a star. This may be partly an image problem, but it's as true of his guitar playing as it is of his looks.

In some ways he's had to work quite hard to arrive at his characteristic uncomplicated directness. The 1973 album *Grinding Stone* contains the massively ill-conceived track called 'Spirit' (you feel he might have called it 'The Spirit Suite', it's that kind of number). It contains about seventeen minutes of guitar playing: riffs, dreamy noises, a Carlos Santana impersonation and a long, building 'emotional' solo where he simply tries too hard. It's ambitious, and ambition isn't to be sneered at, but even in 1973 if you wanted to hear a seventeen-minute guitar track you'd still have dug out 'Voodoo Chile' or 'Spoonful', wouldn't you?

Likewise the 1987 album *Wild Frontier* is a brave enough attempt to combine Celtic folk sounds with heavy guitar rock. Given his background he certainly has every 'right' to attempt this, but parts of it do sound like a rip off of Big Country, though there's no doubt he's a better guitarist than Stuart Adamson or Bruce Watson, and the soloing on 'Over The Hills and Far Away' is superb. Nevertheless, he still sounds more at home with 'Friday On My Mind' than with songs about the coming of the soldiers and the joys of the Wicklow Mountains.

G-Force by contrast were a real, no frills hard working rock band, who didn't aim too high and in one sense succeeded totally. 'White Knuckles' and 'Because Of You' from their 1980 eponymous debut album contains some undeniably lively guitar playing. It's not sophisticated and it's certainly not arty, but guitar playing doesn't have to be.

G-Force always sounded as though they'd be a great band to see after five pints of lager, though the point might be lost if you'd only had a couple of spritzers. *Live At The Marquee*, one of several repackagings of live Gary Moore material, is an album on which you can hear the sweat, the heat, the lack of ventilation, and Moore plays some very hot guitar, for instance on 'Run To Your Mama'.

Moore is one of those guitarists who, in live performance, turns sweating into an artform. He is also a face-puller of international class. And yet there's something not quite convincing about it. Watching Moore on stage you feel that every grimace, every face-pull, almost every bead of sweat, has been rather carefully choreographed. The guitar solos too sound as though they're the result of very careful planning rather than of real fire or passion. You feel that Moore could, and very probably does, produce the same act move for move and note for note every night. This isn't a complete condemnation, Julian Bream doesn't improvise a completely different set every night either, but then Julian Bream isn't trying to come on as a guitar hero. Moore looks as though he is. It's a good act, but it *is* an act rather than the real thing.

Now that *Still Got The Blues* has been a considerable success it's easy to say that the blues was an obvious direction for Gary Moore to move in. Certainly the uncomplicated virtues of the form must have appealed to him. On the other hand, the moment you start playing the blues you inevitably stand to be compared with some formidable players, and you might well feel that those comparisons wouldn't work to Moore's advantage.

I feel that Moore just about gets away with it. His playing is strong and powerful, well within the genre and yet not completely predictable. The power sounds as though it comes courtesy of his guitar and amp set-up as much as from any burning in his soul and it's interesting how overcooked his sound is compared with that of the older blues players Collins and King. Nevertheless, he does have a genuine feel for the blues and the guitar playing on 'Texas Strut' and 'King Of The Blues' is of a quality that isn't to be denied.

Longevity *is* worth something in guitar players. Still to be making records and still to have an appetite for guitar solos after twenty odd years suggests he must be doing something right. And if Moore has never been flavour of the month that very unfashionableness means that he is unlikely ever to be written off as last year's model.

GARY MOORE: SELECTED DISCOGRAPHY

Solo or as band leader: *Grinding Stone* (1973)
  Back On The Streets (1978)

Corridors Of Power (1982)
Live At The Marquee (1983)
Victims Of The Future (1984)
We Want Moore (1984)
Run For Cover (1985)
Rockin'' Every Night (1986)
Wild Frontier (1987)
After The War (1989)
Still Got The Blues (1990)
With Skid Row: *Skid Row* (1970)
Thirty-Four Hours (1971)
With Colosseum: *Strange New Flesh* (1976)
Electric Savage (1977)
War Dance (1977)
With Thin Lizzy: *Black Rose* (1979)
With G-Force: *G-Force* (1980)

Thurston Moore (left) & Lee Ranaldo
Photograph by Michael Lavine
Courtesy of David Geffen Company

THURSTON MOORE

Born 1958, Boca Raton, Florida

& LEE RANALDO

Born 1956, New York City

Twin lead guitarists aren't exactly a new thing. Sometimes they take it in turns, like Tom Verlaine and Richard Lloyd. Sometimes they both play at the same time, like Andy Powell and Ted Turner of Wishbone Ash. Although Thurston Moore and Lee Ranaldo have been known to play and make records separately, within the context of Sonic Youth their playing seems completely inseparable. It is the interplay of the two guitarists that is at the heart of their music, and even though the guitars are the lead instruments in Sonic Youth, neither Moore nor Ranaldo would dream of doing anything so conventional, so 'straight' as 'taking a solo'.

Sonic Youth come out of an early eighties' New York, postpunk, noise-making scene. You can hear elements of the Velvet Underground, of Television, even of the Crass in some of their music. They know their Patti Smith and their Iggy Pop. They collaborate with the likes of Lydia Lunch, Glenn Branca and Chuck D. They know their pop culture. They may not be intellectuals, in fact they'd probably spit on intellectuals, but they're still pretty damn smart.

The guitars of Moore and Ranaldo roar and screech and howl. There are crackles and crashes. Sometimes the guitars are being thrashed, sometimes simply abused. Strings are hit, scrubbed, scraped. Feedback is used extensively. Sometimes the noises they make are tortured and strangulated, but at others they ripple and chime. There is a formidable level of attack, a scorched-earth policy that can result in sounds like *musique concrète* or industrial noise. But the music of Sonic Youth can also be extraordinarily subtle. Sometimes they deal in long, spacious mood pieces. Often the guitars are tuned to strange, unsettling open chords that clang and jangle against each other. Often there is a melancholy, dying fall to their music.

Moore and Ranaldo's methods are consciously low-tech. They're not averse to a bit of fuzz and distortion, but their attempt to find new guitar sounds has nothing to do with the latest effects racks or signal processors. Moore says that some of the guitars they used in their early days were so hopeless they'd only be good for playing one kind of chord or making one kind of sound, so that one thing became the basis of a song. And part of the attraction is that Moore and Ranaldo, in not wanting to sound like anybody else, aren't afraid of sounding thin or weak or indistinct. Theirs is the sound of cheap, battered guitars being wrenched into articulacy. It is not the sound of classic Guilds or Gibsons being coaxed into delicate life. They use any kind of unorthodoxy that suits them and yet you feel that they're involved in some serious enterprise, not just messing about.

Sonic Youth do not make 'good time' music. It's urgent and insistent but it's not something you put on your stereo when you need to cheer yourself up. Their lyrics show a fine unhealthy obsession with drugs, weird sex, death and violence. So, you might say, do the lyrics of many a callow band who haven't got anything real to write about. But even if Sonic Youth remain delinquent, they escape being juvenile. What saves them is a radical sensibility and the fact that they are lavishly endowed with scepticism about the ways and means of popular music. They really don't sound as though they want to be the next Rolling Stones.

It's not always easy to tell whether Sonic Youth are post-modernists or piss-takers, and perhaps at some point these become the same thing. Certainly they are involved in some kind of 'interrogation' of the meanings and importance of rock, and since they're a two-guitar, bass and drum band this involves an interrogation of guitar playing.

The Whitey Album, for example, is one of those 'spin the radio dial' records and as you move from station to station you hear wild guitar screeching, spacey textures, some rap, some Hendrix samples, some very low-grade demos, some dodgy recited prose-poetry, recorded telephone calls, and all of it somehow a parody of a Madonna album. Even on their earliest records Moore and Ranaldo were extracting extraordinary noises from their guitars. 'Protect Me You' from the album *Confusion Is Sex* is full of all sorts of exciting and unusual sounds, off-beat Chinese guitar lines, heavy, trembling bass chords. 'Ghost Bitch' from the album *Bad Moon Rising* begins with wailing, highly eloquent feedback, moves via some crashing chords until a more foghorn-like feedback is interspersed with a sound like sheets of metal being dropped from a great height, then there are spoken vocals, some heavy drumming and it all ends in a storm of thin guitar roaring.

But what made those early albums such hard listening was the terrible, terrible, singing. It is extraordinary how much harder this makes it to appreciate the guitar playing. The early albums were fascinating failures but with *Daydream Nation* not only did they discover how to sing, they created a major work.

Above all, that double album is a startling demonstration of how to tear up the rule book of guitar playing and still produce great guitar music. In some ways it is more conventional than earlier work. The songs are more song-like. The sound is more that of a rock band than of hardcore experimentalists. Nevertheless it takes enormous risks and is utterly radical.

I think it has the status of something like *Trout Mask Replica*, a sprawling masterpiece that is utterly itself, difficult and yet unassailable, the end of the line in its particular direction. It contains the highly ambitious 'Kissability Trilogy' which lasts for the whole of side four, and contains so many ideas, so much invention, so many guitar sounds, textures and colours that it's exhausting to listen to. But my favourite piece from the album is 'Sprawl'. It begins like an 'ordinary' pop song with a verse and a chorus, but soon the two guitars start interweaving and reacting to each other. Sometimes it's quite rock and roll, sometimes it's edgy and atonal. There's brightness and an alertness but also the sound of doomy forboding. It is loose, it meanders and stretches out and yet it is beautifully shaped, and it ends in a long rippling, dying coda, thin, sad rhythm guitar arpeggios with bassy feedback rolling behind them. Moore and Ranaldo deserve a place in rock and roll heaven for that piece alone.

Once in rock and roll heaven they might, of course, encounter Karen Carpenter whom they commemorated on their next album *Goo* on the track 'Tunic (Song For Karen)'. It is delightfully sick and yet contains a certain respect and affection for her.

Goo was Sonic Youth's first album on a major record label (Geffen) but all fears of a sell out seem to have been satisfactorily allayed. It isn't as strong an album as *Daydream Nation* but I think that's an album you can only make once in a career, if you're very lucky. Moore and Ranaldo might argue, of course, that luck had nothing to do with it.

THURSTON MOORE AND LEE RANALDO: SELECTED DISCOGRAPHY

With Sonic Youth: *Confusion Is Sex* (1983)
  Bad Moon Rising (1985)
  Evol (1986)
  Sister (1987)
  Daydream Nation (1988)
  Goo (1990)
  Dirty Boots (1991)
Lee Ranaldo Solo: *From Here → Eternity* (1986)

Photograph courtesy of Atlantic Records

JIMMY PAGE

Born 9 January 1944, Heston, London

Jimmy Page's career and our estimation of his guitar playing is inextricably linked to the success of Led Zeppelin. As I write, Led Zeppelin, after receiving at least a decade of critical scorn, seem suddenly and rather inexplicably to be fashionable again. Fashion is always a hard thing to fathom, but one thing we know for sure; fashions don't last.

To observe the unfolding career of Led Zeppelin was like watching a balloon inflate, getting bigger and bigger, stretched thinner and thinner, puffed up by hot air. Their music became increasingly grandiose and increasingly insubstantial. Page has to take some responsibility for that.

His history pre-Led Zeppelin as a session man and member of the Yardbirds has been told often enough not to need much repeating here; suffice it to say that the guitar part he plays on Joe Cocker's 'With A Little Help From My Friends' displays a passion and an appropriateness that he often found difficult to achieve with Led Zeppelin.

Nobody can reasonably expect guitar playing to be a job for life, but in 1969, the year of the Joe Cocker record, Page was at his peak. He was hot. It was the year of *Led Zeppelin* and *Led Zeppelin II*, and he might have been forgiven for thinking he had a few good years ahead of him. He hadn't. Even if you consider 'Stairway To Heaven' to be a good song (and I consider it to be an abomination) you'll find yourself saying that Page was all washed up by 1972. Even if you find 'Kashmir' bearable (I don't) you'll say he was all washed up by 1976. But a perfectly coherent case can be made out that he was all washed up by the end of 1969.

So what does Jimmy Page do with the rest of his life? Well, given that he owns Aleister Crowley's old house and given his well-publicized taste for whips in the bedroom, we might hazard a guess. It sounds like every suburbanite *News Of The World* reader's idea of being a rock star, but then Led Zeppelin were every suburbanite *News of The World* reader's idea of a rock band.

Zeppelin played three kinds of song. There were the white cock-rock anthems. There were the 'Tolkien' songs about castles and all that. And there were the garbled blues songs.

Let's take these in reverse order. Page and Plant would like you to believe they had a real feel and respect for the blues, but they never convinced anyone of this. They had obviously listened to the music, Page had learned all the riffs, chord changes and blues runs, Plant had learned the words and the mannerisms. Yet they behaved as though all the riffs, chords, runs and lyrics to blues songs were somehow interchangeable. Thus their stage act always featured long, meandering 'blues' songs like 'How Many More Times?' where they could shove in any old blues mannerism that came to hand. A Howlin' Wolf riff, a line from Robert Johnson, a quotation from 'Killing Floor' were all one and the same. The objection isn't that they stole from the blues, because *everyone* steals from the blues. The objection is that they made such little use of what they stole. The blues influence remained a decoration, a badge. They wore the medal without having been in the campaign. Later with 'Rock 'n' Roll' and 'Candystore Rock' they showed they could garble other genres too.

The 'Tolkien' songs reach their apotheosis with 'Stairway to Heaven', but that strain is present as far back as 'What Is And What Should Never Be'. I suppose 'Stairway' might, just might, be tolerable if it weren't for the ludicrous lyrics and Plant's fey vocals; but alas it isn't an instrumental. Sure, Page's guitar sounds nice enough and he didn't personally write those terrible words but his playing can't be separated from the whole concept. It's a song that contains just about everything that was wrong with popular music in the seventies. It is bogus, soft, self-important, meaningless, not very bright . . .

But this too is well-trodden ground. No wonder Zeppelin turned into hate figures for punk. But you didn't have to be a punk to hate them.

Later we were to have 'Kashmir', all Arabic influences and swirling riffs. Again, borrowing from another form of music is fair enough, but it sounds like tourism. It's a soundtrack for a Bob Hope and Bing Crosby movie.

Led Zeppelin's music became increasingly elaborate and increasingly multi-instrumental as it went on. Page's guitar became less important. This might seem inevitable, that a rock band's musical maturity will inevitably take them away from a raw guitar sound (though I wouldn't try telling this to Keith Richards). Yes, there would always be a heavy burden on the guitar player in a band consisting of a power trio and a singer who only rarely played any sort of musical instrument, and when he did it was only a harmonica. But Page shed the burden by loading ever more instruments on to John Paul Jones. This was a mistake. Page's guitar playing was always the most interesting thing about Led Zeppelin, and at this distance it looks like the *only* interesting thing.

And so we come to the cock-rock. It gives me no great pleasure to say this, but Zeppelin were at their best as a guitar riff band who sang about sex with an undeniable urgency. Page's best playing is on 'Whole Lotta Love', 'Communication Breakdown' or 'Heartbreaker'. It is direct and exciting, even if not politically correct, and directness and excitement weren't always present on Led Zeppelin records.

The first two albums are full of wonderfully original and intelligent guitar playing, that takes risks and doesn't get lost in all that Led Zeppelin pomp. 'Whole Lotta Love' remains radical even today; those guitar swoops, the spacey middle section with the treated vocals and weird guitar noise still sounds experimental and defiantly uncommercial. It isn't the simple heavy metal riff that it's remembered as. Alas it's not a very big step from this sort of thing to the more familiar posing, preening and acting like rock royalty that Led Zeppelin became famous for. And, of course, the song shows how much potential there is for long guitar rambles and the sound of Robert Plant faking orgasms. The feeling nevertheless remains that it might all have been very different and so much more interesting.

Apart from remastering some Led Zeppelin tracks, Page's most recent appearance was on his 1988 solo album *Outrider*. This album isn't so much bad as irrelevant. The album features Jason Bonham, Chris Farlow and (on one track) Robert Plant. There are riff-based songs, heavy instrumentals, some blues work-outs, thick layers of guitar texture and some quite tasty noises. It's competent but weary and it sounds old-fashioned in a way that the best early Zeppelin still doesn't. And it manages somehow to sound like a not very exciting garage band that's been too heavily influenced by Led Zeppelin. The opening song is called 'Wasting My Time'. Not only yours Jimmy, not only yours.

JIMMY PAGE: SELECTED DISCOGRAPHY

With Led Zeppelin: *Led Zeppelin* (1969)
  Led Zeppelin II (1969)
  Led Zeppelin III (1970)
  Untitled (known as 'the Runes album') (1971)
  Houses Of The Holy (1973)
  Physical Graffiti (1975)
  Presence (1976)
  The Song Remains The Same (1976)
  In Through The Out Door (1979)
Solo: *Outrider* (1988)
Film Soundtrack: *Death Wish II* (1982)
With The Firm: *The Firm* (1985)
  The Firm Means Business (1986)
With the Honeydrippers: *The Honeydrippers Volume 1* (1984)

Photograph courtesy of Epic Records

VERNON REID

Born 1959, London, raised Brooklyn

If Robert Cray isn't the young black guitarist the world is waiting for, Vernon Reid just possibly is. He is a guitarist of great gifts, knows his music and his history, but whereas Cray is content to be part of a blues tradition, Reid's tradition is that of radicalism. He knows his B.B. King, but he also knows his John Coltrane and his Eric Dolphy. He knows too, and indeed has played with, Public Enemy. The sense of anger and need for confrontation that permeates much rap music is not so very alien to Reid, nor to his band Living Colour.

In 1979 Reid began to play with the Decoding Society and stayed with them for five years until the formation of Living Colour. But throughout his time with them he was moonlighting with the hippest of the New York avant-garde: Defunkt, Bill Frisell, inevitably with John Zorn.

Reid does not make a pretty noise with his guitar. Mellifluous is not a word that springs to mind. Those wanting to hear just how unholy a noise he can make should listen to 'Metamorfosi' on Zorn's *The Big Gundown*, although he's given plenty of help with the unholiness, not least from Diamanda Galas, a woman whose singing would certainly form part of my definition of Hell.

Living Colour are essentially a hard rock band, at times very hard indeed. It took a lot of time for them to get signed to a label, supposedly because they were black. According to the record companies the black audience didn't want to hear hard rock, and the white audience who did want to hear hard rock didn't want it to be played by a bunch of black dudes.

This is the kind of thing that Reid obviously spends a lot of time thinking about. His songs address problems of race and colour. He's part of the Black Rock Coalition. And there is a much-told anecdote about his being a guest at a guitar trade fair where he was sharing a hotel room with a white heavy metal guitarist who, when Reid entered the room, assumed he'd come to clean it.

Reid seems to be not averse to becoming a guitar hero, but it's refreshing to find he has other things on his mind too. Living Colour address real social and political issues and they do it with a great more style and intelligence than the likes of Sting; nevertheless, sometimes it feels like they're working down a list of issues. 'We've done housing and we've done the white appropriation of black music. Now we'd better do a song about safe sex.'

The words to 'Funny Vibe' for instance deal with the casual everyday prejudice experienced by black people, which is in itself a very interesting issue, but the track as a whole is just a chance for Reid to let rip on guitar.

If there is one song that announced Reid's existence to the world it's 'Cult of Personality' from *Vivid*. The premise of the song, that Stalin, Kennedy, Gandhi and Mussolini are all personalities of the same status, seems to me, at best, absurd; but Reid's guitar playing is pretty serious. First there's a fast, grinding, guitar riff that is extremely catchy, and then there's a guitar solo. Oh my, there *is* a guitar solo, and it's magnificent. There are some guitar solos which are spare and elegant, where every note is planned and perfect. This is not Vernon Reid's way with a solo. Some guitarists think less is more. Reid isn't one of them. The solo on 'Cult Of Personality', recorded in one take apparently, is breathtakingly excessive. He goes completely for broke, spraying notes around at dazzling speed like there's no tomorrow. It's wild, noisy, abandoned. It feels reckless, thrown away, uncontrolled, but I'm not entirely sure that it is.

In a recent interview Reid talked about his guitar playing on the song 'This Is The Life'. He said, 'In the solo, the H3000 harmonizes the line with a fourth and I'm spelling out a B maj

7^b5 structure which works really well against the D^b7. I wanted to work within the dominant chord without playing pentatonic scales . . . Instead, I worked with diminished figures.'

Now, this is a conversation that I think you wouldn't have been able to have with Stan Webb or Ted Nugent. The good old boys knew their licks. These young tyros know their scales.

This opens up quite an interesting can of worms. Does knowing your Lydian from your Phrygian actually make you a better guitarist? Does it matter whether or not you know what you're doing? Might not Vernon Reid have played that same solo 'by instinct' even if he didn't know any music theory? Does his theoretical expertise make it a better piece of music? I think the answer has to be, no, it's not a better solo simply *because* he knows the theory, but if the theory helps him to come up with great guitar solos (and it seems to), then who's going to knock it? Certainly at his wildest he sounds as though he's ignoring scales, keys, everything and reaching for some abstract purity of sound. But I suppose there will be those who are reassured that he 'knows what he's doing'.

Reid has been compared with Hendrix and such comparisons are not only odious, they're downright silly. However, there is at least one thing he has in common with Hendrix, and that's the way that, at its best, his playing is a sort of conduit through which passes a whole history of black music and black people. African music is there on 'Solace Of You'. His rhythm playing is alive with James Brown funk, and there's masses of soul and blues, but there's also lots of new high-tech flash like on 'Information Overload'. Yet these aren't merely quotations or references, they're integrated. And when, once in a while, he puts all this together, like on the album version of 'Love Rears Its Ugly Head' the effect is brilliant.

Reid is skilled but he's not always subtle. He likes to thrash and shred. Some of his riffs and chord progressions sound as bone-headed as the most bone-headed heavy rock band. At times listening to Living Colour is like being hit over the skull with a brick, and the fact that the guy hitting you is a skilled craftsman doesn't necessarily make it any pleasanter. Now you could say this is the sound of young, angry, black America expressing its rage. But why does it sometimes sound so much like white, heavy metal America expressing its adolescent angst?

VERNON REID: SELECTED DISCOGRAPHY

With Living Colour: *Vivid* (1988)
   Time's Up (1990)
With John Zorn: *The Big Gundown* (1986)
With Bill Frisell: *Smash and Scatteration* (1985)
With Ronald Shannon Jackson: *Street Priest* (1981)
   Taboo (1991)

Photograph courtesy of Andrew Pothecary

MARC RIBOT

Born 1955

If Marc Ribot didn't exist Tom Waits would very probably have had to invent him. Ribot's skewed, chunky, metallic guitar is the living embodiment of that 'scrapyard orchestra' sound that features on Waits' late albums.

A common response on hearing Marc Ribot play for the first time might be, 'Is it really meant to sound like that?' He sounds a little out of tune, out of step with the rest of the band, if not the whole world. The guitar tone is not one we're accustomed to hearing, neither jazz nor rock, nor anything else you can easily put a name to.

On 'Hang On St Christopher' from *Frank's Wild Years* Ribot plays a floppy, spare, outrageous solo, that doesn't take itself seriously, that consists of almost-but-not-quite bum notes. He contributes skewed, twisted guitar to 'Clap Hands' from *Rain Dogs*, weird, twangy texture to the title track of that album, and his guitar is at the heart of the sound Waits obtains on the live *Big Time*.

There aren't many guitarists who play like Ribot, yet I think his specialness is that of a maverick rather than of a total original. His influences are unusual but he wears them on his sleeve. It's the way he combines them that's startling.

Sometimes he plays like Django Reinhardt, a style which he then subverts to a greater or lesser extent depending on the context. Sometimes he plays hard soul chords, a legacy from a stint with the Real Tones who backed acts like Carla and Rufus Thomas and Chuck Berry. The driving fierceness of his

rhythm playing comes out particularly strongly in live performance. He attacks the guitar like no jazz player ever did. His
solos seem to start from a jazzy premise but soon subside, very
satisfyingly into other, weirder zones. They always occupy that
territory between being all wrong and so wrong they're dead
right. Arto Lindsay's cover notes for *Rootless Cosmopolitans* say
that 'his studies with Haitian classical guitarist and composer
Frantz Cassius' are an important influence. Ribot is happy to
use the old free jazz technique of 'prepared guitar', putting
alligator clips on his strings and then bashing them with a
house key rather than a plectrum. In solo performances he's
been known to alternate lumps of Hot Club jazz with hardcore
feedback.

Now this kind of thing means that he's unlikely to be invited
to play on the next Belinda Carlisle album; but he has his
admirers and those who want him as a sideman on their
recordings; people like Marianne Faithfull, Allen Ginsberg or
Elvis Costello.

'Chewing Gum' from Costello's album *Spike* makes highly
effective use of Ribot's way with mutant soul. 'Pads Paws and
Claws' is far less successful. It is Costello's attempt to sound
like Tom Waits (in itself apparently a step in the right direction)
and Ribot's playing is suitably whacko, but his guitar sounds
grafted on to the song, not an integral part of it. Costello
remains a pop musician and Ribot is something quite different
from that.

His spiritual home is with the New York jazz scene, the
Knitting Factory, along with Zorn, Frisell, Arto Lindsay, John
Lurie *et al*, and in bands like the Lounge Lizards or the Jazz
Passengers, or playing the film score for *Down By Law*. Anyone
coming to this music in search of blistering guitar thrills is
likely to be very disappointed. Nevertheless, on the title track
of the Lounge Lizards' *Voice Of Chunk* he plays a lovely,
extended, fast, fluid, guitar solo in which he's been given lots
of space, been pushed really hard, and he sounds as though
he's enjoying every minute of it. He sounds here too as though
he might slide easily into certain Miles Davis line-ups.

The Rootless Cosmopolitans, however, show Ribot at his
most undiluted. This is his band and his music. The basic
sound is still jazzy with saxes and clarinets, but 'The Cocktail

Party', for instance, contains attacking rhythm guitar interlocking with unlikely guitar lines that might have come out of an incarnation of Beefheart's Magic Band. 'Beak Lunch Manifesto' is full of snapping rhythm guitar, Duane Eddy twangs, James Brown soul chords. It is jumpy, twitchy, complex, angular: the real Marc Ribot.

The album also contains some oddball cover versions: a more or less unrecognizable 'The Wind Cries Mary', an insulting and very witty version of 'While My Guitar Gently Weeps', and rather more respectful assaults on the jazz classics 'I Should Care' and 'Mood Indigo', but they're not all *that* respectful.

Marc Ribot's music is certainly restless if not entirely rootless. Cosmopolitan it certainly is. It is unsettled and unsettling. He is not exactly a guitarist for all seasons but his adventurousness and eccentricity mean there are times when he completely and utterly hits the spot. It's a spot that a lot of guitarists aren't even aware exists.

MARC RIBOT: SELECTED DISCOGRAPHY

With Tom Waits: *Rain Dogs* (1985)
  Frank's Wild Years (1987)
  Big Time (1988)
With the Lounge Lizards: *The Lounge Lizards* (1986)
  No Pain For Cakes (1987)
  Voice of Chunk (1989)
With Elvis Costello: *Spike* (1989)
With Marianne Faithfull: *Blazing Away* (1990)
With the Rootless Cosmopolitans: *The Rootless Cosmopolitans* (1990)
With John Lurie: *Down By Law* (1987)
With Sam Phillips: *Cruel Inventions* (1991)

Photograph by Neal Preston
Courtesy of Virgin Records

KEITH RICHARDS

Born 18 December 1943, Dartford

What on earth would have become of Keith Richards if he hadn't met up with Mick Jagger? It is inconceivable that he wouldn't have been some sort of figure in contemporary music, but without Jagger and the Rolling Stones his status would have been infinitely less. He might very well have ended up a sort of Steve Marriott or Southside Johnny. Without the Stones there is no way he'd have had the opportunity to develop such an heroic drug habit, for instance.

To some extent we're allowed to hear what Richards might have sounded like by way of his solo album *Talk Is Cheap*. He has an interesting non-voice and a lot of the songs feature the unmistakable driving Richards guitar. There's a lovely insistent, yet constantly unpredictable guitar riff that runs through 'Struggle'. But even at their best the songs sound like demos that would be improved if Jagger sang them. Certainly a Keith Richards who didn't have all the Rolling Stones' success behind him would never have been able to round up such a glittering bunch of names to play on his album.

Richards obviously needs collaborators, musicians he trusts and can work with. Wyman and Watts, for all their loyalty to the Stones, have never appeared to be Richards' soulmates; and it must be a major and continuing blow to band morale that Richards sometimes doesn't let Bill Wyman play bass on some tracks, often preferring to let Ron Wood do it. That's probably because Wood is exactly the kind of musical lieutenant he was always looking for. By the end Brian Jones was too unstable, paranoid or stoned to contribute much. Mick Taylor was a good guitarist who was quite obviously never going to fit or be happy in the Stones. You couldn't imagine this cherub-faced blues player being best mates with Richards, and Richards is a guy who needs mates.

The fact that Jagger and Richards are such dazzling live performers has often drawn attention away from their song-writing. It's worth remembering that the Stones began as a largely reverential r & b band who did cover versions of Howlin' Wolf, Muddy Waters and Jimmy Reed songs. All their early hits were with cover versions, including the Beatles' 'I Wanna Be Your Man'. It was surely the example of Lennon and McCartney that led Jagger and Richards to start writing their own songs, albeit with enormous encouragement from Andrew Oldham. That and the realization that there were only so many good, obscure r & b songs around for them to discover. There was also, of course, a lot of money to be made out of composing and publishing royalties.

Even on their earliest records the Stones always had some wonderful guitar sounds. I remember being driven to distraction in 1964 by the opening guitar part to 'All Over Now'. But when Jagger and Richards wrote their own songs the guitar became increasingly central to their records. 'The Last Time' which they regard as their first 'real' song would be nothing without that sliding, distinctive guitar figure. And twenty-five years later that's every bit as true of a song like 'Terrifying' which is built around not much more than an endlessly repeated chord change.

With most Lennon and McCartney songs, so long as you have the melody line and the chords you have the song. This is even true of things like 'I Am The Walrus' or 'Strawberry Fields'. The most humble bedroom guitarist can make a stab at a Beatles song and it won't sound terrible. But this is not true at all of most Jagger and Richards songs. Yes, you can play the riff to 'Satisfaction' or the chords to 'Start Me Up' without being an ace guitarist but somehow that misses the essence of the songs. They aren't just chords and a top line. They're made up of riffs and fills, half chords, arpeggios, blues runs; and to get the essence of those songs you have to play them the way Richards does, and indeed sing them the way

Jagger does. This is why a lot of people cover Beatles songs and why covers of Rolling Stones songs usually sound redundant.

Richards is one of the few important guitarists who has gained a reputation essentially by playing rhythm guitar. In fact there was a time when he dismissed the distinction between rhythm and lead. He and Ron Wood both played both, he claimed, and if one of them missed something the other would fill in. Certainly there are few moments in Rolling Stones records where the music becomes merely 'backing' for a guitar solo. And yet, on the Urban Jungle tour there was a fair bit of Richards coming down to the front of the stage and playing, if not a solo, some very long 'lead lines'; and they weren't the most tuneful or relevant lead lines a guitarist has ever played.

And again, even though Richards' guitar is generally held to be the core of the Stones sound, in live performance he seems to be able to stop playing altogether from time to time and the overall band sound remains unchanged.

Richards is surely the only major rock guitarist ever to have fallen asleep on stage during a performance (after playing the solo on 'Fool To Cry' at a gig in Germany in 1976). You feel that many sidemen have probably been kicked off stage by Chuck Berry for playing too loud. The fact that it happened to Richards, even given that Berry claims not to have known who he was, in some peculiar way seems to add to both their legends.

Richards has served as a role model for hundreds of ill-looking, dangerous, hard-living, drugged-up, rock stars. You could hardly call this a pose. He really was a heroin addict, he really did carry a gun, keep nocturnal hours and pass out a lot. And yet Richards is clever enough to know that this kind of image sells tickets and Richards has never been anything if not image-conscious. There is nothing fake about the image but it is neither ingenuous nor unstudied.

Richards ought to be some terrible warning to us all. We ought to be able to look at him and see the terrible effect a lifetime of excess has on a creative artist. Yet we can't do that. You couldn't exactly claim that drink and drugs have helped Richards' music, but he is living proof that twenty-five years of bodily abuse may damage your health but won't necessarily make you a worse guitar player.

KEITH RICHARDS: SELECTED DISCOGRAPHY

Solo: *Talk Is Cheap* (1988)
With the Rolling Stones: *The Rolling Stones* (1964)
    Aftermath (1966)
    Their Satanic Majesties Request (1967)
    Beggars Banquet (1968)
    Let It Bleed (1969)
    Sticky Fingers (1971)
    Exile On Main Street (1972)
    Goat's Head Soup (1973)
    It's Only Rock 'n' Roll (1974)
    Black and Blue (1976)
    Some Girls (1978)
    Emotional Rescue (1980)
    Tattoo You (1981)
    Under Cover (1983)
    Dirty Work (1986)
    Steel Wheels (1989)

Photograph courtesy of CBS Records

CARLOS SANTANA

Born 20 July 1947, Autlan, Mexico

Here's a piece of advice for guitar players everywhere. If John McLaughlin phones and asks you to play on his next record, you should say, 'OK John, but only if we can record plenty of *slow* numbers.'

Carlos Santana obviously didn't say this, and therefore the album he made with McLaughlin, called *Love, Devotion, Surrender* is full of really fast guitar playing. The problem is that not many people can play as fast or with as much feeling as McLaughlin (in 1973 when the album was made probably nobody could). And certainly Santana doesn't. In consequence Santana gets well and truly blown off the record, even though McLaughlin actually sounds a bit below par. That record gets dismissed as being 'self-indulgent', but I think that's unfair. OK, so the two of them play guitar solos for forty minutes, but they're guitarists, what else are they supposed to do, mess about with synthesizers? But the album doesn't allow Santana to do what he does best, in fact the only thing he does at all, and that's be Santana.

I saw Santana in a gym at the University of California in Santa Barbara at about this time and he was still in his John McLaughlin phase: drug-free, dressed all in white, and he came on stage and said as an opening remark, 'We're going to play what you want us to play for as long as you want us to play it, but first a minute's silence so we can really get into it.'

Even in California this was regarded as ludicrously

pretentious and as Carlos stood silently for a minute, head bowed, eyes closed, elements in the crowd whistled and jeered and suggested he get on with it rather than into it. But this, I suppose, indicates the fact that Carlos Santana demands a spiritual dimension to his music. Yes, he is a sixties character. He was even at Woodstock.

Watching his performance in that film from a modern perspective, as he plays 'Soul Sacrifice' the first question you ask is, Is all that grimacing really necessary? Given the facial agonies he goes through you'd think he was playing something mind-bogglingly difficult, but when you hear the notes, if you watch his fingers, you're struck by the effective simplicity of what he plays. He keeps going, keeps playing the right thing, keeps inventing without becoming lost or unnecessarily complicated.

Nobody else sounds like Santana, and Santana always sounds pretty much the same. There are the Latin rhythms, the congas, the chanting in Spanish, then his piercing, sustaining guitar tone. There have been well over thirty different line-ups of Santana, the band, but the essential sound has remained the same for some twenty years.

Yet listen to his early records and you'll find his backings have more life than most records made in the late sixties. Although he was a sixties act, he wasn't a sixties act the way Love or Quicksilver Messenger Service were sixties acts. His was always a one-off sound and perhaps that's why it hasn't dated. Latin music, despite Madonna and Gloria Estafan, remains a minority taste, and one can make out a good case that Santana was playing world music long before it became fashionable. In fact, he is influenced by Cuban and Puerto Rican music as much as by that of his native Mexico. But in the end the Latin influence provides only a backdrop. His guitar is pure rock.

What's more it's pure Santana, and in a way he might be more 'influential' if he hadn't so completely perfected his own sound. What up and coming guitarist is going to use Latin rhythms knowing that he'll be instantly compared with Carlos Santana? Not that he's difficult to imitate. Zappa did it on 'Variations On The Carlos Santana Secret Chord Progression' but few have Zappa's nerve.

Santana is not much of a composer and his search for material leads him on the one hand to seek out Latin American classics like 'Jingo' and 'Oye Como Va' and on the other to rework pop songs like 'Black Magic Woman' and 'She's Not There' that lend themselves to a Latin interpretation. Unfortunately there seem to be few songs that can be reworked that way. The song 'The Healer' on the John Lee Hooker album of that name, is attributed to Hooker and Santana, but Santana has swamped the material so completely that it sounds like a Santana song on which Hooker is simply guest vocalist.

I believe you can learn a lot about artists from their less good work. I own a strange Santana cassette called *As The Years Go By*, bought cheaply – but not nearly cheaply enough – in a Woolworths bargain bin. There's a ten-minute version of 'La Puerta Del Sol', an eleven-minute version of 'Jingo', a twelve-minute version of 'El Corazon Manda'. Carlos plays what he always plays, he has the same old Latin rhythms going in the background, it's typical, possibly classical, Santana and yet these numbers feel as though they go on pointlessly and forever.

There's also the dire *Carlos Santana & Buddy Miles! Live!* (it's those two exclamation marks that tell you it's going to be really terrible). It's described, I kid you not, as 'Energy for the Universe from the centre of a Volcano'. Basically it's Buddy Miles lousing up another album by showing how much soul he's got, and it contains a gem called 'Free Form Funkadelic Filth', a twenty-five-minute (it seems much longer) session of abject, jazzy time-wasting. It sounds a little like Miles Davis might have sounded in the early seventies if he had no musical ability, sense of dynamics or skills as a band leader. It proves, if proof were required, that a rhythm, a riff and a guitar solo are necessary but not sufficient.

In 1990, however, he released *Viva Santana!* (still the exclamation mark, but only one of them), a startling collection of live performances, recorded rehearsals, jams and unreleased songs.

Although some of it falls into the category of research material, the real Santana is there in abundance. On 'Open Invitation' or on 'Jungle Strut' (on the latter Neal Schon also plays guitar) his playing goes up a gear and he combines excitement and feeling in a way that is both moving and uplifting. It's a sort of greatest-hits collection but it's also his attempt to stake his claim to be a great guitarist and I find it very convincing.

CARLOS SANTANA: SELECTED DISCOGRAPHY

Solo or as band leader: *Santana* (1969)
  Abraxas (1970)
  Santana III (1972)
  Caravanserai (1972)
  Welcome (1973)
  Borboletta (1974)
  Amigos (1976)
  Inner Secrets (1978)
  Zebop! (1981)
  Shango (1982)
  Havana Moon (1985)
  Freedom (1987)
  Blues for Salvador (1987)
  Viva Santana! (1990)
With Buddy Miles: *Carlos Santana and Buddy Miles! Live!* (1972)
With John McLaughlin: *Love, Devotion, Surrender* (1973)
With Alice Coltrane: *Illuminations* (1974)

Photograph courtesy of Music For Nations

JOE SATRIANI

Born 1957, Long Island

If you read any of those glossy American guitar magazines with all the colour pictures of guitars and guitarists you'll find that they take it as a matter of unchallengeable wisdom that Joe Satriani is one of *the* great guitarists. And as you thumb through the magazine you'll see Joe's picture staring out at you from all those advertisements where he's endorsing Ibanez guitars, DiMarzio pickups and D'Addario strings, so you know it must be true. As it happens, it very probably is.

Satriani only has one real problem and that is Steve Vai. Now nobody would really deny that Joe Satriani is not as good a guitarist as Steve Vai. And there's no shame in that, few people are. But Satriani would like to be. His music has that same high-tech gloss, that same sub-heavy metal attack, that technical wizardry, that same naff way with a title, only less so. You feel that if Satriani realized all his ambitions and fulfilled his potential he still wouldn't quite be as good as Vai.

His technique, however formidable, is not quite as formidable as Vai's. However impressive Satriani's degree of invention and range of sounds, Vai is more impressive still. And there's an image problem here too. Satriani's cheekbones are high but they're not as high as Vai's, the dark brooding looks are not nearly as dark and brooding as Vai's. Vai even has better taste in leather jackets. And whereas Ibanez are prepared to provide Satriani with a special chrome-plated guitar, they're prepared to redesign from scratch a brand new seven-string model for Vai. What must be the worst thing of all for Satriani is that he used to *teach* Steve Vai.

However, despite these odious comparisons, Joe Satriani is his own man and certainly there are times when you'd rather hear him than Steve Vai. His playing, for all its technical virtuosity, is very good at avoiding unnecessary complication. It's not 'fussy'. You wouldn't find Satriani composing a tinkly little tune like Vai's 'Ballerina 12/24' and you couldn't imagine him playing anything quite as silly as 'The Audience Is Listening'. In three albums I don't think he's come up with a bum track.

At its best his playing is both flash and melodic. Sometimes his guitar playing is almost incomprehensibly fast and yet the title tracks of both *Surfing With The Alien* and *Not Of This Earth* are, at least in parts, hummable. At its worst his playing sounds like somebody playing scales very, very fast. (Even so this is still preferable to a whole new breed of metal guitarists who sound as if they're playing scales all the time.)

These outer-space titles Satriani goes for seem to me wildly inappropriate. OK, finding titles for instrumentals is never easy, but some of us admire Satriani because he sounds like a real down-to-earth guy, not like some kind of space cadet.

Occasionally some of the accompaniments to Satriani's playing seem unnecessarily leaden. On 'Hordes Of Locusts' from the first album he performs all kinds of guitar wonders yet they are played over a ploddingly obvious heavy metal riff. I wonder if this has something to do with the fact that Satriani plays ninety per cent of the instruments on his records, including bass, keyboards and percussion. This must avoid arguments with fellow musicians but it means he never gets the spark that comes from the chemistry of collaboration. However, let's be positive. On such pieces as 'Circles' and 'Lords of Karma' from *Surfing With The Alien* he has the balance between well-crafted composition and bravura showing-off just about perfect for my taste.

Listening to Satriani's first two albums I was reminded of the David Byrne quip that 'Singing is a trick to get people to listen to music for longer than they would ordinarily.' Words, hooks, choruses are great mnemonics. They make music more memorable, and I guess I found some of Satriani's early work a little unmemorable. Which I think is to say that some of his music sounds like heavy metal songs with the words, hooks and choruses left off. Given the intellectual and emotional content of most heavy metal lyrics you might be glad to be without them, but still . . .

Then along came the third album, *Flying In A Blue Dream*, and suddenly Joe was singing. Not on every track, but often enough that you had to consider it seriously. He sings songs about how he likes driving in his car, how he likes riding his motorbikes, how he sometimes feels strange because of 'the big bad moon', while at other times he feels strange and he doesn't know why at all. Actually his video for 'Big Bad Moon' is as dumb as anything you're ever likely to see on MTV but at least he isn't going on about his phallic endowment or about dungeons and dragons. And as a matter of fact, the song 'Strange' is a real winner with a Prince-style soulful rhythm guitar overlayed with heavy guitar bursts and solos. It's heavy but it's not metal, if you know what I mean.

Flying In A Blue Dream is a consciously more sprawling and adventurous album than his first two. Whereas they contained ten tracks each of more or less standard length, *Flying* has eighteen tracks, some of which are designated parts one and two of the same piece, and four of which are only about a minute in length. Some of the one-minute tracks, like 'Bells Of Lal (Part One)' and 'The Forgotten (Part One)' are actually more interesting than some of the longer guitar extravaganzas. He's prepared to take one-minute risks, but he won't take five-minute risks. But he still has the capacity to go for broke as on 'One Big Rush' or 'The Forgotten (Part Two)'.

Above all Satriani still likes to rock, and he still seems to be in love with the sound of his guitar. It's surprising how many 'major' guitarists you couldn't say that about.

JOE SATRIANI: SELECTED DISCOGRAPHY

Not Of This Earth (1986)
Surfing With The Alien (1987)
Flying In A Blue Dream (1989)

Photograph by Jim Hagopian
Courtesy of Music For Nations

STEVE VAI

Born 6 June 1960, Long Island

Even if Steve Vai could only play three chords, he would still command a place in many a rock band, so convincingly, not to say archetypically, does he look the part. He has the long black hair with blond streaks, the tattoos, the cheekbones, a whippy, amphetamine leanness, though he says he doesn't do drugs at all. Then there are the high kicks, the squats, the pirouettes and any number of other hot-guitar moves. This makes him sound like every other American heavy metal-ish guitar player. But Steve Vai can play.

His earliest claim to fame was, while a music student, doing transcriptions of Frank Zappa's improvised guitar solos. These he sent to Zappa, and although Zappa thought it was a weird thing for anybody to do, he liked the idea, and eventually Vai was taken on as a guitarist. He appears on Zappa albums from *Tinsel Town Rebellion* through to *Jazz From Hell*. He is sometimes credited as rhythm guitarist, sometimes as player of 'impossible guitar parts'. Generally, however, he is inaudible.

It was certainly Vai's Satanic good looks that got him the part as the Devil's guitarist in the movie *Crossroads*. This is a confused and confusing film. At its climax a guitar duel takes place between the Devil's guitarist and the film's cleancut young hero. Vai plays all his snarling licks, works all his stage wizardry but is defeated when the kid plays a load of strictly non-bluesy classical guitar stuff on his Telecaster. If there is a moral in this, it escapes me.

Looks aside, Vai plays blindingly fast, metal guitar. He gets all the requisite heavy metal sounds, but also a few more besides. His playing is consciously flashy, consciously technical, and yet it does have a soul. For someone in the heavy metal camp he has a great delicacy. Although he makes some convincingly dirty noises, he generally avoids simple grunge in favour of speedy accuracy. His sound has a hard, bright, glossy surface, has edge, and yet has moments of great melody and lyricism.

He released an early home-made solo album called *Flex-Able*, but his real claims to heroic stature reside in *Passion And Warfare*. It's a naff title and in interview Vai has explained at length that it is based on a series of dreams, out-of-the-body experiences, astral travel, that stuff.

It sounds like a recipe for jejune failure, and certainly *Passion And Warfare* is an album full of great guitar playing rather than a great album. This is complex, difficult-to-play music, full of varying, complex guitar sounds. Some of it is bombastic, like 'Liberty'; some of it is silly, like 'The Audience Is Listening'; but there are some consummate moments.

The best of these occur on the dodgily titled 'For The Love Of God'. The story is Vai fasted for four days before recording the solo, and that his hands bled while playing it; but it was worth it. A soaring, whining, sustained guitar playing Lydian scales against an E minor backing is always going to get the tear ducts moving, but this does seem to be an occasion on the album when Vai's formidable technique and his spiritual aspirations actually coincide.

When Vai goes it alone he seems to get there. But all too often he is just a sideman, a hired gun. If you can tell a man by the company he keeps, Vai looks to be in trouble. He replaced Yngwie Malmsteen in the deathly Alcatrazz, and he has done stretches with David Lee Roth and Whitesnake.

He has always denied that he's doing these gigs in the spirit of take the money and run. He insists he loves playing in Whitesnake. You can sort of see why. Roth and Coverdale are masters of style over content, and their music would appear to leave room for Vai simply to do his stuff and show off nicely.

He played all the guitar parts on *Slip Of The Tongue* following Adrian Vandenberg's inability to play at all due to overzealous practice. Vandenberg and Coverdale wrote the whole album and it's not entirely clear to what extent Vai is playing under orders. He produces shimmering little guitar breaks throughout the album and yet he is peculiarly marginalized; his playing is pushed to the edges, so that it becomes decoration rather than substance.

It seems idle to protest about sexism in heavy metal, yet you don't have to be Andrea Dworkin to find huge chunks of Whitesnake offensive. Maybe guitar playing ought to be neutral, abstract, but it's not. For example, Vai makes some tasty guitar noise on 'Cheap An' Nasty' but it's not easy to enjoy a song which celebrates cheapness and nastiness as desirable female traits, and exhorts the lady not to speak with her mouth full. Oh dear. Being a gem set in fustian is all very well, but why doesn't Vai play in a more interesting context?

On one occasion he did. He appeared, uncredited, on the Bill Laswell-produced, Public Image Ltd *Album*, and for me it shows Vai at his very best, if only briefly. He discovers a wildness, an adventurousness here that he shies away from even on his own albums.

The middle guitar passage, one hesitates to call it a solo, on 'Fishing' sounds as though he's just discovered a whammy bar for the first time, and he plays guitar with a real unforced, untutored freedom. It isn't exactly the cutting edge of experimentalism but it'd leave your average Whitesnake fan befuddled.

And the outro on 'Ease' sees him just going for broke, freed from the glitzy precision of his heavy metal mode. Of course, he can't resist throwing in some scorchingly fast runs, but at its best it's as though he's been forced to go beyond what he knows and knows works, and to approach the instrument afresh, to play it as a primitive. It is wonderful.

Some of us could put up with a lot more of this. We're the same people who hope the best of Steve Vai is yet to come.

STEVE VAI: SELECTED DISCOGRAPHY

Solo: *Flex-Able* (1984)
  Passion And Warfare (1990)
With Whitesnake: *Slip Of The Tongue* (1989)
With David Lee Roth: *Eat 'Em And Smile* (1986)
With Alcatrazz: *Disturbing The Peace*
With PIL: *Album* (1986)

Photograph by Mark Weiss
Courtesy of Idols

EDWARD VAN HALEN

Born 1957, Amsterdam, moved to Pasadena, 1968

There are those who would have you believe that round about 1978 with the release of the album *Van Halen*, Edward of that ilk completely reinvented the nature of rock guitar, and they're probably right. There is a sense in which guitar playing divides itself into pre- and post-Van Halen. Pre-Van Halen you might have been able to accept someone like, say, Paul Kossoff as a guitarist, post-Van Halen the Paul Kossoffs of this world looked like triflers. Van Halen put down a blueprint of what guitar playing could be in terms of sheer speed and dexterity. If you couldn't do that stuff, then what claims could you have to be a guitarist?

Edward Van Halen plays very, very fast, very flashy metal guitar. The sound is overdriven, abrasive, uses feedback, lots of whammy bar, and lots of two-handed tapping on the fretboard to achieve the relentless, rippling, seamless chains of notes that characterize his playing. Today a whole school of guitarists (from Steve Vai via Vinnie Moore to Reb Beach) regards this as standard. In 1978 it looked miraculous.

As far as we Brits were concerned 1978 wasn't much of a time to be reinventing the guitar. In 1978 Mick Jones's guitar playing felt much more relevant than Eric Clapton's; some would say it still does. OK, so punk never meant much to America, but even in 1978 a band specializing in flares, permed hair and bare chests was starting to look *passé*.

It didn't help that Van Halen played a form of heavy metal, although they were probably on the borderline where heavy metal meets hard rock. True they had a sense of humour and a sense of the absurd, but at their worst they seemed both plodding and inconsequential. Nor has heavy metal ever exactly been a hotbed of experiment and innovation.

The track 'Eruption' is generally regarded as the guitar solo that changed the world and it remains a more or less unchallengeable piece of showing off of its own kind. The first thing to say about it is that it's very short: one minute and forty-two seconds according to the record label. It's a solo in the simplest sense that apart from a little drumming the rest of the band don't play on it. It's noisy, consists of a great number of notes, most of them played at an astounding rate, and it's unmelodic, or indeed anti-melodic. It's exciting and impressive, but it doesn't really have a shape. It has different parts but not a structure, and it ends when you're expecting it to move on to something even more exciting. It *is* a great bit of guitar playing but that's all it is, a great *bit*, not a great whole.

This turned out to be Edward Van Halen's standard pattern. On 'Spanish Fly' from *Van Halen II* he shows he can be fast and flashy on acoustic guitar as well. This lasts fifty-six seconds. On the introduction to 'Women In Love' he plays another chunk of wild, extraordinary guitar, but it doesn't relate to the song it's an introduction to, and might just as well be the introduction to almost any other Van Halen song.

Great guitar playing needs to be coherent. Great guitar players make substantial pieces of music, not detachable nuggets of blazing noise, however bold and thrilling they may be. This, however, seems to have escaped both Edward Van Halen and his fans.

Constantly his guitar playing is pushed to the margins; a wild fill, a tasty intro, a quick, storming solo. And even when the guitar playing is at the centre of the song, it will be on some dodgy number like 'Everybody Wants Some' from *Women And Children First*. Nice song, shame about the vocals, the lyrics, the sexual politics.

It's tempting to blame David Lee Roth for a lot of this. Roth is a great something or other, but not a great singer. He certainly has personality, some charm, and a pop sensibility. He doesn't look like the British idea of a serious singer. To the British serious singers look like Van Morrison or Joe Cocker.

And he doesn't take himself seriously either, which sounds fine, but he makes rather heavy weather of being frivolous. He lacks lightness and I guess that it was Roth's instincts that led the band to do some rather weary versions of pop classics.

'Intruder' from *Diver Down* shows Edward Van Halen at his very best. There's lots of eccentric guitar noise, by no means a predictable heavy metal noise. It's almost restrained, and certainly it's very cleverly controlled. But it doesn't last very long and then we're into a version of 'Pretty Woman'. The guitar noise itself is of a kind Adrian Belew might be proud of, and although Belew has been known to do cover versions as well, when *he* does one he gives the song a real mauling in keeping with the wildness of the guitar. With Van Halen it feels like a case of, 'OK, so I've done the wild guitar bit, now let's get back to something commercial.' I'm obviously not saying that he should go on stage and make weird guitar noise for a couple of hours, but there's a feeling that the conservative nature of Van Halen, the band, is at odds with the originality of Van Halen, the man. The departure of Roth and the arrival of Sammy Hagar (a man who had covered 'A Whiter Shade Of Pale') has done little to resolve this contradiction. Neither did his playing and arranging with Michael Jackson produce any surprises. Now if he were to play with Thurston Moore . . . but, of course, he won't.

The problem for anyone who changes the face of anything is knowing what to do next. Although Edward Van Halen was an original, an entire generation of American guitarists has found him surprisingly easy to copy. A lot of people have caught up, leaving him with nowhere to go. This could probably have been predicted. Technical ability is not so hard to copy once someone has shown you what's possible. A lot of players have spent a lot of time watching and listening to Van Halen. They can now do what he does. What can't be copied is something more personal, some sort of feeling that comes from the heart, and finally I think you have to say that Edward Van Halen's playing comes from the fingers rather than the heart.

His importance is that he showed that there was more possible with the electric guitar than a lot of people had dreamed of. He established a range of sounds and techniques that were in themselves staggering but had to leave it to others (Vai, Satriani) to use those things in a way that was truly satisfying.

EDWARD VAN HALEN: SELECTED DISCOGRAPHY

With Van Halen: *Van Halen* (1978)
  Van Halen II (1979)
  Women And Children First (1980)
  Fair Warning (1981)
  Diver Down (1982)
  1984 (1984)
  5150 (1985)
  For Unlawful Carnal Knowledge (1991)

Photograph by George Bodnar
Courtesy of Idols

ANGUS YOUNG

Born 31 March 1959, Glasgow

Once, about 1979, I had the misfortune to see AC/DC at Wembley Stadium. (I also had the misfortune to see The Who headlining the same bill, but that's another story.) Wembley Stadium is not the right venue for AC/DC. You need to see them in a horrible, packed basement club with condensation running down the walls, but Wembley it had to be. My 'date' (an American girl called Margaret) and I positioned ourselves well forward in the crowd so that we were standing immediately in front of a group of callow AC/DC fans. I offered the opinion that callow AC/DC fans weren't the kind of guys anyone would want to be standing in front of, but Margaret thought it was a great spot and why should we move? Why indeed? She continued to think it was a great spot until the AC/DC fans started to pinch her bottom with sustained boyish fervour. She told them to stop. They didn't. I told them to stop. They didn't. Push came to shove. Being a chivalrous man I offered to knock out the teeth of the smallest, weediest AC/DC fan and then made a strategic withdrawal to the comfy seats at the side of the stadium.

Now, from what I hear, Angus Young is a quiet, retiring flower off stage, drinks nothing stronger than tea and is by no means a bottom-pincher; but *on* stage he looks and behaves like the kind of guy who'd chew a girl's bottom as soon as look at her. And even if it wasn't exactly Angus Young's fault that Margaret had her bottom pinched, I bet it wouldn't have happened at a John Abercrombie gig.

AC/DC want to look like bad lads, and Angus Young wants to look like a ratty, hyperactive schoolboy. Now in his thirties he's still pretty successful at this.

It must be an indication of something that in Australia a band can call itself AC/DC and this is seen as a purely electrical term. Anywhere else in the Western world it would surely be a proclamation of sexual versatility, but no, these are straight bad lads, and AC/DC fans can watch a lead guitarist stripped down to his shorts, drenched in sweat, careering around the stage doing a very fair impression of sexual frenzy, and yet still feel entirely secure in their adolescent sexuality.

Angus Young is at least as much athlete as he is guitar player. His physical vocabulary (like his musical one) is not extensive, but it's employed with such manic conviction you have to admire it.

First there's the head-nodding, verging on head-banging, two to the left, two to the right, the co-ordinated leg twitches, the deep bend forward with the guitar. Then there's the sprinting from one side of the stage to the other, head and hair flailing, mouth gaping, and there's the falling down on stage, the legs wriggling like a dying wasp. Young's sweating is indeed world class, and after he's been writhing on his back he leaves a pool of sweat behind him on the boards. He is in constant, frantic motion, dashing off stage once in a while to get a blast from the oxygen cylinder placed there to keep him going.

That he can play guitar at all at the same time as doing all the above is so amazing that to carp about the quality of the playing seems a little churlish. He may not be a phenomenally good guitarist but he is certainly a guitar phenomenon.

His solos never exactly take you by surprise, yet they have a rightness about them, an inevitable quality that stays just the right side of predictability. You couldn't claim that they're brilliantly original but within the context of AC/DC they're just what's required.

I used to wonder whether AC/DC's music was written to fit around Angus Young's style of movement or whether he moved that way because of the music. Apparently it's the latter. The movement developed to help him keep in time with the music. It obviously worked.

Certainly it's hard to think of a band that keeps such a hard, consistent beat without sounding entirely moronic. And it's difficult to think of any comparable band that has such a clean, crisp production sound. AC/DC occupy the high ground between hard rock and heavy metal. The sexist posturing remains intact. 'Heatseeker', if not the ultimate song about phallocratic imperialism, will certainly do for now. But even when they sing about a 'Highway to Hell' you know the lyrics aren't going to start twittering about satanism and crucifixes.

Although they're essentially a live band they're also a singles band. To list their singles is to list their best work: 'You Shook Me All Night Long', 'If You Want Blood', 'Let's Get It Up', etc., etc. Of course the lyrical content of these songs varies from the crass to the pernicious but lyrical content is not what AC/DC are about.

If Angus Young's guitar playing is technically unremarkable there are few who can match his, and AC/DC's, way with an intro. Typically these start out with an unaccompanied guitar riff, which is joined by a lean drum part for a few bars, after which the rest of the band kicks in and the music hits that hard familiar groove. You can hear this kind of intro through-out AC/DC's records, but 'Highway To Hell' or 'Let Me Put My Love Into You' would be good examples.

Of course, nobody goes to see and hear AC/DC for the subtlety of their intros, nor I suspect for their songs, or for any other reason except to see Angus do his stuff. And he doesn't disappoint. He comes up with what's expected. It's a minor talent but he's perfected it and it's one to cherish. If you want to see a guitarist sweat and go crazy who ya gonna call, Pete Townsend?

The punchline to the Margaret bottom-pinching story is that Pete Townsend was determined the all-day concert should finish promptly at ten o'clock sharp so as not to irritate the locals and so that everybody could catch their last bus home (*very* rock and roll, Pete). However, earlier in the evening a bus conductor had been beaten up by one of his passengers (not an AC/DC fan as far as I know) and all London Transport workers had gone out on strike in sympathy. We had to walk the ten miles home from Wembley. It was not the end of a perfect day.

ANGUS YOUNG: SELECTED DISCOGRAPHY

With AC/DC: *High Voltage* (1976)
  Dirty Deeds Done Dirt Cheap (1976)
  Let There Be Rock (1977)
  If You Want Blood (1978)
  Highway To Hell (1979)
  Back In Black (1980)
  For Those About To Rock (1981)
  Who Made Who (1986)
  Blow Up Your Video (1988)

Photograph by Mike Hashimoto
Courtesy of Reprise Records

NEIL YOUNG

Born 12 November 1945, Toronto

There are times in a man's life when nothing will do but a Neil Young album. Depending on the life and the man these times will occur with greater or lesser frequency, but generally they occur late at night after you've imbibed a consciousness changing amount of something or other, when the motor coordination has begun to slip, and after your girlfriend has said, 'Oh no, not Neil Young again.' But you don't care. You rifle ham-fistedly through your record collection. You know it's here somewhere, and finally you come up with *Tonight's The Night* and you too, in the comfort of your own living-room, can wallow in edgy, drug-fringed angst. And when Neil cranks up his guitar and plays one of those frazzled one-note solos . . . but wait, no he doesn't play too much of that on *Tonight's The Night*, what you really need is *Zuma* or *Rust Never Sleeps* or, the ultimate, *Live Rust*. Suddenly it is several hours later and you seem to have played half your Neil Young collection, the girlfriend has gone to bed, and is that the bass drum sounding particularly good tonight on 'Like A Hurricane' or is it the neighbours pounding on the wall?

Neil Young seems to be not even slightly interested in technical flashiness for its own sake, and certainly not in showing how fast he can play. Who needs that when you have Young's capacity to play the right, telling, melancholy tear-jerking note? His solos, however wild, seem to emerge organically out of the song he's playing and are never just tacked on.

Young is one of those sixties figures who, having survived

some professional doldrums, has developed a 'late style'. His work is still recognizably that of the same man who wrote 'The Loner' or 'Expecting To Fly' and although it consciously rejects attempts to be fashionable, it is relevant and modern. His guitar playing too has gone through changes.

When he plays the guitar solo at the end of 'Southern Man' on *After The Goldrush* he sounds like a guy who can't really play the guitar but has found a way of making highly effective noise with it. By the time of *Live Rust* he sounds like a guy who can really play and has incorporated that noise-making into a highly sophisticated technique.

I use that word sophisticated deliberately, since it's easy to see *Live Rust* as a series of extended versions of Young's greatest hits played with a sort of garage-band malevolent enthusiasm. Certainly the sound is raw: great, thick distorted chords and then fierce, trebly solos that cut through like a chain-saw. The album has an enormous freshness about it and I know of no live album on which a band sounds so sharp and vital. But this kind of spontaneity is only achieved through a great deal of sophistication. There is nothing haphazard or primitive about it. I would pick the version here of 'Cortez The Killer' as one of Neil Young's greatest moments (more precisely, one of his greatest seven and a half minutes). I'm not sure that the song amounts to much as an indictment of Spanish colonialism, and yet Young's searing, yearning guitar speaks very eloquently indeed about nostalgia and loss.

Young has, to say the least, a reputation for eccentric behaviour, like disappearing for months at a time with only his credit card for company, like rejecting sponsorship for his tours; and you don't get much more eccentric than that in America today. He has also suffered from polio, diabetes and epilepsy. Sometimes it's easy to convince yourself that this is partly what you hear in a Neil Young guitar solo: a weird, not very healthy shakiness. Of course, you hear something of the same thing in his voice.

He is, of course, a singer/songwriter and in one guise, say at Live Aid, he is a solo performer strumming an acoustic guitar and singing 'folk songs' with easy chords. Yet he's also this guy who likes to thrash his guitar and make your ears bleed. It is part of Young's genius that these two traits complement rather than contradict each other. And with 'Hey Hey My My' (among others) he shows that the same song can work either way.

Young manages to have a social conscience without being a complete wimp, which is not to say that he doesn't have wimpish tendencies; you can take your pick of examples: 'Heart of Gold', 'Old Man', 'Wrecking Ball', etc., etc. It is precisely his electric guitar playing that saves him. It is hard to play the sensitive folkie with an overdriven Les Paul in your hands. It's this that stops him turning into, say, Graham Nash. And Neil Young is the only thing that makes Crosby, Stills, Nash and Young listenable these days.

Unusually for a lead guitarist, Young is remarkably little influenced by the blues. Certainly he's influenced by Hendrix but it's the Hendrix of 'Star Spangled Banner' rather than the Hendrix of 'Red House'. The nearest he gets to the blues is the album *This Note's For You*, which even then is more r & b than straight blues. And his playing on that album is, by his own standards, very restrained. Which is not to say it isn't very effective. The guitar on 'Twilight', particularly at the end, shows what he can do with a more or less clear tone.

His 1990 album *Ragged Glory* has something of the same feel as *Tonight's The Night*; boys getting together late at night and making some unwholesome din. But this time Young's guitar playing is given all the room it wants. 'Fuckin' Up' proceeds through layers and filaments of changing guitar sound to a gorgeous ending of moaning, grunting feedback, but then quite a lot of the songs end that way.

I'm still not sure if the song 'Mother Earth' is sublime or ridiculous, but either way it is quintessential Neil Young. His guitar tone is pretty much that of Hendrix's Woodstock 'Star Spangled Banner', and he plays a melody that sounds like a cross between 'Amazing Grace' and 'Home On The Range', over which a many-voiced and much over-dubbed choir sings ethereal harmonies about what might loosely be called ecology. Without the guitar it would make you want to scream.

Ragged Glory is the freer, rockier, more unbuttoned companion piece to *Freedom* but it is this latter record which contains Young's most radical playing. On 'Don't Cry', a basically mawkish song complete with bell chimes, the narrator tells his sweet girl not to cry even though he's just kicked her out of the house. Mercifully the song is transformed, partly by Young's deliberately untidy vocals, and crucially by thunderous eruptions of guitar which are gloriously off the wall and completely 'inappropriate'.

'On Broadway' is an extraordinary example of a song revitalized by taking its premises seriously and literally. Young takes the slick Leiber and Stoller (and Mann and Weil) hit and asks very simply, well, what's it actually like on Broadway these days? Pretty rough, is the answer, and the guitar solo, which the song says will make him a star is as rough and manic as the meanest of streets. It has a painful, desperate, inarticulateness, that the bums and whores of Broadway know only too well. The surprising, and wonderful, thing is that Young knows it too. You feel that most rock musicians who have been successful for as long as Neil Young have neither the desire nor the ability to express that kind of pain.

NEIL YOUNG: SELECTED DISCOGRAPHY

Neil Young (1968)
Everybody Knows This Is Nowhere (1969)
After The Goldrush (1970)
Harvest (1971)
On The Beach (1974)
Tonight's The Night (1975)
Zuma (1975)
American Stars 'n' Bars (1977)
Comes A Time (1978)
Rust Never Sleeps (1979)
Live Rust (1979)
Hawks and Doves (1980)
RE-AC-TOR (1981)
Trans (1982)
Old Ways (1984)
Landing On Water (1986)
This Note's For You (1988)
Freedom (1989)

Ragged Glory (1990)
With Buffalo Springfield: *Buffalo Springfield* (1986)
  Again (1967)
  Last Time Around (1968)
With Crosby, Stills, Nash & Young: *Déjà Vu* (1970)
With Stills-Young Band: *Long May You Run* (1976)

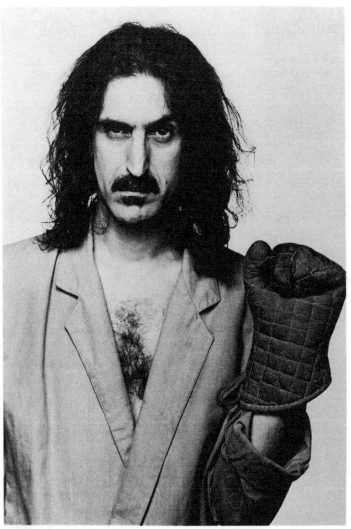

Photograph by Steve Schapiro
Courtesy of EMI

FRANK ZAPPA

Born 1940, Baltimore, Maryland

In the early 1960s Frank Zappa recorded three songs with Don Van Vliet, later to be known as Captain Beefheart. They called themselves the Soots and the songs were 'Slippin' And Slidin'', 'Cheryl's Canyon' and 'Metal Man Has Won His Wings'. They went along to Dot Records and tried to get them to buy and release the recordings. They got short shrift. 'We can't release these,' the guy said. 'The guitar is distorted.'

This must surely rate as one of rock and roll's all-time stupid remarks and it seems only appropriate that Zappa should have been on the receiving end of it. He (and everyone else) has been distorting ever since.

Even in the earliest days, Zappa's Mothers of Invention came across as a bunch of serious musicians who didn't take themselves, or the world, entirely seriously. You knew they could *really play*, even if most of the time they chose not to.

They were social satirists, musical anarchists, and Zappa decided there was no room in the band for anyone who wanted to come over as a guitar wizard. He wasn't about to do anything so unironic as get on down and express himself, but even so there are enterprising guitar solos on recordings as diverse as 'Stuff Up The Cracks' on *Cruising With Ruben and the Jets* or 'Nine Types of Industrial Pollution' on *Uncle Meat*.

It wasn't until *Hot Rats* that he made his bid to be thought of as a *real* guitarist, and it worked. Today his playing on that album sounds surprisingly thin and passionless, but at the time it felt like the real McCoy. 'Willie the Pimp' is probably as close to a boogy as Zappa is ever likely to get, and it was certainly a dozen times more interesting and effective than the various boogyings of contemporaries such as, say, Alvin Lee.

The term jazz-rock has seldom been a compliment, but there's a considerable jazz influence on *Hot Rats*, especially from the other musicians such as Ian Underwood and Jean-Luc Ponty. But if Zappa is not your average rock guitarist he isn't *any* kind of jazz guitarist. He names his influences as Johnny 'Guitar' Watson, Clarence 'Gatemouth' Brown and Guitar Slim. These influences are not always immediately obvious. And although he says he is an admirer of Clapton and Beck his sound is remarkably uninfluenced by their kind of playing too.

If you want to hear the type of rock guitarist he might have become if he hadn't had such a weird head listen to 'Out to Get You' by Grand Funk Railroad. Zappa produced the record and plays the first solo. It is a great 'straight' solo and it is recognizably Zappa, but it doesn't sound like *proper* Zappa.

He has never been afraid to surround himself with great musicians, including guitarists. Adrian Belew, Steve Vai and Johnny 'Guitar' Watson have all been in the band at one time or another.

Zappa has always had more on his mind than has the average guitar bum. He also has a highly developed sense of irony. Neither of these things is a guaranteed passport to success in the world of rock. But Zappa has always wanted us to know he's more than just a rock and roll guitar player, hence his compositions for orchestra, his work with Pierre Boulez, his championing of Varese, his excursions into film. The popular imagination has always had trouble with people who want to be more than one thing.

Recently Zappa has been something of a victim of his own prolific nature. It might be easier to be a fan of his music if there was a little less music to have to deal with. Regular releases of double and triple albums, rereleases on CD, releases of archive material, means there's just too much to keep track of. In the first seven months of 1991 he released eleven albums – admittedly eight of these were repackaged bootlegs, but it still suggests that the Zappa product does not obey conventional notions of supply and demand.

At the same time, Zappa the absurdist seems to have become Zappa the 'Practical Conservative' and this is simply less interesting. Zappa has always been, in the broadest sense, political and becoming Trade and Culture Emissary for the Czech government seemed like a good Dadaist joke. Yet I find it infinitely depressing that he has commissioned a 'feasibility study' to see whether he's a viable Presidential candidate. OK, it's not as depressing as some of Sting's 'political' gestures, but you get the feeling that Zappa actually wants to *be* President and that's the worst joke of all. Some of us were kind of glad when he decided to shut up 'n play his guitar.

The triple album called *Shut Up 'n' Play Yer Guitar* and the later *Guitar* are simply collections of live guitar solos culled from concerts between 1977 and 1984. The CD of *Guitar* contains thirty-two such pieces. These are the twin peaks on which Zappa's reputation as a guitarist rests.

Generally the band lays down a moody, complex but repetitive riff or chord sequence and Zappa just *plays* over the top. It is almost entirely improvised. It is what he calls 'structured spontaneous entertainment'. There are huge sweeps and expanses of sound, endless flurries of notes, an awesome, whining sustain. One can certainly imagine guitarists who play faster or more accurately and improvise more melodically, but nobody makes a noise quite *like that*. Certainly if you wanted someone to make an ugly subversive noise to save your life, Zappa's your man. His guitar still sounds as though it wants to kill something and most mothers still wouldn't like it.

But he also makes some wonderfully, soaring, moving and, I'll admit it, spiritual noises too. If 'Watermelon in Easter Hay' doesn't bring a tear to your eye then you have no soul.

There appears to be some doubt as to how much guitar playing Zappa intends to do in the future. 'Jazz From Hell' was composed and performed on a Synclavier and he apparently found the experience liberating. In *The Real Frank Zappa Book* he talks at length about the frustrations of having to use live musicians, and it may just be that he feels he's played enough guitar solos for one lifetime, but I'm not so sure. Once a killer axeman, always a killer axeman. Keep watching the skies.

FRANK ZAPPA: SELECTED DISCOGRAPHY

Freak Out (1966)
We're Only In It For The Money (1968)
Cruising With Ruben And The Jets (1969)
Uncle Meat (1969)
Hot Rats (1969)
The Mothers: Fillmore East, June 1971 (1971)
200 Motels (1971)
Grand Wazoo (1972)
Overnite Sensation (1973)
One Size Fits All (1975)
Bongo Fury (1975)
Zoot Allures (1976)
Sheik Yerbouti (1979)
Shut Up 'n' Play Yer Guitar (1981)
Ship Arriving Too Late To Save A Drowning Witch (1982)
The Man From Utopia (1983)
Thing Fish (1985)
Jazz From Hell (1986)
Guitar (1988)
Broadway The Hard Way (1989)
The Best Band You Never Heard in Your Life (1991)
Make a Jazz Noise Here (1991)

ONE HUNDRED MORE MIGHTY GUITAR MOMENTS

The thirty-seven guitarists I've dealt with in this book are, as you know, but the tip of the tip of the iceberg. Just to prove, if proof were required, that every dog has his day and that great guitar playing isn't all that rare a phenomenon – in fact, in some cases, can turn up in the most unlikely locations – here are one hundred mighty (and magical) guitar moments, each played by a different guitarist. Not all of them are strictly rock and roll but they're all worth a listen.

Of course, this still leaves plenty of iceberg submerged, and I realize I've probably still not included your own favourite guitar hero. Sorry, nothing personal, that's just the way it is with icebergs.

Here, in no particular order, we go.

1. **ROBERT JOHNSON** – 'Come On In My Kitchen'
2. **ALBERT KING** – 'For The Love Of A Woman'
3. **BUDDY GUY** – 'In My Younger Days'
4. **TOM VERLAINE** – 'Marquee Moon' (Television)
5. **RICHARD LLOYD** – 'See No Evil' (Television)
6. **ROBERT QUINE** – 'Love Comes In Spurts' (Richard Hell and the Voidoids)
7. **JOHN CANN** – 'Sleeping For Years' (Atomic Rooster)
8. **CHARLIE CHRISTIAN** – 'Blues In B'
9. **TONY McPHEE** – 'Split Part II' (Groundhogs)
10. **DAVID T. CHASTAINE** – 'Pantheon'
11. **PETER GREEN** – 'Albatross' (Fleetwood Mac)
12. **JOE WALSH** – 'Life's Been Good'

13. **VINNIE MOORE** – 'Beyond The Door'
14. **SUNNY ADE** – 'Chief Lekan Salami'
15. **SCOTTY MOORE** – 'That's All Right [Mama]' (Elvis Presley)
16. **STEVE HUNTER** – 'No Regrets' (Walker Brothers)
17. **PAUL KOSSOFF** – 'Mr Big' (Free)
18. **REEVES GABRELS** – 'Working Class Hero' (Tin Machine)
19. **TED NUGENT** – 'Cat Scratch Fever'
20. **DAVID BOWIE** – 'Rebel Rebel'
21. **STEVE RAY VAUGHAN** – 'Superstitious'
22. **EDDIE MARTINEZ** – 'Simply Irresistible' (Robert Palmer)
23. **ELMORE JAMES** – 'The Sky Is Cryin'
24. **BILLY GIBBONS** – 'Gimme All Your Lovin' (ZZ Top)
25. **PETER FRAMPTON** – 'Show Me The Way'
26. **NILS LOFGREN** – 'Tunnel Of Love' (Bruce Springsteen)
27. **PETE TOWNSEND** – 'Young Man Blues' (Who)
28. **RANDY RHOADS** – 'Suicide Solution' (Ozzie Osbourne)
29. **CHRIS SPEDDING** – 'Morning Story' (Jack Bruce)
30. **JOHNNY MARR** – 'Death of A Disco Dancer' (Smiths)
31. **MICHAEL SCHENKER** – 'Courvoisier Concerto'
32. **HANK MARVIN** – 'Apache' (Shadows)
33. **FREDDIE KING** – 'I'm Tore Down'
34. **PAUL WELLER** – 'Eton Rifles' (The Jam)
35. **JOHN PERRY** – 'The Beast' (Only Ones)
36. **NILE RODGERS** – 'Good Times' (Chic)
37. **ROY BUCHANAN** – 'Sweet Dreams'
38. **TONY IOMMI** – 'Paranoid' (Black Sabbath)
39. **JOHNNY WINTER** – 'Highway 61'
40. **JOHN SCOFIELD** – 'One Phone Call/Street Scene' (Miles Davis)
41. **DUANE ALLMAN** – 'Whipping Post' (Allman Brothers)
42. **DUANE EDDY** – 'Rebel Rouser'
43. **JOHNNY 'GUITAR' WATSON** – 'Hit The Highway'
44. **MICK JONES** – 'Should I Stay Or Should I Go?' (Clash)
45. **RANDY CALIFORNIA** – 'I Got A Line On You' (Spirit)
46. **JJ CALE** – 'Cocaine'
47. **BILL NELSON** – 'Furniture Music'
48. **DAVID EDMUNDS** – 'Sabre Dance' (Love Sculpture)
49. **ZAL CLEMINSON** – 'Vambo' (SAHB)

50. **ROGER McGUINN** – 'Eight Miles High' (Byrds)
51. **EDDIE COCHRAN** – 'Summertime Blues'
52. **MARSHALL CRENSHAW** – 'Some Day Some Way'
53. **HUGH CORNWALL** – 'No Mercy' (Stranglers)
54. **JOHN LEE HOOKER** – 'Boom Boom'
55. **ADRIAN GURVITZ** – 'Race With The Devil' (The Gun)
56. **STEVE HOWE** – 'The Clap' (Yes)
57. **WILKO JOHNSON** – 'She Does It Right' (Dr Feelgood)
58. **PETER BUCK** – 'Orange Crush' (REM)
59. **BO DIDDLEY** – 'Mumblin' Guitar'
60. **MIDGE URE** – 'No Regrets'
61. **LONNIE MACK** – 'Memphis'
62. **ROBIN TROWER** – 'Bridge Of Sighs'
63. **LESLIE WEST** – 'Nantucket Sleighride' (Mountain)
64. **RONNIE MONTROSE** – 'Bad Motor Scooter' (Montrose)
65. **FRED FRITH** – 'Hello Music'
66. **SLASH** – 'Sweet Child O' Mine' (Guns 'n' Roses)
67. **HARVEY MANDEL** – 'Unanswered Questions' (John Mayall)
68. **BUDDY HOLLY** – 'Peggy Sue'
69. **STANLEY JORDAN** – 'Eleanor Rigby'
70. **BILLY DUFFY** – 'Little Devil' (Cult)
71. **DON WILSON & BOB BOGLE** – 'Walk Don't Run' (Ventures)
72. **BERT WEEDON** – 'Guitar Boogie Shuffle'
73. **EUGENE CHADBOURNE** – 'The List Is Too Long'
74. **JAN AKKERMAN** – 'Well Done' from 'Hamburger Concerto' (Focus)
75. **STEVE CROPPER** – 'Soul Man' (Sam and Dave)
76. **PRINCE** – 'I Could Never Take The Place Of Your Man'
77. **DJANGO REINHARDT** – 'Limehouse Blues'
78. **BERNARD SUMNER** – 'New Dawn Fades' (Joy Division)
79. **ALVIN LEE** – 'Love Like A Man' (Ten Years After)
80. **LES PAUL** – 'The World Is Waiting For The Sunshine' (With Mary Ford)
81. **ANDY SUMMERS** – 'Message In A Bottle' (Police)
82. **MICK RONSON** – 'You Shook Me Cold' (David Bowie)
83. **ZOOT HORN ROLLO** – 'Moonlight On Vermont' (Captain Beefheart)
84. **LOWELL GEORGE** – 'Tripe Face Boogie' (Little Feat)

85. **RORY GALLAGHER** – 'Bullfrog Blues'
86. **ANDY POWELL & TED TURNER** – 'Blowin' Free' (Wishbone Ash)
87. **GLENN BRANCA** – 'Symphony Number 6'
88. **MICK ABRAHAMS** – 'Ain't Ya Coming Home Babe?' (Blodwyn Pig)
89. **MIKE RATHKE** – 'Busload Of Faith' (Lou Reed)
90. **MICK BOX** – 'Gypsy' (Uriah Heep)
91. **TONY HICKS** – 'I Can't Let Go' (Hollies)
92. **GEORGE THOROGOOD** – 'Bad To The Bone'
93. **MICK TAYLOR** – 'Walkin' On Sunset'
94. **ALBERT LEE** – 'Luxury Liner' (Emmylou Harris)
95. **PAT METHENY** – 'Electric Counterpoint' (Steve Reich)
96. **ZAKK WYLDE** – 'War Pigs' (Ozzy Osbourne)
97. **LENNY KAYE** – 'Pumping [My Heart]' (Patti Smith Group)
98. **ROBERT SMITH** – 'Boys Don't Cry' (The Cure)
99. **MICK HARVEY** – 'The Singer' (Nick Cave)
100. **JOHN SQUIRE** – 'Fools Gold' (Stone Roses)

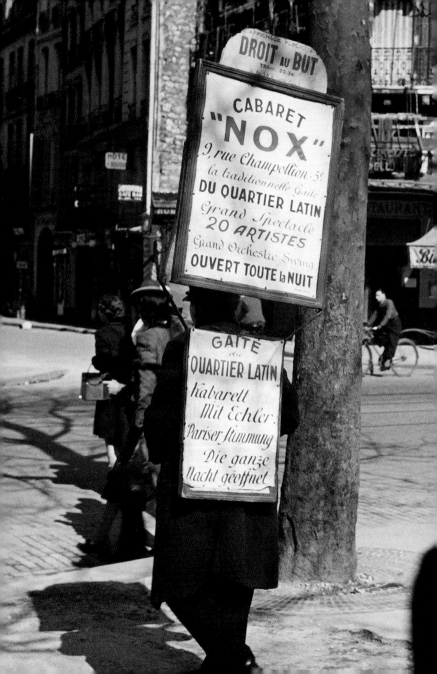

STUDIO 28

VILLE DORÉE

SOMMAIRE

LA VIE CULTURELLE
DANS LA FRANCE OCCUPÉE

Olivier Barrot et Raymond Chirat

PROPAGANDASTAFFEL PARIS

DER PROP.-ABTEILUNG FRANKREICH

GRUPPE PRESSE
Referat 5

DÉCOUVERTES GALLIMARD
HISTOIRE

Juin 1940 : l'armistice arrête la déroute, stoppe la grande pagaille et découpe le pays en deux tranches. Vichy devient capitale de la zone libre. La République liquidée, l'État français légifère. Il déifie son chef, le maréchal Pétain, dénonce et moralise. En zone occupée, Paris se soumet à la censure militaire et subit la pression de l'ambassade d'Allemagne pour une collaboration active.

CHAPITRE 1

LA FRANCE OCCUPÉE

15 juin 1940, au petit matin, la méditation du vainqueur devant le désert de la rue de Rivoli. Ni piétons, ni chiens, ni voitures. Seul l'étendard nazi aussitôt déployé trouble de ses frissons le silence de la ville (à gauche). Une époque commence, lourde de contraintes, comme le laissez-passer obligatoire pour la circulation et les passages aux frontières des deux zones (à droite, celui d'un inspecteur des Messageries Hachette).

1940, l'armistice et ses conditions

Depuis plusieurs semaines, le déferlement des divisions allemandes, soutenues efficacement par l'aviation, terrorise les populations françaises en fuite par millions. Le 14 juin, la Wehrmacht est à Paris. Le 16, le président du Conseil Paul Reynaud démissionne. Un gouvernement de la dernière heure est mis en place. Le maréchal Pétain en est le président, le général Weygand le ministre de la Défense. Soucieux de préserver l'honneur de l'armée, hostile à la capitulation, il insiste pour solliciter un armistice. Tandis que Charles de Gaulle, sous-secrétaire d'État à la Guerre dans l'ancien gouvernement, s'envole pour Londres, le Maréchal annonce, le 17 juin, aux Français « le cœur serré, qu'il faut cesser le combat ». Le lendemain, 18 juin, le général de Gaulle lance, sur les ondes anglaises, son premier appel à la résistance.

Le 22 juin 1940, l'armistice entre la France et l'Allemagne est signé à Rethondes. Il morcelle la France en deux zones, l'une libre, l'autre occupée. La zone occupée par l'Allemagne correspond aux trois cinquièmes du pays. Elle est définie par une ligne de démarcation, frontière contrôlée de 1 000 kilomètres qui serpente de l'Espagne à la Suisse et englobe toutes les façades maritimes à l'exception des côtes méditerranéennes. Le reste, ou zone libre, est la portion consentie au nouveau territoire français. De plus, un million et demi de prisonniers sont parqués en Allemagne et le paiement des frais d'entretien des troupes occupantes est demandé à la France, ce qui bouleverse l'économie du pays. Mais, Hitler étant favorable à un gouvernement français en zone libre, l'armistice est jugé acceptable par le gouvernement : pas d'annexion, pas de mainmise sur l'empire colonial,

La France se brise en deux morceaux (ci-dessous). La zone occupée englobe Paris, descend jusqu'à l'Allier, annexe les côtes de l'Atlantique, de la Manche et celles de la mer du Nord. Elle s'étale des Landes aux provinces de l'Est, victimes de dispositions

particulières en Alsace-Lorraine. Les départements du Nord sont décrétés zone interdite. Le pourtour méditerranéen est le seul épargné et Vichy devient capitale de l'État français. La Kommandantur impose aux Parisiens un calendrier officiel. Seul le statut de la France d'outre-mer n'est pas modifié.

Les multiples services de la Kommandantur (signalés en caractères gothiques) s'installent au centre de Paris, près de l'Opéra (ci-contre). La capitale se plie à l'heure de Berlin (une heure en moins), et ses artères se hérissent de pancartes et de poteaux indicateurs en allemand, destinés à guider dans la ville les troupes d'occupation (ci-dessous).

pas de livraison de la flotte seulement désarmée. Le 25 juin, les vingt-quatre articles approuvés entrent en vigueur.

Paris, centre de la France occupée

Paris, capitale enviée par Hitler qui la visite rapidement, se soumet à l'autorité militaire allemande. Les bureaux du commandant du « Gross Paris » s'installent au Palais-Bourbon. Le palais du Luxembourg accueille le quartier général de la Luftwaffe et les réquisitions affectent près de 400 hôtels (dont le Meurice, résidence de Von Choltitz, commandant du Gross Paris, et le Majestic, siège du commandement militaire en France). Les trois couleurs françaises s'éclipsent, la croix gammée déferle et les pancartes de signalisation en allemand jalonnent les vingt arrondissements. Paris devient à la fois ville de garnison et ville de détente pour les militaires.

À partir de septembre 1940, les premières

ordonnances raciales sont promulguées, qui « définissent » les Juifs, les excluent de certaines professions et les dépossèdent de leurs biens dans le cadre de l'aryanisation.

Les courriers à en-tête des organismes de contrôle vont proliférer et réglementer les moindres détails de la vie culturelle. Ici, tampon du département Culture de la Propaganda Staffel de Paris (à gauche); en-tête du département de la Propaganda Abteilung au ministère de la Propagande du Reich (au centre); en-tête du Deutsches Institut de Paris (ci-dessous).

Culture, censure et propagande

Pour l'Allemagne, la suprématie culturelle de la France doit s'effacer devant le rayonnement

```
An die
Propaganda-Abteilung beim
Militärbefehlshaber in Frankreich
Hôtel Majestic

P a r i s
```

DEUTSCHES INSTITUT
57, RUE SAINT DOMINIQUE
1, RUE TALLEYRAND
PARIS 7ᵉ
TEL. INVALIDES 60·80 bis 85

allemand. L'occupant veut également extirper de la culture française toute influence juive, maçonnique ou anti-allemande. La censure s'appuie d'un côté sur la MBF et en particulier la Propaganda Abteilung, délégation du ministère de la Propagande du Reich. Fief de Goebbels, ministre de la Propagande en Allemagne, dirigée à Paris par le capitaine Schmidtke et divisée régionalement en quatre Propaganda Staffeln (dont la principale est celle de Paris), elle est responsable de la lutte contre les Juifs et les francs-maçons et de la surveillance des menées anti-allemandes. Ses services (*Referaten*) contrôlent la presse, l'édition, la radio, les actualités cinématographiques et les films.

L'autre pôle de contrôle de la culture se trouve à l'ambassade. Otto Abetz, ambassadeur d'Allemagne, entend garder la haute main sur la propagande. Il se targue d'affinités avec les Français. Bel homme, décoratif, le francophile Abetz règne sur les échanges culturels, même si la prépondérance de l'armée s'impose tout au long de l'Occupation. Il amorce une véritable « collaboration intellectuelle », puissamment aidé par le directeur de l'Institut allemand. Karl Epting, national-socialiste bon teint,

préconise une réconciliation franco-allemande et une multiplication des échanges entre les deux pays. L'Institut organise des voyages culturels dans le Grand Reich et de multiples conférences en France, servi par des conférenciers convaincants tels que Friedrich Sieburg et Helmut Grimm.

Otto Abetz remplit parfaitement son rôle. Il affirmera plus tard que ses invitations furent toujours honorées aussi bien par une élite intellectuelle que par les acteurs et artistes en vogue côtoyant quelques grands noms du Paris mondain. Soucieux d'offrir la meilleure image du vainqueur, il multiplie galas, rencontres, sorties de films. Toutes manifestations entraînant les énergies françaises dans la spirale collaborationniste qui va bientôt s'infiltrer en province.

Otto Abetz s'installe dès août 1940, au 78, rue de Lille, dans l'hôtel de Beauharnais, siège de l'ambassade d'Allemagne. Il connaît Paris de longue date, y a vécu, s'y est marié

avec une Française, d'où de nombreux amis dont il va profiter pour mener à bien son projet de rassemblement culturel. Attaché à ses prérogatives vis-à-vis de la Kommandantur, il se conforme pourtant strictement aux décisions du Führer. Ci-contre, Otto Abetz quittant l'hôtel Majestic, avenue Kléber, siège de la Propaganda Abteilung. Ci-dessus, de gauche à droite : Karl Epting, directeur du Deutsches Institut, Jacques Benoist-Méchin, secrétaire d'État à la vice-présidence du Conseil de l'État français, et le docteur Conti, la plus haute autorité médicale du Reich, qui vient de donner une conférence.

Deux casques ennemis réunis par une branche de laurier symbolisent les intentions pacifiques d'Otto Abetz (ci-contre). Ses armes : les conférences, concerts et réceptions somptueuses où se rend une certaine élite artistique et littéraire. Quelques exemples ici : conférence du professeur Schumann au palais d'Orsay, avec, au premier rang, Otto Abetz et Rudolf Schleier, son adjoint (page de gauche, en haut); dîner de la presse à l'ambassade – Schleier à la gauche de Jean Luchaire (debout), le directeur du Groupement de la presse quotidienne (à gauche, en bas); Abetz et son épouse, Suzanne de Bruycker, recevant les acteurs français et la troupe du Schiller Theater, venue jouer à la Comédie-Française en 1942 (ci-dessous).

ACTUALITÉ

MONSIEUR & MADAME ABETZ ONT INVITÉ LES ACTEURS FRANÇAIS ET LE

DANS LE HALL, M. ET Mme ABETZ REÇOIVENT LES INVITÉS

LE CONSUL GÉNÉRAL SCHLEIER ET G. UHLEN, DU SCHILLER THEATER.

VEDETTES DE *Paris* EN ALLEMAGNE

L'Institut allemand multiplie les voyages vers le Grand Reich. Page de gauche, en haut, en mars 1942, les actrices Viviane Romance et Danielle Darrieux, Suzy Delair et Junie Astor au départ du train les emmenant à Berlin présenter le film *Premier Rendez-vous*. Quelques mois plus tôt, c'était le tour des artistes, Despiau, Othon Friesz, Dunoyer de Segonzac, Vlaminck, Van Dongen et Derain (page de gauche, en bas). Les écrivains, deux fois sollicités, s'extasièrent sur l'accueil reçu (ci-dessous, une page de *Signal*, en janvier 1942). D'autres voyages mobilisèrent, jusqu'en 1944, des troupes de music-hall (ci-contre).

Les Lettres françaises accueillies en Allemagne

Sur invitation du Dr Goebbels, ministre du Reich, des écrivains et poètes français se sont rendus en Allemagne. Les voici dans le studio d'Arno Breker, le célèbre sculpteur allemand

M. ABEL BONNARD, de l'Académie Française, est, parmi les auteurs philosophiques, un des plus connus pour l'élégance de son style. Il est ici en conversation animée avec le professeur Breker et un autre écrivain français, M. André Fraigneau (au centre)

Vichy, siège du gouvernement de la zone libre

Le 29 juin 1940, gouvernement, sénateurs et députés emménagent à Vichy et s'installent tant bien que mal dans les hôtels de la ville où chaque chambre va devenir bureau ministériel (les Hôtels du Parc et Majestic accueillent le Maréchal et ses services ainsi que ceux des Affaires étrangères).

La confusion règne. Certains élus, partisans de continuer la lutte en Afrique du Nord et embarqués

Sur le perron de l'hôtel du Parc : le maréchal Pétain (au centre), Pierre Laval (à sa droite), Fernand de Brinon (délégué général du gouvernement à Paris ; en costume clair), René Bousquet, secrétaire général de la Police (à gauche, sur la marche). Le salut au drapeau, le défilé d'une maigre

sur le *Massilia*, sont appréhendés à leur arrivée à Casablanca. Les machinations de Pierre Laval, alors vice-président du Conseil des ministres du gouvernement Pétain (futur vice-président du Conseil et secrétaire d'État aux Affaires étrangères de l'État français) précipitent l'autosabordage des parlementaires. Réunis au Petit Casino de Vichy et à la salle des Sociétés médicales, épouvantés par l'affrontement franco-anglais et la destruction de la flotte à Mers el-Kebir, les deux chambres votent, le 10 juillet 1940 par 549 voix sur 669 votants, les pleins pouvoirs à Philippe Pétain.

Pétain, chef de l'État français : révolution nationale et collaboration d'État

Un ordre nouveau commence. La République est remplacée par l'État français. À la devise « Liberté,

participation militaire tolérée par les conventions d'armistice, la présence insidieuse des représentants de la police composent les réjouissances scandant la vie de la station thermale devenue capitale de l'État français. Manquent sur le cliché quelques ecclésiastiques vénérant en Pétain, le chef aux yeux clairs, la « divine surprise », selon l'écrivain royaliste Charles Maurras. Un État qualifié par certains de « communauté réduite aux caquets ».

Égalité,
Fraternité », se substitue
« Travail, Famille,
Patrie ». Le Maréchal arpente le
territoire qui lui est concédé,
profitant de la confiance sans limites d'une
population à la fois soulagée de la misère des
combats et confiante dans les étoiles de son guide.
Le chef de l'État va répétant inlassablement sa
confiance dans les moissons futures, sa bienveillance
pour les provinces, sa prédilection pour le folklore
et sa volonté de redorer les traditions oubliées.
Il prêche avant tout la contrition régénératrice :
la France doit se relever, il la soutient, aidé par les
vétérans de la Grande Guerre, réunis dès le 29 août
en Légion des combattants. Le drapeau n'est plus en
berne, le coq recommence à chanter !

Pétain multiplie les voyages en zone libre. Impavide, la main au képi, les lèvres sur l'étendard, il scande de sa canne les défilés des combattants fiers de porter son emblème, la francisque (ci-dessus, à Toulouse en juin 1942; au centre, le nouvel emblème et sa devise). Il accepte avec dignité les vivats de la foule. Selon le cardinal Gerlier, primat des Gaules, « les cris de vive l'armée, vive la France, vive la paix se confondent, car la France c'est Pétain ».

Les premières lois raciales sont édictées par l'État français : dès le 22 juillet 1940, c'est la révision des naturalisations, le 3 octobre, le statut des Juifs, plus radical qu'en zone occupée dans la « définition » et l'exclusion. Des lois applicables dans les deux zones, et qui se conjuguent avec les mesures allemandes.

Dans le gouvernement de Vichy, trois ministres vont se consacrer à la culture. Dès février 1941, Paul Marion devient secrétaire général à l'Information et à la Propagande. Il croit à une construction européenne sous l'égide de l'Allemagne et est obsédé par l'idée d'un ralliement de l'opinion autour du Maréchal. Il n'atteint pas son but. À la même date, Jérôme Carcopino est nommé ministre de l'Éducation nationale et de la Jeunesse (et ministre de tutelle du secrétariat général aux Beaux-Arts), favorisant l'École libre tout en ménageant la laïcité. Il est supplanté en 1942 par Abel Bonnard, habitué des salons

grande salle de jeux a été divisée en cellules. Il y a quelques mois, ces cellules étaient séparées par les décors du théâtre, aujourd'hui remplacés par des cloisons. A droite, vue de la même salle avant-guerre.

LE CASINO DE VICHY EST DEVENU LE MINISTÈRE DE LA JEUNESSE

Avant la guerre, le Casino de Vichy était l'un des plus célèbres du monde. Il abrite provisoirement le Secrétariat général à la Jeunesse. Aux termes de la loi du 23 avril 1941, qui l'a réorganisé, le Secrétariat général à la Jeunesse « contrôle la formation morale, sociale, civique et professionnelle des jeunes ». Son titulaire est M. Georges Lamirand, né le 12 juin 1895, fils d'un inspecteur général de l'enseignement, ancien élève de Centrale, ingénieur de l'industrie charbonnière et métallurgique, puis ... une usine de papiers peints, chef du per-

parisiens, membre de l'Académie française, qui va virer à un collaborationnisme forcené entretenu par son ami Otto Abetz.

Un chantre de la collaboration franco-allemande, Fernand de Brinon, devient délégué général du gouvernement – ambassadeur – pour les territoires occupés. Malgré tout, Otto Abetz se méfie des intentions revanchardes qu'il prête à l'entourage militaire du chef de l'État français et se conforme aux directives de Ribbentrop, ministre des Affaires étrangères du Reich : l'Allemagne victorieuse doit évincer la France en quelque domaine que ce soit.

La France occupée

Les violences antisémites, entamées dès le 7 juin 1942 par l'obligation faite aux Juifs d'arborer l'étoile jaune à six pointes, s'accentuent. Leur arrestation en masse par les Allemands va se faire grâce aux différents fichiers, après entente avec René Bousquet, secrétaire général de la Police du gouvernement de Vichy et avec participation de la police française.

Le 11 novembre 1942, pour riposter au débarquement des Alliés en Afrique du Nord, les Allemands envahissent la zone Sud et occupent tout le territoire. Dès lors dans l'Hexagone occupé, face à une collaboration extrême, vont proliférer les mouvements de résistance, y compris dans le milieu culturel.

Vue aérienne de la métamorphose du casino de Vichy en secrétariat général de la Jeunesse, placé sous la tutelle du ministre de l'Éducation nationale : les tables de la roulette ont cédé la place à des alvéoles ministérielles semblables à celles qui encombrent les chambres d'hôtel (au centre). De gauche à droite, photographiés dans leurs bureaux improvisés : Paul Marion, secrétaire à l'Information et à la Propagande ; Abel Bonnard, ministre de l'Éducation nationale en 1942 ; Fernand de Brinon, premier journaliste français à avoir interviewé Hitler en 1933, est le délégué général du gouvernement à Paris. Enfin le secrétaire à la vice-présidence du Conseil, Jacques Benoist-Méchin, auteur, en 1933, d'une *Histoire de l'armée allemande*, et désireux d'associer la France à la direction d'une « Nouvelle Europe ».

Drôle d'époque, que le recul rend difficile à comprendre. Des Parisiens trouvent ces Allemands fréquentables, jusqu'à ce qu'ils se heurtent à d'insoutenables difficultés de survie. Officiellement, on n'hésite pas à devancer les exigences de l'occupant, les salles de spectacle ne désemplissent pas, Paris sera toujours Paris, capitale d'une mode en ersatz. On chante, on danse, on joue la comédie. Mais la Propaganda sévit et la spoliation des biens juifs a commencé.

CHAPITRE 2

L'AIR DU TEMPS

Repos du guerrier pour les troupes allemandes qui savourent leur victoire en admirant les spectacles des boîtes de nuit, en progression constante (à gauche, au Moulin de la Galette). Cependant la propagande virulente voue à l'exécration les Juifs, le bolchevisme et la franc-maçonnerie, et cela à Lyon autant qu'à Paris (ci-contre, en mars 1943 à Lyon, l'exposition « Le bolchevisme contre l'Europe »).

Propagande et « amitié franco-allemande »

La plus brillante manifestation de propagande, celle qui fit battre à l'unisson les cœurs acquis à la collaboration, reste la rencontre des visiteurs avec les œuvres d'Arno Breker, sculpteur allemand chantre du héros aryen, au musée de l'Orangerie, le 15 mai 1942. Grâce aux efforts d'Otto Abetz et de Jacques Benoist-Méchin, secrétaire d'État auprès du gouvernement de Vichy et organisateur de l'événement, le rassemblement France-Allemagne s'impose à l'ombre de ses statues colossales. Breker, choyé par Hitler, a du goût pour la France dont il apprécie et vante les artistes. Le ministre de l'Éducation nationale et à la Jeunesse, Abel Bonnard, et

La fine fleur de la Collaboration à l'inauguration de l'exposition Breker. De gauche à droite : A. Bonnard, J. Benoist-Méchin, Mᵐᵉ Breker, A. Breker, F. de Brinon, C. Magny (préfet de la Seine) et le général von Barckhausen.

SALUT A BREKER

par Jean COCTEAU

JE VOUS SALUE, BREKER. JE VOUS SALUE DE LA HAUTE PATRIE DES POÈTES, PATRIE OÙ LES PATRIES N'EXISTENT PAS, SAUF DANS LA MESURE OÙ CHACUN Y APPORTE LE TRÉSOR DU TRAVAIL NATIONAL.

JE VOUS SALUE, PARCE QUE VOUS RÉHABILITEZ LES MILLE RELIEFS DONT UN ARBRE COMPOSE SA GRANDEUR.

PARCE QUE VOUS REGARDEZ VOS MODÈLES COMME DES ARBRES ET QUE, LOIN DE SACRIFIER AUX VOLUMES, VOUS DOUE VOS BRONZES ET VOS PLÂTRES D'UNE SÈVE DÉLICATE QUI TOU MENTE LE BOUCLIER D'ACHILLE DE LEURS GENOUX, QUI FA SYSTÈME FLUVIAL DE LEURS VEINES, QUI FRISE

Benoist-Méchin déroulent leurs discours, l'intelligentsia les savoure et le sculpteur Maillol, sortant de sa retraite, les cautionne. Cocteau adresse, le 23 mai, en lettres capitales et en première page de l'hebdomadaire *Comœdia*, un vibrant salut à Breker.

Un feu roulant de mondanités lui fait écho. Le musée Rodin, l'ambassade, le Ritz, la librairie Rive Gauche y participent. Brasillach, rédacteur en chef du très collaborationniste *Je suis partout*, donne une conférence, un concert réunit les pianistes Alfred Cortot et Wilhem Kempf, et la cantatrice Germaine Lubin. Sacha Guitry s'exclame : « Si les statues de Breker entraient en érection, on ne pourrait plus circuler. »

Fernand de Brinon, ambassadeur de l'État français à Paris, préside la clôture en présence des couturiers à la mode entourés de leurs plus fidèles clientes : Josée de Chambrun, fille de Pierre Laval, Arletty…

Des expositions sont organisées qui, avec tout le savoir-faire de la propagande, adressent aux occupés deux messages essentiels : ils partagent, avec le vainqueur, des ennemis communs ; leur avenir, c'est l'insertion volontaire de la France dans l'Europe allemande. À la fin de 1941, la curiosité et la gratuité des entrées attirent un million de personnes au Petit Palais où sont dénoncés les méfaits de la franc-maçonnerie. En mai 1941, il y aura 635 000 visiteurs au Grand Palais à la rencontre de « La France européenne ». La Propaganda, qui dénonce en septembre « Le Juif et la France » au palais Berlitz, stigmatise le bolchevisme en 1942 salle Wagram, finit par lasser le public. Celui-ci, déjà, n'avait guère été ému par le retour des cendres de l'Aiglon effectué majestueusement aux Invalides, en décembre 1940.

En mai 1942, au terme des hommages répétés au sculpteur allemand (au centre, le salut de Cocteau à Breker), l'intelligentsia se retrouve à l'ombre des statues colossales pour un concert destiné à séduire les mélomanes. Il réunit Germaine Lubin, auréolée par son triomphe à Bayreuth, le pianiste allemand Wilhelm Kempf et le Français Alfred Cortot (ci-dessus). Ce dernier, bien en cour à Vichy, admirateur inconditionnel de Hitler, avait déjà participé au festival Mozart organisé par l'occupant en décembre 1941 à Paris.

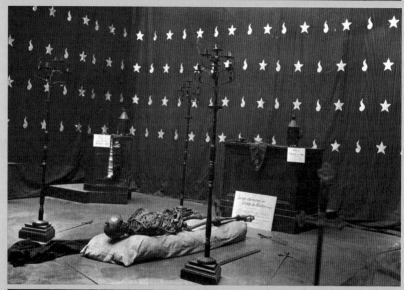

Jusqu'en 1942, les expositions organisées par les Français, financées et orientées en coulisse par la Propaganda Staffel et l'ambassade se succèdent à Paris et en zone libre. En octobre 1940, les rites de la franc-maçonnerie sont mis en scène au Petit Palais, sous la férule de Jacques de Lesdin et Jean Marquès-Rivière. « Acte de foi et d'énergie » selon Fernand de Brinon, l'exposition « France européenne » offre en juin 1941 la démonstration d'une France prête à participer volontairement à l'édifice européen, où Hitler a laissé entendre qu'elle occuperait la seconde place (ci-contre, en bas, le commandant des forces d'occupation, H. von Stülpnagel, sort du Grand Palais). En septembre 1941, c'est l'« emprise » des Juifs en France qui est dénoncée au palais Berlitz. Manifestation organisée par l'Institut d'études des questions juives, à grand renfort de caricatures haineuses et d'affiches provocatrices (ci-contre, en haut, signée Michel Jacquot). Le 6 mars 1942, « La France contre le bolchevisme », organisée cette fois par la Propaganda, est inaugurée par Schleier, de Brinon et Marion (page de gauche, en bas, sous la fresque illustrant la poignée de main entre Hitler et Pétain à Montoire).

L'art entre spoliation et exposition, pillage et vernissage

Le recensement des collections juives démarre le 30 juin 1940. En octobre, commence le pillage. Un pillage très rapide, puisque, fin 1941, l'essentiel des œuvres a été confisqué. Les stocks des grands marchands de tableaux comme Wildenstein, Seligmann, Paul Rosenberg ou Bernheim-Jeune se retrouvent d'abord à l'ambassade. Soixante-dix-neuf collections, dont celles des Rothschild, d'Albert Kahn, de David-Weil, de Seligmann, de Lévy-Benzion, sont saisies, avec l'aide de la police française. Goering, qui s'est réservé la part du lion, fait parade au Jeu de paume des œuvres d'art qu'il a spoliées.

La vie artistique n'est pas morte pour autant. La peinture sera

Alfred Rosenberg, responsable, à Berlin, du service en charge du pillage des collections juives (ERR), masque ces razzias sous l'idéologie de la lutte contre le judaïsme. Hermann Goering, lui, s'en réjouit. Il choisit le musée du Jeu de paume pour étaler sans vergogne les rapines

Je tiens à attirer votre attention sur le fait que le Musée du Jeu de Paume a été réquisitionné depuis le début de l'occupation par les autorités allemandes qui l'utilisent comme dépôt des collections juives. Un personnel de gardiennage des musées nationaux y demeure pour assurer le service de sécurité et de nettoyage;

constamment à l'honneur sous l'Occupation. Les galeries gardent leur attrait, aussi bien les anciennes que les nouvelles : Charpentier rend hommage aux paysagistes français, de Corot à nos jours, Louis Carré expose aussi Maillol. Plus récente, la Galerie de France regroupera en février 1943 des œuvres de Bazaine, Villon, Fougeron. La galerie parisienne de Jeanne Bucher, qui a déjà exposé Pignon, Bazaine, Lapicque et Max Ernst, se distingue en 1942 par son obstination et son courage en exposant Kandinsky et Nicolas de Staël, une action jugée provocatrice par les Allemands.

effectuées sur les collections d'Albert Kahn et de bien d'autres. Dès novembre 1940, les murs de la salle des Martyrs sont tapissés des trésors confisqués (en haut; ci-dessus, lettre au responsable vichyssois des Beaux-Arts signalant le travail de gardiennage des collections juives exigé du personnel du musée par les Allemands).

Si Maillol reste fidèle aux environs de Banyuls, si Matisse travaille près d'Avignon, Paris, en dépit de l'éloignement de Kisling, Chagall, Léger ou Mondrian, connaît toujours l'effervescence artistique symbolisée par Picasso. Sans exposer, celui-ci n'arrête pas de peindre. Il profite de sa renommée, se targue de la confiance de Cocteau, de l'amitié de Serge Lifar. Il reçoit le francophile Ernst Jünger, évite de trop parler et trouve un défenseur de poids avec Arno Breker qui, à Berlin, exalte le talent de ce représentant de l'« art dégénéré ».

À Paris, le salon d'Automne rassemble ses fidèles à Chaillot dès novembre 1940. Le vernissage des Indépendants provoque en 1941 d'acerbes critiques. Dans *Je suis partout*, Lucien Rebatet propose même d'inscrire « la liquidation des Indépendants » « dans le grand nettoyage de la France ». Le 6 août 1942, a lieu l'inauguration du palais de Tokyo qui doit, selon Louis Hautecœur, secrétaire d'État aux Beaux-Arts et chantre vichyste du nationalisme artistique, exalter « l'art, fleur de la nation ». Une façon de montrer que la France a su conserver son prestige artistique malgré la défaite.

Au Louvre (ci-dessus), dans les salles du séquestre (six en tout) – véritable enclave allemande reflétant l'ampleur et la systématisation du pillage –, s'empile la masse du butin, des tas de tableaux retournés, avec ou sans cadre selon leur destination. La plupart des transporteurs parisiens ont été réquisitionnés pour déplacer des œuvres spoliées. Les tableaux sont inventoriés et numérotés par des historiens d'art sous contrôle policier. Il s'agit d'abord du personnel du Louvre, remplacé dès le 26 octobre 1940 par des Allemands. Un registre clandestin et partiel est cependant constitué.

Touristes en uniforme

L'ayant catalogué Luna Park de l'Europe, Goebbels voue Paris aux plaisirs du militaire et du permissionnaire. On affecte à leur intention des brasseries (*Soldaten-Heim*), des salles de théâtre (*Soldaten-Theater*), des salles de cinéma (*Soldaten-Kino*) dont le Rex et le Marignan, le Paris.

   Une centaine d'établissements éparpillés entre Montmartre, Montparnasse et les Champs-Élysées proposent leurs programmes – *Paris bei Nacht* –, plus suivis que les visites culturelles proposées au Louvre ou à Versailles. Deux music-halls, l'Alcazar et l'ABC, obtempèrent et invitent, en allemand, les soldats à savourer un aspect du repos du guerrier. De Montmartre à Montparnasse, que choisir ? Tout se ressemble : *Vive Paris, Toujours Paris, Fleurs de Paris, Paris je t'aime*… et rapidement les cinémas de quartier vont s'efforcer d'offrir en attraction des numéros de chanteurs, de clowns, d'acrobates. À la fin de l'année 1940, les Folies-Bergère trépident à bureau fermé. À minuit, les bouchons de champagne sautent. Enterrons l'an 40. La guerre, connais pas. L'occupation – allons donc – Paris sera toujours Paris.

Divertir l'occupant et l'occupé : une nécessité

La puissance occupante l'exige : Paris, ex-Ville lumière, doit retrouver son auréole. Les courses

En ordre parfait, marquant la cadence, les troupes allemandes au repos pénètrent dans les salles de cinéma à elles seules réservées. D'autres militaires montent en vagues épaisses à l'assaut de la basilique du Sacré-Cœur (à droite, au centre).

Goebbels, qui avait trouvé Paris triste, veut ranimer « à tout prix l'activité et la gaieté ». La capitale s'accroche à sa légende. Le soir, les Folies-Bergère, quintessence des nuits parisiennes, offrent aux vainqueurs leurs bouquets de jolies filles (à droite, détail d'une affichette en allemand). Le Moulin Rouge, le Casino de Paris et d'autres établissements se hâtent d'aguicher ce nouveau public. Le désastre de juin 1940 s'estompe, la capitale recommence à respirer.

hippiques constituent, paraît-il, un élément indispensable au bon moral de la capitale. Longchamp rouvre en 1941 : succès immédiat. Auteuil, Chantilly, Maisons-Laffitte drainent turfistes et élégantes. Jean Guéhenno se scandalise qu'après le bombardement des usines

Die Bekannten

FOLIES BERGÈRE

AUS PARIS

Renault (le 3 mars 1942), les cadavres n'arrêtent pas les épreuves à Longchamp et que, le lendemain, les journaux publient, en même temps que les listes des victimes, le résultat des courses. Le PMU ne transige pas.

Bringen die Grosse Revue

FOLIES IN BLUMEN

  Les boîtes de nuit et cabarets prolifèrent. L'annuaire du spectacle de 1942 recense pas moins de cent deux boîtes de nuit ouvertes.

À La Vie parisienne, qui mélange tous les soirs Allemands de passage et Français désinvoltes, Suzy Solidor soupire *Lily Marlène* avant d'imposer ses refrains de marins, pressée de se faire remarquer à la radio et d'enchaîner avec un autre cabaret pour y reprendre *Lily Marlène*. Lucienne Boyer reçoit Chez Elle. Elle en écarte les Juifs, mais refusera plus tard de se produire en Allemagne. Léo Marjane reste parisienne : à Sheherazade, « *das pariser Kabarett* », elle clame sa nostalgie et contourne, nonchalante, les gradés à la croix de fer. Le répertoire proposé déplore l'absence du prisonnier (*Si tu revois Paris*), s'attendrit sur la solitude (*Seule ce soir*). Plus tard, Ginette Leclerc, qui mise sur son image de femme fatale, inaugure le Baccara, club politique réservé aux artistes.

Dans les guinguettes, les bistros, les petits bals, la chanson populaire ne manque ni d'éclat ni d'entrain. Georgius tourne en dérision les obsessions alimentaires. Les chansonniers montmartrois, inquiets de leurs couplets anti-hitlériens pendant la Drôle de Guerre, ont mis de l'eau dans leur vin. Moins acides qu'autrefois, ils parviennent au hasard de leurs compositions à se moquer parfois des Fridolins. La censure se montre libérale. Un Martini, un Léon Michel, soumis à la Propaganda radiophonique qui se prodigue dans l'émission « Au rythme du temps », demeurent des exceptions.

« Complices ou inconscients ? »

Dès 1941, les rentrées se succèdent : Charles Trenet, prêt à rénover la France par la joie, effectue la sienne à l'Avenue mais doit faire la preuve de ses qualités de pur aryen. Mistinguett espère atténuer la dureté des

La firme Continental produit des films, mais édite aussi en petits formats les refrains à la mode qu'on chante au coin des rues (ci-dessus). On les retrouve à la fin des banquets où l'on imite Suzy Solidor, Léo Marjane et Maurice le titi parisien.

Dès juillet 1940, le Casino de Paris rouvre des portes sur lesquelles on peut lire « Interdit aux Juifs et aux Chiens ». Mistinguett, la vedette féminine la plus populaire de France, y fait sa rentrée. En janvier 1942, sur la même scène, Mistinguett, toujours, en panache, les boys en frac et les girls ondulantes mènent la sarabande et chantent la gloire d'un Montmartre en carton-pâte et paillettes (ci-contre, dernier tableau d'une revue au titre révélateur « Toujours Paris »).

temps par sa présence. Maurice Chevalier reparaît au Casino de Paris, mais soucieux de protéger sa compagne, l'indésirable Nita Raya, s'avance prudemment dans les studios de Radio-Paris. À Bobino, Piaf chante *L'Accordéoniste*, car « son boulot, c'est de chanter quoi qu'il arrive », l'occupation en tant que telle lui est indifférente. Tino Rossi se prépare à chanter pour les galas de la France européenne ; en 1943, ce sera au bénéfice des Légionnaires contre le bolchevisme. Aucune de ces vedettes ne souffre de voir les uniformes verts remplir les fauteuils d'orchestre.

Dans tous ces spectacles et revues, le public vient chercher sa part d'illusion et l'occasion d'oublier un

Quartier de l'Opéra, au Café de la Paix, à l'heure de l'apéritif, on doit s'habituer à la promiscuité des terrasses, favorable aux demoiselles de petite vertu sensibles au prestige de l'uniforme. Tous les grades de la Wehrmacht sont représentés (ci-dessous). L'usager paisible se retrouve « en étrange pays dans son pays lui-même » (Aragon).

soir la morosité. Serpentins et confettis, toute cette gaieté plaquée sur la misère ambiante, cette frénésie de parties fines qui contaminent aussi Megève et Cannes, surprennent et inquiètent. André Weil-Curiel (auteur de *Le jour se lève à Londres*, 1945), interrogé plus tard, répondra à André Halimi (réalisateur de *Chantons sous l'Occupation*, 1976) : « Les Français qui ont chanté sous l'Occupation n'ont été ni des complices ni des lâches, mais avant tout des inconscients. Pour eux, la guerre n'existait plus et ils acceptaient l'ordre nouveau voulu par les nazis. » Comme l'a dit le décorateur de revue Michel Gyarmati, « on ne pouvait pas rester sans rien faire, la maison fermée, car les

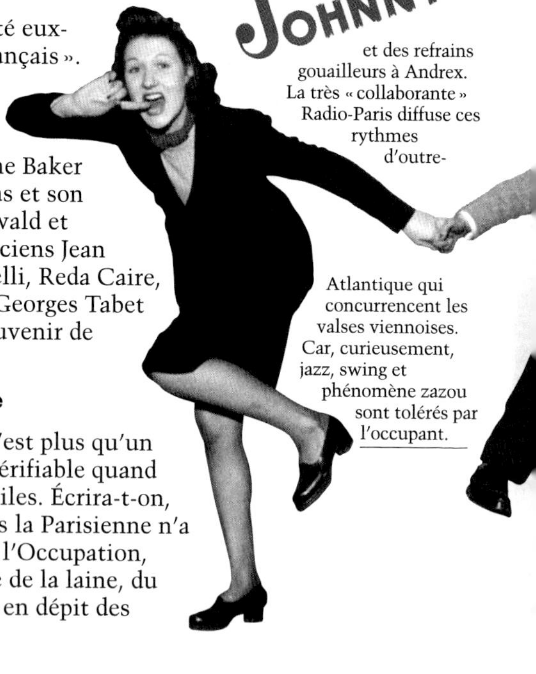

La vogue du swing, variation très prisée du jazz, fait fureur. Radio et cinéma s'en emparent. Entre musique et mode, le phénomène « zazou » amuse une jeunesse désabusée (en bas). Il inspire des couplets narquois à Johnny Hess (« Je suis swing », « Ils sont zazous » ; ci-dessous)

ILS SONT ZAZOUS

JOHNNY HESS

Allemands auraient exploité eux-mêmes avec des artistes français ».

Cependant, certaines vedettes du music-hall et de la musique aimées du public ont émigré. Joséphine Baker et ses bananes, Marie Dubas et son *Légionnaire*, Marianne Oswald et Germaine Sablon, les musiciens Jean Wiener et Stéphane Grappelli, Reda Caire, Ray Ventura, Jean Sablon, Georges Tabet entretiennent au loin le souvenir de Paris.

et des refrains gouailleurs à Andrex. La très « collaborante » Radio-Paris diffuse ces rythmes d'outre-Atlantique qui concurrencent les valses viennoises. Car, curieusement, jazz, swing et phénomène zazou sont tolérés par l'occupant.

La mode fait de la résistance

Paris sera toujours Paris. C'est plus qu'un truisme, mais une réalité vérifiable quand se profilent les temps difficiles. Écrira-t-on, parodiant Sartre, que jamais la Parisienne n'a été aussi élégante que sous l'Occupation, malgré la raréfaction rapide de la laine, du coton, de la soie et du cuir, en dépit des

LUTTONS CONTRE LE FROID!

Entretenir la flamme dans le domaine de la mode, c'est une façon de rester français. D'où l'ingéniosité assez prodigieuse des créateurs malgré la pénurie, mais aussi le rôle dévolu aux femmes au foyer, également solidaires de cette revendication nationale qu'est la continuité de la femme française dans son image et son élégance en dépit des épreuves (ci-dessous, les conseils du magazine *Elle*) Qu'importe si étoffes textiles nouveaux à base de crin de cheval, de poil de lapin ou de cheveux humains ? En tout cas le souci de tenir son rang apparaît aussi comme une façon, modeste certes, de résister, d'afficher comme un patriotisme de fidélité. La mode, quoi qu'il advienne, ne sera jamais dictée depuis Berlin, et demeure un incontestable apanage parisien et français.

À preuve la première collection de l'Occupation à l'automne 1940, à la présentation de laquelle se presse l'état-major ennemi en poste à Paris. Les grands couturiers, Chanel, Maggy Rouff, Piguet, Lanvin, Nina Ricci, Madeleine Vionnet, Lucien Lelong, Balenciaga, Jacques Fath, Schiaparelli, Molyneux, Rochas, anticipant la dureté annoncée de l'époque et les frimas hivernaux, privilégient le fonctionnel et le confortable.

et fourrures ne sont qu'ersatz et substituts. Les talons des Parisiennes claquent toujours sur les trottoirs, et les forces d'occupation ne sont pas les dernières à se retourner sur ces silhouettes. Un film comme *Falbalas* de Jacques Becker, tourné en 1944 dans le monde de la mode, donne la mesure de cette frivolité d'apparence (en haut, les coulisses d'un défilé de mode de Jacques Fath à Paris en 1942).

On insiste également sur le recyclage de vêtements passés de mode, justement, mais encore mettables, au prix d'ajustements astucieux que les magazines de mode exposent avec prodigalité. Toutes, mesdames, vous pouvez vous muer en couturières expertes ; et de toute façon, vous n'avez guère le choix ! Les semelles de bois et de liège apparaissent bientôt, comme les coutures fictives des bas, dessinées à même la peau. Pour les plus favorisées, la fourrure reste en vente libre, tandis que l'acquisition des autres pièces d'habillement s'effectue avec des points textiles et donne le choix entre des tissus chimiques aux noms aussi exotiques que le rutabaga ou le topinambour en matière d'alimentation : voici le flamangore, l'operamil, le filigrin…

Il faut bien pourtant que la vie se poursuive : malgré les restrictions, un modèle drapé trop majestueux de Madame Grès vaut à celle-ci une interdiction professionnelle, qu'une pétition signée par Cocteau, Derain, Guitry, Sauguet finira par faire lever. La profession, consciente de ses devoirs et de ses intérêts, réagit, prenant à témoin la presse spécialisée : c'est un acte véritablement politique

Escouade de charme : cinquante-quatre mannequins parisiens arrivent à Lyon pour une présentation de la mode 1942 (ci-dessus). Certains porteront cette étonnante sandale à semelle compensée en bois évidé, avec un talon en volute, le tout doublé de caoutchouc ci-dessous).

que le défilé du printemps 1942, organisé par la Chambre syndicale en zone libre, à Lyon. La haute couture française, son artisanat d'exception ne disparaîtront pas. Et bien que sinistrés, les chausseurs, modistes et gantiers s'efforcent de s'organiser, ou de se reconvertir : les premiers s'adonnent à une sorte de menuiserie pour armaturer de bois les souliers de leurs clientes. Le noir, la taille mince, les jupes courtes se répandent pour des raisons d'économie. Il n'est pas jusqu'à la haute coiffure qui ne subit les épreuves de la pénurie : cheveux courts et accessoires spectaculaires. Paraître, c'est être, on le ressent avec évidence quand on voit les films de l'époque, notamment les productions en costumes, où la mise des comédiennes continue d'éblouir et d'influencer les collections : *Les Visiteurs du soir*, *Pontcarral*, *La Duchesse de Langeais*, *Douce*. Quant aux reportages photographiques des étés de l'Occupation, ils traduisent une compréhensible volonté d'insouciance, et un sens du chic que le temps non seulement n'a nullement démodé, mais parfois consacré ou réadopté.

Des manifestations d'un genre nouveau suivent les directives des Français libres. Pour le 14 juillet 1941, la radio de Londres donne consigne à l'ensemble de la population de se promener en arborant dans ses tenues le souvenir du drapeau tricolore. Jean Guéhenno note, dans son *Journal des années noires* : « Que d'ingéniosité pour rassembler de quelque manière les trois couleurs interdites. Les souliers bleus, les bas blancs, la robe rouge. Que d'efforts dérisoires mais non pas perdus après tout. L'attention des uns aux autres finissait par créer la joie d'une communion. »

Sur l'injonction du ministère de la Production industrielle, on recycle tous les textiles contre des « points textiles » (ci-dessous). Tout est rationné (en bas, carte de ravitaillement).

La propagande du Maréchal

Dans la zone libre, le Maréchal, à sa vive satisfaction, assiste à la reproduction de sa personne et des accessoires qui l'accompagnent : képi, bâton, étoiles se multiplient. Trois artistes sont préposés à cette prolifération : Cogné pour la statuaire,

Lallemand pour étudier le style « Maréchal », Ambroselli pour l'imagerie. Mais plus qu'à la fête des Mères, instaurée le 25 mai 1941, ou à celle des Provinces, le chef de l'État, glorifié au musée Galliera, est sensible aux dessins d'enfants qui lui sont envoyés pour Noël 1940 ou à l'hommage que lui rendent en 1942 les écoles parisiennes.

Dans le domaine de la mode, il faut aussi compter avec les recommandations du gouvernement, qui songe à interdire le pantalon aux femmes et préconise les culottes courtes pour les garçons jusqu'à quinze ans. L'ordre moral nouveau sévit, la femme fauteuse de troubles, d'abandon, de luxure se voit stigmatisée. Que

Écoliers et maître écoutent religieusement un discours du Maréchal à la radio (ci-dessus, à Paris en 1941). Avec un sens accompli de ce qui ne s'appelle pas encore communication, mais bien propagande, le régime mène une efficace campagne de sanctification du « sauveur de la France », comme le chante si

MARÉCHAL

désormais la noble figure du Maréchal orne les foulards, ou à défaut les feuilles de chêne de son auguste képi ! Réhabilitons les tissus simples, comme celui que l'on dénomme opportunément… Vichy.

Le répertoire folklorique de l'État français, diffusé par toutes les chorales, rabâche les prescriptions à la mode : joies du travail et de l'effort prometteuses d'un pays régénéré. L'agriculture ne manque plus de bras : « Vive la terre de France », et les mamans garantissent le bloc familial privé de son chef, le drapeau tricolore claque au vent

bien le nouvel hymne national (ci-dessus). Il faut abolir tout esprit critique (en haut à droite, une histoire édifiante du Maréchal). Le pays, abasourdi par la défaite, obscurément honteux de cette débâcle, accepte cette prise en main. Très peu de Français en mesurent les excès ou s'en insurgent.

PALUEL-MARMONT

IL ÉTAIT UNE FOIS un MARÉCHAL de FRANCE...

IMAGES DE
PIERRE ROUSSEAU

Éditions et Publications Françaises

TRAVAIL PATRIE FAMILLE

76, Rue de Vaugirard Paris-6e

Le culte du maréchal Pétain s'appuie sur la diffusion de son image, portraits officiels, statuettes (ci-dessous, des bustes produits en série, destinés à remplacer ceux de Marianne dans les mairies et institutions publiques). Des affiches aussi, dont l'État français veille à ce qu'elles soient bientôt diffusées en zone occupée où les affiches allemandes ont pourtant priorité. Les Allemands les utilisent en effet comme des armes de propagande massive. La population les arrache, les lacère ou les détourne. Acte de sabotage en zone occupée, délit en zone Sud. Une véritable guerre des affiches se déroule sur les murs de France, où se liront bientôt celles collées par la Résistance.

NOUS VOILA!

nouveau. Beaux jours de l'été 1940 quand André Dassary chante à pleins poumons son serment d'allégeance à Philippe Pétain : « Maréchal, nous voilà… » Au fil des saisons l'hymne s'essouffle. Anna Marly martèle sourdement un chant de Libération. La parenthèse de Vichy se ferme tandis que s'impose définitivement ce qui devient le *Chant des partisans.*

C'est le monde de l'imprimé, celui des livres et des journaux, qui a fourni la contribution la plus visible et la plus symbolique aux activités culturelles de la France occupée. De Brasillach à Vercors, la gamme est large et perdure dans les mémoires : normal, l'écrit reflète au plus près les interrogations intimes, celles qui portent sur la conscience.

CHAPITRE 3

L'IMPRIMÉ

Une Parisienne séduisante plongée dans la lecture entre deux éventaires de bouquinistes : cette photo d'André Zucca (à gauche) traduit à sa façon l'importance de l'écrit. S'il est des « ouvrages littéraires non désirables en France » – ceux de la fameuse liste Otto –, la vie des livres et des journaux connaît une exceptionnelle densité (ci-contre, 3e liste Otto du 10 mai 1943, avec, en annexe, le nom de 739 écrivains juifs).

SUPPLÉMENT
AU BULLETIN DE L'INSTRUCTION PRIMAIRE
N° 166

Ouvrages Littéraires

non désirables

en France

Une presse contrôlée

La presse était déjà sous contrôle français depuis juin 1939, contrôle qui avait aussi prévalu lors du premier conflit mondial. Il s'agit de prévenir toute atteinte au sacro-saint moral des troupes, dont on s'est peu à peu convaincu qu'elles ne pouvaient être défaites. Jean Giraudoux, puis Ludovic-Oscar Frossard et enfin Jean Prouvost dirigent un Commissariat général à l'information largement inféodé aux directives de l'état-major. On voit des placards blancs, c'est-à-dire censurés, dans les journaux de la Drôle de Guerre, on interdit la presse communiste après la signature du pacte germano-soviétique (août 1939), on veille scrupuleusement à combattre un pacifisme rampant, accru par l'immobilité de l'armée et le retour des mobilisés dans leurs foyers. La hantise, c'est cette mystérieuse Cinquième Colonne à la solde de Berlin, ou peut-être de Moscou, ou encore de Londres, ces « oreilles ennemies [qui] nous écoutent », stigmatisées par les affiches de Paul Colin.

De nouvelles règles du jeu

Toutes précautions balayées en juin 1940. Certains titres interrompent purement et simplement leur activité (on dit alors qu'ils se « sabordent »), les quotidiens *L'Intransigeant*, indépendant, *L'Aube*, chrétien démocrate, *Le Populaire*, socialiste, les régionaux *La Croix du Nord*, *L'Est républicain*, et l'hebdomadaire

Une administration est spécialement créée pour distribuer le papier à la presse et à l'édition (ci-dessous). Étape d'une censure qui en connaît beaucoup d'autres (en bas, l'œil ct les ciseaux des censeurs allemands). Autre moyen de contrôle, la carte professionnelle délivrée par l'administration allemande (à gauche, celle de Brasillach, rédacteur en chef de *Je suis partout*).

OFFICE DES PAPIERS DE PRESSE ET D'ÉDITION

S. A. R. L. 50.000 fr.

31. RUE TRON...

PARI...

Le Canard enchaîné. D'autres demeurent à Paris sous l'autorité allemande, ou émigrent en zone libre sous le regard de Vichy.

Mais les règles du jeu journalistique ont partout changé du tout au tout. À Paris, les autorités allemandes instaurent la censure préalable jusqu'à 1943, puis un nouveau « contrat de confiance » qui donne une bonne idée de la docilité des publications de la capitale. Ils contrôlent aussi l'agence Havas, rebaptisée Office français d'information (OFI) ainsi que l'officine obligée Inter France, et acquièrent tout ou partie du capital des titres qui restent à Paris, via le « trust » de Gerhard Hibbelen.

Le Dr Dietrich, chef de la presse du Reich, réunit régulièrement les directeurs des principaux journaux parisiens lors de conférences « d'orientation ». Sur cette photographie, prise au Ritz, publiée dans *La Semaine* du 12 décembre 1940 (ci-dessus), on peut voir, de gauche à droite : le Dr Dietrich, Henri Lèbre du *Cri du peuple*, le directeur de *Paris-Soir*, Marcel Déat de *L'Œuvre*, Guy Zuccarelli des *Nouveaux Temps*, Fernand de Brinon et, de dos, Georges Suarez d'*Aujourd'hui*.

À partir de 1941, l'organisation de la censure en zone Sud porte la marque de Paul Marion, ministre de l'Information. C'est l'Office français d'information qui donne ses consignes à la presse. Ici, en avril 1942, Marion répond aux journalistes (au centre; à gauche, René Bousquet, secrétaire général de la police). En décembre 1942, René Bonnefoy le remplace. Il propose une certaine souplesse de la censure contre un « soutien » à la politique de Vichy.

À Vichy, Pierre Laval et les responsables de l'information, Paul Marion, puis René Bonnefoy, diligentent la célébration des mérites de la politique du Maréchal et interdisent toute référence à de Gaulle; à la fin de la zone Sud en 1942, la mainmise de Berlin s'y généralise tout naturellement.

Au Nord, une presse collaborationniste ou servile

Le paysage journalistique français se divise en deux zones inégales et contrastées. En zone Nord, *Le Matin* et *Le Petit Parisien* ont reparu, journaux populaires et influents dont la direction a changé, assurée désormais par de « nouveaux messieurs », sympathisants du régime vainqueur. *Paris-Soir* s'étant transporté à Lyon, l'occupant choisit pittoresquement d'en publier une version parisienne à lui.

De nouveaux quotidiens voient le jour : *Aujourd'hui*, fréquemment ironique à l'endroit du pouvoir, notamment sous la plume de son premier

Deux affiches de presse collaborationniste illustrées par Ralph Soupault : *Au pilori*, avec des caricatures de Daladier, Blum, Herriot, Geneviève Tabouis (ci-dessus); *Le Cri du peuple*, dont le directeur, Jacques Doriot, leader du PPF, soutient jusqu'en 1942 la politique du Maréchal (à droite, en haut). Taxé de mollesse, il adopte ensuite des positions pro-nazies.

rédacteur en chef Henri Jeanson (bientôt remplacé par Georges Suarez), et les « collaborationnistes » *Le Cri du peuple* de Jacques Doriot et *Les Nouveaux Temps* de Jean Luchaire, intime d'Abetz et régent de fait des attributions de papier et autres facilités.

À quoi s'ajoutent les hebdomadaires dont on a peine de nos jours à mesurer l'immonde servilité en même temps que la haine criminelle : *La Gerbe* d'Alphonse de Châteaubriant, « hebdomadaire de la volonté française », *Au Pilori* de Robert Pierret et Jean Drault,

_voilà le cri du peuple.

LISEZ

LE CRI du PEUPLE DE PARIS

DIRECTEUR JACQUES DORIOT

GRAND QUOTIDIEN D'INFORMATION

« hebdomadaire de combat contre la judéo-maçonnerie », *La Révolution nationale* d'Eugène Deloncle, *Je suis partout* de Robert Brasillach et de ses amis Rebatet, Cousteau, Laubreaux et consorts, unis dans l'abjection. Sans oublier le quotidien allemand *Pariser Zeitung*, installé dans les locaux de *Paris-Soir*, rue Réaumur.

Jean Luchaire (ci-contre), directeur des *Nouveaux Temps*, devient le relais des autorités allemandes. Avec l'aide d'Abetz, il crée le Groupement corporatif de la presse quotidienne parisienne, puis la Corporation nationale de la presse française et contrôle ainsi toute la presse de la zone Nord.

Au Sud, résistance et clandestinité

Le Temps, le vrai *Paris-Soir* de Jean Prouvost, *Le Figaro*, réputé anglophile, *L'Action française* de Charles Maurras, bientôt interdit car imprévisible, se replient à Lyon, *La Croix* s'installe à Limoges, *Le Petit Journal* à Clermont-Ferrand, *Le Jour-L'Écho de Paris* à Marseille. Mais la presse parisienne repliée doit, comme la presse régionale, suivre les consignes de l'OFI et se soumettre à la censure de

Vichy. Quand, à la fin 1942, le territoire est entièrement occupé, trois titres parmi les plus significatifs refusent de paraître sous contrôle allemand et interrompent leur publication : *Le Figaro* se saborde le 11 novembre, *Le Temps* le 30 novembre et *Paris-Soir* en mai 1943.

La presse pourtant ne saurait se limiter aux feuilles politiques installées. Si les périodiques féminins (*Le Petit Écho de la mode*), sentimentaux (*Pour Elle, Notre Cœur*) et de jeunesse (*Benjamin*) connaissent des étiages proches de ceux de l'avant-guerre, la volonté de résister à l'énorme entreprise de mise au pas voit naître dès octobre 1940 la première publication clandestine, *Pantagruel*, que son fondateur Raymond Deiss paiera de sa vie. Elle est bientôt suivie de *Résistance* (Boris Vildé et le groupe du musée de l'Homme).

L'esprit de résistance se fait jour, manifesté en des organes portant le plus souvent le titre du réseau dont ils émanent, *Libération-Nord* (Christian Pineau), *Libération-Sud* (Emmanuel d'Astier), *Défense de la France* (Robert Salmon et Philippe Viannay), *Cahiers du témoignage chrétien* (père

La photographe Denise Bellon a consacré tout un reportage à la presse lyonnaise et à la presse parisienne repliée à Lyon. Ci-dessus, à l'angle des rues Childebert et David-Girin, les bureaux de *L'Effort*, *L'Auto* et *Lyon républicain*. Page de droite, *Le Figaro* hébergé dans les locaux du *Nouvelliste*. En haut, Pierre Brisson, son directeur ; en bas, l'équipe de rédaction avec, de gauche à droite, Jean-Baptiste Séverac, James de Coquet, Louis-Gabriel Robinet et Georges Ravon. L'équipement journalistique lyonnais profite aussi à la presse clandestine qui utilise souvent le matériel légal pour imprimer ses tracts ou ses journaux.

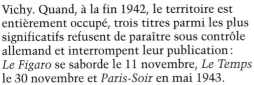

Pierre Chaillet), *Franc-Tireur* (Jean-Pierre Lévy), *Combat* (Henri Frenay) qui tous se mueront en journaux classiques à la Libération. Ou encore *Les Lettres françaises*, conçu à Paris par Jacques Decour et rassemblant un prodigieux ensemble d'écrivains (Aragon, Sartre, Eluard, Paulhan, Queneau, etc.), toutes entreprises menées selon les risques mortels de la clandestinité, et dont l'emprise sur les consciences ne cessera de croître, plus encore à partir de 1942.

PANTAGRUEL

FEUILLE D'INFORMATIONS

...Jamais ne se tourmentait, jamais ne se scandalisait. Ainsi eût-il été

...orissu du ...amour de raison, et autrement se fût contristé ou altéré

Car tous ...... la terre contient en toutes ses

dimensions ...

esprits ...

...

No 1

PANTAGRUEL est ...

la diffusion des nouvelles ...

Mais il est tout de ...

victoire de l'Angleterre ...

economique, et de l'inf...

L'Angleterre, ne l'ou...

grité territoriale dont pers...

allem ... dent personne ...

de ... servi ...

cor ...

[handwritten note across top] ... et dessus un ramassé d'ennuis pour compléter votre documentation. Si j'en avais pas eu peur de subir le sort de votre Terasilier du Bois, je vous aurais écrit plus longuement ... J'aurai signé. Octobre 1942 — N° 12

LE FRANC-TIREUR

Mensuel dans la mesure du possible et par la grâce de la police de Pierre Laval

LIBERTÉ — ÉGALITÉ — FRATERNITÉ

C'EST LA CHASSE AUX FRANÇAIS

Le commencement de la fin

Voilà où ils nous ont mené, à force d'abandons, de lâcheté, de trahison.
On veut faire de nous, Français, la chair à travail d'Hitler. On relève un fiasco. Laval menace. On s'aperçoit ...

pour 50 ouvriers, un contremaître pour 25. Les ouvriers qui refusent de partir s'exposent à mourir de faim d'abord et ...

N° 51   15 NOVEMBRE 1943

Un seul chef : DE GAULLE

Un seul combat :
pour NOS LIBERTÉS

Autres organes des
Mouvements Unis de Résistance
LIBÉRATION FRANC-TIREUR

¢ombat

Dans la guerre comme dans la paix, le dernier mot est à ceux qui ne se rendent jamais. Clemenceau.

ORGANE DES MOUVEMENTS UNIS DE RÉSISTANCE

HOMMES DU S.T.O., GARE AU PIÈGE !

La déportation des jeunes Français va être suspendue jusqu'à la fin de 1943.
Succès de la politique Laval ? Non.
Victoire de la Résistance ! L'intimidation n'ayant pas réussi, le Reich n'a pas cru possible d'engager maintenant des opérations de force contre nos maquis. La guerre en Russie, la guerre en Italie, la guérilla en Yougoslavie offrent déjà à la Wehrmacht plus de fil que ses outils émoussés peuvent retordre.
Victoire des Alliés ! Car en raison du bombardement des villes allemandes, l'industrie allemande doit moins songer à utiliser de nouveaux ouvriers, qu'à déplacer au plus vite ce qui reste de ses usines et à employer la main-d'œuvre dans des régions moins atteintes.
Où transporter les industries allemandes bombardées ? N'est-ce pas dans les territoires occupés qu'elles courraient le moins de risques ? Et si les Alliés viennent les y attaquer, quel élément pour la propagande nazie ?
De toutes façons, il s'agit de faire travailler notre jeunesse pour les boches en présentant l'affaire de telle sorte que, si les jeunes gens persistent dans leur résolution de ne pas servir l'ennemi, on puisse encore les accuser de n'être que des paresseux, qui refusent l'ouvrage qu'on leur propose chez eux, en France.
Mais cette propagande n'obtiendra pas plus de succès que n'en avaient obtenu les appels pour le travail en Allemagne, pour la L.V.F. ou pour les Waffen S.S. L'embarigadement et la servitude qu'on prétend ...
Loin d'accepter chez eux l'embrigadement à l'étranger, les 80.000 jeunes réfractaires persévéreront dans leur attitude "Le succès qu'ils ont déjà obtenu les y encourage. C'est en exploitant leur victoire, qu'ils aideront à la Victoire.

MISE AU POINT

SUR LE VOYAGE
de quelques parlementaires

Nous avons reçu des protestations indignées contre l'envoi à Londres et à Alger, comme membres de la « Résistance » de représentants de cet ancien « régime » qui a conduit la France au désastre et la République au suicide.

Et, nous dit-on aux généraux de la défaite et aux financiers de la vieille économie capitaliste, introduits à la faveur du premier — compromis —, on ajoute maintenant les coupeurs de cheveux en quatre des anciennes coulisses parlementaires, c'est l'association du conservatisme politique et du conservatisme social, et il faut désespérer de tout renouveau...

Une mise au point est nécessaire.
Les hommes de l'ancienne politique partis pour Alger ne représentent pas la « Résistance ». La Résistance est un tout. Elle groupe les hommes qui se battent réellement pour la France et la République et qui ont oublié les distinctions chinoises d'étiquettes et les anciens nègre-blanc. Demain éclatant au grand jour dans ses premiers congrès, elle ralliera dans un grand mouvement, l'immense masse des Français qui attendent avec confiance la rénovation promise par de Gaulle. De nouveaux chefs, une nouvelle élite politique se feront jour, fruit de beaucoup d'efforts et de beaucoup de dévouement. Elle comprendra des hommes nouveaux et les meilleurs des anciens ...

LA REFONTE DU C.F.L.N.

N° 27

LIBÉRATION

1ᵉʳ MAI 1943   EDITION SUD   N° Spécial

ORGANE DES MOUVEMENTS DE RESISTANCE UNIS

Un seul chef : DE GAULLE
Une seule lutte : pour nos Libertés

Notre seul but est de rendre la parole au Peuple Français Général DE GAULLE

1ᵉʳ Mai 1943 : Fête Nationale du sabotage contre l'Ennemi

Vive le 1ᵉʳ Mai

1ᵉʳ Mai est traditionnellement un jour de fête et de pour la classe ouvrière. Que ce quatrième premier guerre manifeste clairement à nos amis et à nos unis et inébranlable, rangés désormais notre français — loin d'être abattu — […]

FÉVRIER 1941

vos organisations de résistance. Le 1ᵉʳ mai 1943, vous manifesterez par tous les moyens contre l'oppression nazie, contre la déportation de vos frères en Allemagne, pour vos droits humains les plus élémentaires. […]

l'Humanité

ORGANE CENTRAL DU PARTI COMMUNISTE FRANÇAIS

Fondateur Jean JAURÈS   Rédacteur en Chef 1926-1937 : Paul Vaillant-Couturier

C'est au Peuple français de fixer le destin de la France
A bas le Conseil National des traîtres !
Place à un Gouvernement du Peuple !

LE COMMUNISME, SEUL ESPOIR DE LA FRANCE

• Si les classes ouvrières comme main-tiens, leurs contrôle du risque de voir les Français des générations […]
— 5 février 1941

En voici aucun Français sérieux ne soit-que l'Etat […]

Il n'y a rien de change. Sous les […]

Sous le drapeau de LÉNINE - STALINE

A l'occasion de la 18ᵉ conférence du Parti bolchevik, convoquée à Moscou le 15 février, le Parti qui ont fondé Léni-ne et Staline […]

COURRIER FRANÇAIS DU TÉMOIGNAGE CHRÉTIEN

NUMÉRO 10   LIEN DU FRONT DE RÉSISTANCE SPIRITUELLE   NUMÉRO 10

LE MAQUIS A LA PLAINE

Frères,

Libération et discipline

L'évasion a commencé pour chacun hors de France l'envahisseur et rendre à la patrie sa liberté et sa grandeur. […]

POUR LE MAQUIS… CONTRE LE TERRORISME

Trahir en paroles, n'est pas moins trahir. […]

Formation du mythe : TERRORISME.

LA PLAINE AU MAQUIS

La presse résistante et clandestine est distribuée de la main à la main. Le numéro 1 du premier de ces journaux, *Pantagruel* (page de gauche, en haut), diffuse les « nouvelles venues d'Angleterre par radio ». *Le Franc-Tireur*, *Combat* (page de gauche, au centre et en bas) et *Libération* (ci-contre, en haut) portent le nom des réseaux de Résistance qui les éditent et survivront à la fin de la guerre sous forme de quotidiens. Le journal communiste *L'Humanité* (ci-contre, au centre), n'ayant pu reparaître après la défaite, revoit le jour clandestinement sous l'autorité de Jacques Duclos – Maurice Thorez, secrétaire général du parti, s'étant réfugié à Moscou. *Témoignage chrétien* apporte une dimension spirituelle à l'activité des maquis. Très tôt, cette presse combattante unifie et agrège. Il est frappant de constater que la tonalité évidemment patriotique de ces organes s'abstient cependant de toute manifestation de haine à l'égard de l'Allemagne. Il s'agit de préparer la réconciliation du pays et sa reconstruction sous l'autorité du général de Gaulle et du Parti.

Le contrôle de la vie littéraire par les Allemands

Bien sûr depuis août 1939, le Commissariat général à l'Information exerçait déjà une certaine censure. Mais les combats ont cessé, les écrivains ont payé leur tribut à la guerre, Paul Nizan est tombé les armes à la main, Saint-Pol Roux lors d'un attentat crapuleux. Sartre et Brasillach sont prisonniers.

Dès l'été 1940, l'occupant prend le relais avec ses deux organismes de contrôle concurrents, l'un lié au commandement militaire, l'autre à l'ambassade du Reich, avec Otto Abetz. Ce dernier est l'intime de maints écrivains et journalistes parisiens, Jean Luchaire comme Paul Morand, Jacques Benoist-Méchin aussi bien que Jules Romains. Tandis que le directeur de l'Institut allemand, Karl Epting, proche entre autres de Giraudoux, Montherlant, Cocteau, Giono et Valéry, explique qu'« il faut que les intellectuels français renoncent à l'universel ».

Et Gerhard Heller, Berlinois éclairé responsable du secteur littéraire de la Propagandastaffel qui prend à son séjour parisien un plaisir extrême, adore jouer des contradictions de ses amis français, partagés entre ce qui leur reste d'esprit national, de soumission à Pétain et d'admiration explicite pour la soldatesque en uniforme feldgrau.

« Liste Bernhard » et « liste Otto »

Dès août 1940, un décret empêche la diffusion des œuvres de « littérature anti-allemande », celle des E. M. Remarque, Vicky Baum, Heinrich Mann, Carl Gustav Jung, Lion Feuchtwanger, Erich Kästner, ainsi que toutes les œuvres qui touchent au Führer et au Duce. Une première liste d'environ 150 ouvrages est établie. C'est la « liste Bernhard » où figurent tous les livres traduits de l'allemand évoquant le IIIᵉ Reich – y compris *Mein Kampf* parce que seulement disponible en morceaux choisis –, ainsi que des textes de futurs opposants tels Jacques Decour ou André Malraux.

En septembre, une autre nomenclature (qui sera enrichie deux fois jusqu'à 1943), la « liste Otto »

La liste Bernhard (ci-dessous) précède la liste Otto. C'est une liste sommaire de 143 ouvrages interdits. Paradoxalement, un bon nombre des ouvrages interdits proviennent de maisons d'édition qui vont se déclarer ouvertement « collaborationnistes », telles Sorlot ou Grasset ou Denoël. L'occupant interdit surtout et systématiquement tout ce qui a trait à l'Allemagne, faute d'en avoir contrôlé l'orientation idéologique.

LIST

1. ACHARD Paul :
2. ALLARD Paul, :
3. *** : A
4. ALPARI J. : Di
5. ANDLER Charle
   Paris : Ed. F
6. ANDLER Charl
   l'Allemagne."
7. *** : Anklag
   Prozesses. (N
8. APFEL Alfred :
9. APPUHN Chr. :
10. ARAGON Louis
11. AZANA Manue

(comme le prénom de l'ambassadeur du Reich à Paris) complète considérablement la mesure. Elle est précédée de l'éclairant préambule : « Désireux de contribuer à la création d'une atmosphère plus saine et dans le souci d'établir les conditions nécessaires à une appréciation plus juste et objective des problèmes européens, les éditeurs français ont décidé de retirer des librairies et de la vente les œuvres qui figurent sur les listes suivantes et sur des listes analogues qui pourraient être publiées plus tard. Il s'agit de livres qui, par leur esprit mensonger et tendancieux, ont systématiquement empoisonné l'opinion publique française ; sont visées en particulier les publications de réfugiés

Gerhard Heller (ci-dessous) sème le trouble dans les consciences grâce à sa francophilie rouée. Ainsi, en juillet 1942, il a reçu au restaurant Drieu La Rochelle, René Drouin (le galeriste), Brasillach, Jean Paulhan, Marcel Arland, André Bay et René Delange (note de frais, ci-contre).

E BERNHARD

aris : Ed. des lettres françaises, 21, Place des Vosges.
Hitler espionne la France. Paris : Les Editions de France.
agne parle. Que veut-elle ? Paris : Paillard 1934.
en sind gefallen. Paris : Ed. Prométhée 1938.
minorités raciales, religieuses et politiques. Coll. „Documents sur l'Allemagne .
Sorlot.
socialisme impérialiste dans l'Allemagne contemporaine. Coll. „Documents sur
Ed. Fernand Sorlot.
n die Anklaeger. Die Widerlegung der geheimen Anklageschrift des Reichstagsbrand-
zum Braunbuch I). Paris : Ed. du Carrefour 1933.
ssous de la Justice allemande. Paris : Ed. Gallimard.
„Mcin Kampf" par luimême. Paris : Jacques Haumont, 139, rue Broca.
Glocken von Basel.(Les Cloches de Bâle) Paris : Ed. du Carrefour 1936.
a spricht. Paris : Ed. du Carrefour 1937.
Steele 1936.

politiques ou d'écrivains juifs qui, trahissant l'hospitalité que la France leur avait accordée, ont sans scrupule poussé à une guerre dont ils espéraient tirer profit pour leurs buts égoïstes. Les autorités allemandes ont enregistré avec satisfaction l'initiative des éditeurs français et ont de leur côté pris les mesures nécessaires. » Suivent des centaines d'auteurs, classés par ordre alphabétique d'éditeur, parmi lesquels Carco, Dorgelès, Koestler, de Gaulle, Loti, Aragon, Bainville, Neruda, Blum, Kessel, Béraud, Engels, Dekobra, Einstein, Daladier, Mounier, Trotsky, Duhamel, Freud, Claudel, Benda, Chesterton, Griaule, Lénine, Nizan, Freud, Maurois, Aron, Döblin, Massis, Schnitzler, Bruant, Zangwill, Simenon, Rivière, Gide, Istrati… Farandole cosmopolite et anachronique de signataires d'un ou plusieurs ouvrages jugés contraires aux préceptes désormais en vigueur.

Mais c'est évidemment la mention de cette « initiative des éditeurs français » qui vaut d'être soulignée : le vaincu va au-delà des exigences du vainqueur, dans ce domaine comme dans d'autres. Comment se comporter quand son pays est envahi ?

Des éditeurs juifs ou « enjuivés »

Difficile d'imaginer que de tels édits passent inaperçus ou laissent indifférents, que l'on soit concerné ou non, d'autant que le statut des Juifs promulgué en octobre précise s'il en était besoin le nouveau racisme d'État. Toutes mesures qui n'empêchent nullement une reprise rapide et autorisée de l'activité éditoriale. Une « Convention de censure » est signée en septembre 1940, sorte de code de « bonne conduite » vis-à-vis de l'occupant. Pour l'écrivain Pierre Assouline, « l'éditeur saisi par le doute a néanmoins la faculté de faire lire ses manuscrits par la censure qui lui indiquera ce qu'il faut en penser. La contrepartie de l'autocensure, c'est l'attribution du contingent de papier ».

Les grandes figures égaillées sur le territoire après la défaite regagnent la capitale après un éventuel

La Convention sur la censure des livres, signée par la Propaganda Staffel et le Syndicat des éditeurs, régit les conditions de reprise d'activité des maisons d'édition en zone occupée (ci-dessus); tout ouvrage à paraître, susceptible ou non de « nuire au prestige et aux intérêts allemands », doit être envoyé, pour examen, au groupe littérature à la Propaganda Staffel. À droite, une page de la liste Otto révisée de juillet 1942 concernant les livres interdits des éditions Gallimard : y sont inscrits en nombre des auteurs germaniques renommés (Breitbach, Döblin, Freud, Henrich Mann, Thomas Mann, Remarque, Joseph Roth, Ungar, Wassermann), des écrivains juifs ou soupçonnés d'anti-germanisme (Aron, Benda, Blum, Churchill, Chesterton, Gide, Malraux, Mauriac, Nizan, Rivière). À droite, en bas, au Cercle de la Librairie, les fichiers des livres mis à l'index par les listes Bernhard et Otto.

BEDEL Maurice. — *Monsieur Hitler* (1937).

BENDA J. — *Appositions* (1938).
» *Délices d'Eleuthère*.
» *Discours à la nation européenne* (1933).
» *Essai d'un discours cohérent sur les rapports de Dieu et du monde* (1931).
» *Esquisse d'une histoire des Français* (1932).
» *La fin de l'Eternel* (1929).
» *La jeunesse d'un clerc*.
» *Précision 1930-1936*.
» *Mon premier testament* (1928).
» *Un régulier dans le siècle*.

BENÈS Edouard. — *La France et la nouvelle Europe*.

BERNARD Marc. — *La conquête de la Méditerranée* (1939).

BLUM Léon. — *L'exercice du pouvoir* (1937).
» *Nouvelles conversations de Gœthe avec Eckermann*.
» *Souvenirs sur l'Affaire* (1935).

BONAYGUE et REBER. — *Vienne porte de la guerre* (1934).

BOPP Léon. — *Liaisons du monde* (1938).

BREITBACH Joseph. — *Rival et rivale* (1935).

BROWN Lewis. — *La vie des Juifs* (1939).

GRATELION. — *Moldagne*.

CHESTERTON. — *La barbarie de Berlin* (1938).

CHURCHILL Winston. — *Les grands contemporains*.

CILIGA A. — *Au pays du grand mensonge*.

CLAUDEL Paul. — *Ainsi donc encore une fois* (1940).
» *Contacts et circonstances* (1940).

CURIE Eve. — *Madame Curie*.

DAVID André. — *Mon père, répondez-moi*.

DECOUR Jacques. — *Philizterburg*.

DELAVIGNETTE. — *Les vrais Chefs de l'Empire*.

DOBLIN Alfred. — *Berlin Alexanderplatz* (1933).
» *Voyage Babylonien* (1937).

DOMELA. — *Doméla par lui-même*.

EFFEL Jean. — *Ritournelle, I* (1938).
» *Ritournelle, II* (1938).

FELLER Arthur. — *L'expérience du bolchevisme* (1934).

FINK Georges. — *J'ai faim* (1935).

FLEG Edmond). — *I. Eternel est notre Dieu*.
» *Israël et moi*.

FRANÇOIS J. — *L'affaire Roehm-Hitler* (1935).

FREUD Sigmund. — *Délire et rêve* (1931).
» *Essais de psychanalyse appliquée* (1936).
» *Ma vie et la psychanalyse* (1938).
» *Métapsychologie* (1940).
» *Le moi et ses rapports avec l'inconscient*.
» *Nouvelles ... psycha- nalyse ...*
» *Le r...*
» *Trois ... sexu...*

» *De la Sainte-Russie à l'U.R.S.S.* (1938).
» *Jacques Aron : tome II L'Adieu* (1932).
» *Ville qui n'a pas de fin* (1932).
» *Votre tour viendra* (1930).

GIDE André. — *Retour de l'U.R.S.S.*
» *Retouches à mon retour de l'U.R. S.S.*

GRAF Oscar-Maria. — *Nous sommes prisonniers* (1930).

GRAHAM Stéphen. — *Sarajévo* (1933).

GRIADLE (Maurice). — *La peau de l'ours*.

GUERIN Daniel. — *Fascisme et grand capital* (1936).

GUERIN Paul. — *Le problème français* (1939).

GUMBEL E.-J. — *Les crimes politiques en Allemagne*.

HEGEMANN Werner. — *Le Grand Frédéric* (1934).

HIRSCHFELD Magnus. — *L'âme et l'amour* (1935).
» *Le corps et l'amour* (1937).
» *Le tour du monde d'un sexologue* (1938).

HOOVER Calvin-B. — *L'Allemagne IIIe Empire* (1934).

KAUS. — *Demain neuf heures*.
» *Les Sœurs Kleh*.

LAST Jef. — *Zuyderzée*.

KEUN Irmgard. — *La jeune fille en soie artificielle* (1933).

KISCH E-E. — *La Chine secrète* (1935).

KRACAUER. — *Genêt* (1933).

LACHIN Maurice. — *L'Ethiopie et son destin* (1935).

LAST Jef. — *Lettres d'Espagne* (1938).

LENINE. — *Cahiers sur la dialectique de Hegel*.

LEWINSOHN Richard. — *L'argent dans la politique* (1931).

LUDWIG Emil. — *Dirigeants de l'Europe* (1938).
» *Le meurtre de Davos* (1936).
» *La nouvelle Sainte-Alliance* (1938).
» *La Prusse et l'Europe* (1943).

LUSSU Emilio. — *La marche sur Rome*.

MALRAUX André. — *L'espoir* (1937).
» *Le temps du mépris* (1935).

MANN Heinrich. — *La haine* (1933).

MANN Thomas. — *Avertissement à l'Europe* (1937).
» *Les histoires de Jacob : Joseph et ses frères* (1935).
» *Le jeune Joseph* (1938).
» *Joseph en Egypte* (1938).
» *La victoire finale de la démocratie* (1939).

MARX Karl. — *Morceaux choisis*.

MAUROIS André. — *Les origines de la guerre de 1939*.

MAZELINE Guy. — *Scènes de la vie hitlérienne* (1938).

MULLER H.-J. — *Hors de la nuit*.

NIZAN Paul. — *Chronique de Septembre* (1939).

NOLLET (Général). — *Une expérience du désarmement* (1932).

NOTH E-E. — *Le désert* (1939).

... Rudolf. — *Stresemann* (1932).

...ESSON W, d'. — *La confiance en Allemagne?* (1928).

RATHENEAU Walther. — *Le Kaiser*.

RAUSCHNING. — *La révolution du nihilisme* (1940).

REBER. — *Vienne porte de la guerre*.

REMARQUE E.-M. — *Après* (1931).
» *Les camarades* (1938).

REYNAUD Paul. — *Jeunesse, quelle France veux-tu?* (1938).

RIVIERE Jacques. — *L'Allemand* (1938).

ROLLAN Henri. — *Apocalypse de notre temps* (1939).

ROSE Pascal. — *La vie de famille* (1935).

ROSSI A. — *La naissance du fascisme*.

ROSTAND Jean. — *Hérédité et racisme* (1939).

ROTH Joseph. — *La fuite sans fin* (1929).

ROUGEMONT Denis de. — *Journal d'Allemagne* (1938).

SAAGER Adolf. — *Mussolini* (1935).

SALVEMINI. — *La terreur fasciste* (1930).

SCHARRER Adam. — *Les sans Patrie* (1931).

SCHERMANN Raphaël. — *L'écriture ne ment pas* (1935).

SELINKO A.-M. — *Demain tout ira mieux*.
» *J'étais une jeune fille laide*.

SFORZA. — *Les bâtisseurs de l'Europe moderne* (1931).
» *Dictateurs et dictatures* (1931).
» *Les frères ennemis*.
» *Pachitch et l'Union des Yougoslaves* (1938).
» *Synthèse de l'Europe* (1937).

STEKEL. — *L'éducation des parents*.
» *La femme frigide*.
» *Lettres à une mère*.

STOWE Leland. — *Hitler est-ce la guerre?* (1934).

TREFUSIS Violet. — *Il court... il court...*
» *Les causes perdues*.

TRINTZIUS. — *Deutschland*.

TCHAKHOTINE Serge. — *Le viol des foules par la propagande politique* (1939).

UNGAR Hermann. — *Enfants et meurtriers* (1928).
» *Les sous-hommes* (1928).

URBANITZKY C. Von. — *Mara*.

VALLENTIN A. — *Henri Heine* (1934).

VERMEIL Edmond). — *L'Allemagne* (1940).
» *Hitler et le christianisme* (1940).

WASSERMANN Jacob. — *La vie de Christophe Colomb* (1938).

WEIL Bruno. — *L'affaire Dreyfus* (1940).

YVON. — *L'U.R.S.S. telle qu'elle est*.

LA NOUVELLE SOCIÉTÉ D'ÉDITION

CARTIER Ra...
» *croix ...*

CREMIEUX ...
» *Forza ...*
» *Fosse ...*
» *La gr...*
» *Jours...*

SPEYER W ...

WASSERMANN ...
années ...

NOUVE...

XXX. — *Oe...*
kommiss...

détour par Vichy, ou prolongent leur séjour en zone libre. Jean Fayard est à Lyon, Fernand Sorlot à Clermont-Ferrand, Robert Denoël, Bernard Grasset, Robert Esménard (Albin Michel) et Gaston Gallimard sont revenus à Paris.

Une question de fond surgit, celle des maisons d'édition et des librairies appartenant à des Juifs, en employant, ou soupçonnées de pensées, voire de menées anti-allemandes, ces critères pouvant se cumuler. La librairie Kra est vandalisée, les éditions Ferenczi, Nathan et Calmann-Lévy sont « aryanisées » – le vocable lui-même fait frémir –, c'est-à-dire que les propriétaires sont dépouillés de leurs parts de capital revendues à des concurrents aryens. Calmann-Lévy, la plus ancienne et la plus prestigieuse des trois, est l'objet de diverses propositions de rachat, de la part

L'aryanisation des entreprises culturelles, et en particulier de l'édition, est menée conjointement et concurremment par l'occupant allemand et le régime de Vichy. La dépossession des Juifs est d'ailleurs inscrite au cahier des charges du Commissariat général aux questions juives, créé par Vichy. Ci-dessous, son secrétaire général demande au Bureau de la Propaganda Staffel de lui transférer du papier entreposé à la maison Geismar et Lévy, « maison juive ».

Monsieur le Docteur,

J'ai l'honneur de porter à votre connaissance qu'il nous a été signalé qu'un important stock de papier pour impressions existait à la maison Geismar et Lévy, Quai de Valmy, N° 187, Paris.

Cette maison étant une maison juive, nous pensons qu'il vous serait possible de vous assurer la disposition de ce papier et, sur ce stock, de vouloir bien réserver à notre revue les quantités qui lui sont nécessaires.

notamment de Fayard et de Gallimard. Intégrée au trust allemand Hibbelen, la maison est rebaptisée « Éditions Balzac ». À sa tête, des Aryens incontestés : Albert Lejeune, Henry Jamet, responsable de la librairie Rive Gauche, tous deux candidats d'Abetz.

Gallimard et la *Nouvelle Revue Française*

Gallimard représente un autre enjeu. La grande maison n'est pas propriété juive, mais « enjuivée » d'autant plus gravement qu'elle exerce une forte influence intellectuelle, de par sa production livresque mais aussi par la revue qu'elle publie. « Il y a trois puissances en France : la banque, le parti communiste et la NRF », aurait affirmé Abetz, à moins que ce soit Paulhan lui-même. Gaston

L'aryanisation de l'édition ne concerne pas seulement les propriétaires et les dirigeants. En 1941, Gerhard Heller envoie à toutes les maisons d'édition un questionnaire concernant leur personnel. Il demande d'y ajouter « une déclaration de chaque personne nommée [...], affirmant que la personne et son conjoint sont d'origine aryenne (c'est-à-dire descendante de quatre grands-parents aryens).

Pierre Drieu la Rochelle (ci-contre), dont les sentiments pro-allemands sont avérés, succède à Jean Paulhan à la tête de *La Nouvelle Revue française*, qui reparaît dans une continuité assumée dès le 1er décembre 1940 (ci-dessous). Figure à ce premier sommaire la fine fleur des tenants de la Nouvelle Europe. Des neutres aussi, Audiberti, Aymé, Giono, Alain, Auric. Mais aucun opposant déclaré au régime. Un incontestable sentiment de malaise sourd de cette renaissance, accentué encore par l'éditorial sans équivoque de Drieu la Rochelle.

Gallimard, absent au moment de la publication de la liste Otto, refuse toute entrée de capitaux allemands dans l'entreprise. Mais il doit accepter de confier les rênes de *La Nouvelle Revue française* à Pierre Drieu la Rochelle, un écrivain clairement en faveur de la « nouvelle Europe », nommé avec l'agrément fervent des services allemands, qui remplace un Jean Paulhan désireux de s'éloigner, et de se consacrer à son action clandestine au sein de la Résistance.

Au sommaire du premier numéro de cette nouvelle époque (mais cependant numéroté 322, 1er décembre 1940), pour lequel Drieu et Paulhan ont battu le rappel des bonnes volontés, une majorité d'écrivains très air du temps, très en faveur de la collaboration franco-allemande, Jouhandeau, Chardonne, Fabre-Luce, Morand, Fernandez, Petitjean, Fraigneau…

LIBRAIRIE GALLIMARD

nrf Ch. postal 169.33 — Téléph. : Littré 28-91 à 28-95

Société anonyme au capital de 4.800.000 fr.

REGISTRE DU COMMERCE DE LA SEINE N° 35.801 — PRODUCTEUR SEINE C. A. 1.043

5, rue Sébastien-Bottin (ancᵗ 43, rue de Beaune), PARIS-VIIᵉ

ADRESSE TÉLÉGRAPHIQUE : ENEREFENE PARIS'

le 10 mai 1941

Monsieur Marcel Drouin
Cuverville en Caux
par Criquetot-Lesneval
Seine Inférieur.

Monsieur,

J'ai été content de voir adressés à la
Revue quelque mots d'un homme qui a été si important
dans ses beaux débuts.

Certes, je publierai cette page d'huma-
nisme très pur avec une sorte d'émotion, que je connai...
depuis quelque temps déjà , car il m'arrive dans ce bu...
reau où m'ont porté des circonstances si démesurées,de...
rouvrir les recueils de 1908, 1909 et de rêver sur vou...
tous .

André Gide, tiraillé par diverses influ...
ces , m'a récemment fait savoir qu'il m'écrirait plus à...
la Revue . Je déplore ce mouvement qui ne peut que par...
inconsidéré et ingrat car j'ai recommencé la Revue ava...
tout pour protéger des oeuvres aussi menacées dans le...
présents que celles de Gide . Et quand je dis menacées...
veux dire encore plus par certains éléments français ...
par les Allemands .

Du reste,on m'a annoncé depuis que Gid...
grettait la carte de rupture qu'il m'avait adressée à ...
vers cette terrible ligne de démarcation .

Je souhaite un jour causer avec vous, ...
sieur,et je vous prie de croire à une considération q...
commencé quand j'avais dix-huit ans, que j'étais jeun...
teur de la Revue .

P. Drieu La Rochelle.

P Drieu la Rochelle

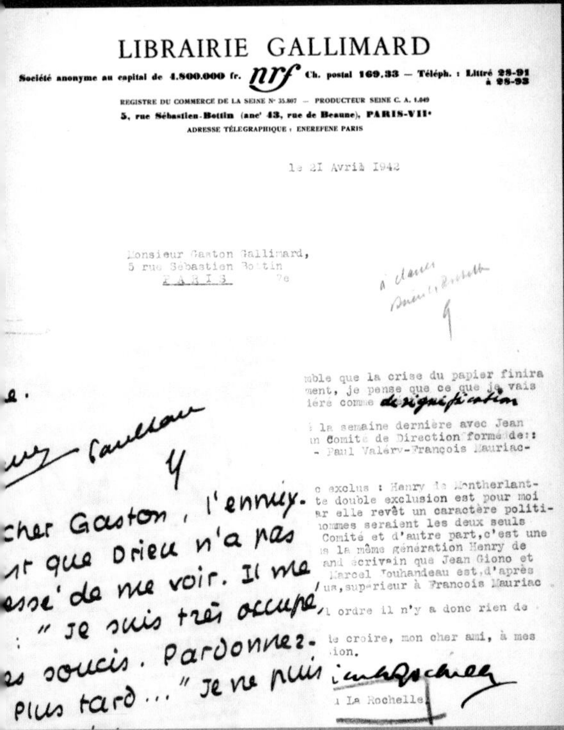

LIBRAIRIE GALLIMARD

Société anonyme au capital de 4.800.000 fr. **nrf** Ch. postal 169.33 – Téléph. : Littré 28-91 à 95-93

REGISTRE DU COMMERCE DE LA SEINE N° 35.807 — PRODUCTEUR SEINE C. A. 1.040

5, rue Sébastien-Bottin (anc' 43, rue de Beaune), PARIS-VII

ADRESSE TÉLÉGRAPHIQUE : ENEREFENE PARIS

le 21 Avril 1942

Monsieur Gaston Gallimard,
5 rue Sébastien Bottin
P A R I S

à classer
Drieu la Rochelle

...ble que la crise du papier finira
...ment. Je pense que ce que je vais
...iers comme **dé signification**

...la semaine dernière avec Jean
...n Comité de Direction formé de :
...- Paul Valéry-François Mauriac-

...c exclus : Henry de Montherlant-
...te double exclusion est pour moi
...ar elle revêt un caractère politi-
...hommes seraient les deux seuls
...Comité et d'autre part, c'est une
...la même génération Henry de
...ani écrivain que Jean Giono et
...Marcel Jouhandeau est d'après
...ua, supérieur à François Mauriac

...ordre il n'y a donc rien de

...la croire, mon cher ami, à mes
...ion.

Drieu la Rochelle.

cher Gaston, l'ennuy.
...t que Drieu n'a pas
...essé de me voir. Il me
... "je suis très occupé
... soucis. Pardonnez-
plus tard... " Je ne puis

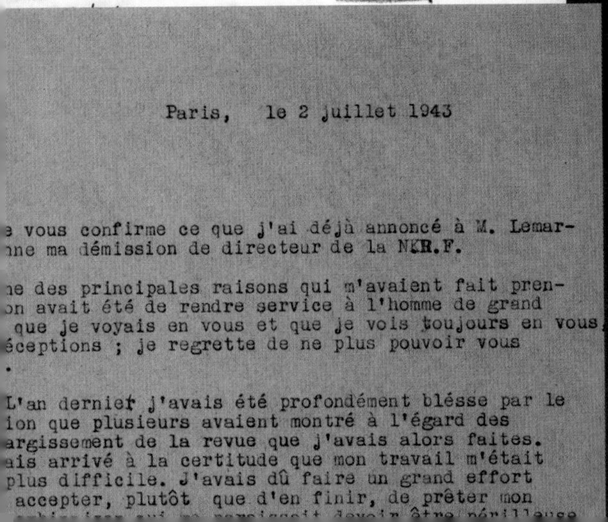

Paris, le 2 Juillet 1943

...e vous confirme ce que j'ai déjà annoncé à M. Lemar-
...nne ma démission de directeur de la N.R.F.

...ne des principales raisons qui m'avaient fait pren-
...on avait été de rendre service à l'homme de grand
...que je voyais en vous et que je vois toujours en vous
...ceptions ; je regrette de ne plus pouvoir vous

...L'an dernier j'avais été profondément blessé par le
...ion que plusieurs avaient montré à l'égard de la
...argissement de la revue que j'avais alors faites.
...ais arrivé à la certitude que mon travail m'était
...plus difficile. J'avais dû faire un grand effort
...accepter, plutôt que d'en finir, de prêter mon

La *NRF* reparaît en décembre 1940, sous la direction de Drieu la Rochelle. Sous la pression des autorités d'occupation, Gaston Gallimard s'était résolu à « abandonner » sa revue à cette tutelle pro-allemande, à deux conditions : le maintien de l'indépendance capitalistique et commerciale des Éditions et l'assurance que la revue ne serait que littéraire. Mais des auteurs d'importance, comme Gide et Mauriac, qui envisageaient d'écrire encore dans la *NRF*, se rendent vite à l'évidence ; la revue n'est pas neutre, mieux vaut ne pas s'y compromettre (page de droite, en haut, lettre de Mauriac à Drieu du 30 décembre 1940 ; en bas, lettre de Drieu à Marcel Drouin relatant le refus de Gide, 10 mai 1941). Malgré l'aide souterraine du résistant Paulhan et la fidélité de quelques auteurs, Drieu ne peut maintenir la revue à niveau. En avril 1942, Paulhan lui propose un comité de direction avec Gide, Claudel, Valéry, Mauriac et Giono, mais excluant Jouhandeau et Montherlant. Drieu refuse et proteste auprès de Gaston Gallimard (ci-contre, en haut ; au centre, un billet de Paulhan à Gaston Gallimard). Se sentant manipulé, Drieu démissionne (ci-contre, sa lettre du 2 juillet 1943).

La haine

L'éditeur Robert Denoël « profite », c'est bien le mot, du nouveau statut des Juifs pour lancer une « collection d'intérêt national » fiévreusement antisémite, où paraissent notamment dès 1940 l'édifiant *Comment reconnaître le Juif* de George Montandon, professeur d'université, et le non moins abject *Les Tribus du cinéma et du théâtre* de Lucien Rebatet. Le même Rebatet connaît en 1942 l'un des authentiques succès de librairie du temps avec son pavé *Les Décombres*, vendu à 65 000 exemplaires toujours par Denoël, et qui aligne dans le désordre les responsables à ses yeux de la débâcle nationale, les juifs et le Maréchal, les communistes et l'Action française, l'Église et les francs-maçons, l'Armée et les bourgeois, ce qui fait beaucoup de monde. Céline en rajoute dans la violence haineuse : *Les Beaux Draps* accable les Juifs et le régime de Vichy qui n'a pas su les abattre une fois pour toutes. Ce qui n'empêche pas Denoël de publier à la même époque Aragon, Elsa Triolet et… les discours de Hitler. Morale de l'ambiguïté ?

Grasset, Plon, Mercure de France, d'autres maisons de moindre notoriété multiplient les publications pétainistes et racistes, encouragés par le climat de haine raciale et d'appels au meurtre lancés impunément par des feuilles obsédées de violence, telles *Au pilori*, *Je suis partout* ou *L'Appel*. Plusieurs traduisent les auteurs allemands contemporains, Wiechert, Carossa, Jünger, Sieburg, Fallada.

Dans *Les Décombres*, Lucien Rebatet attaque avec férocité ceux qui ont mis la France dans l'état de ruine où elle se trouve. Prônant un régime anti-juif, anti-parlementaire, anti-bolchevique, anti-maçonnique, anti-clérical…, il aspire à une alliance totale entre la France et l'Allemagne nazie (ci-dessous, *Les Décombres* et Rebatet dédicaçant son livre à la librairie allemande Rive Gauche).

Victoire idéologique allemande? Berlin s'en donne l'ambition. Ses représentants à Paris, tous épris du pays conquis, ne manquent ni d'intelligence, ni d'entregent, ni de moyens. Ils ont entrevu les zones de friabilité et les personnalités récupérables : à cet égard, le travail de Gerhard Heller paraît exemplaire, quand il convie en octobre 1941 à Weimar, la ville de Goethe le grand Européen, un groupe de Français qui participent à un Congrès des écrivains du Vieux Continent. Aucun effort n'est épargné pour éblouir les invités, Drieu, Brasillach, Fernandez, Chardonne, Jouhandeau, Fraigneau, Bonnard, brochette identitaire de la Collaboration. Parmi les ténors, ne manquent qu'Alphonse de Châteaubriant, illuminé par Hitler qu'il assimile à une divinité, Céline, Montherlant, Béraud, Rebatet, Thérive, Benoist-Méchin, Hermant et quelques moindres fusils.

Les Beaux Draps de Céline (en haut, à gauche) sont publiés par Robert Denoël en 1941 aux Nouvelles Éditions françaises qu'il a créées pour éditer des textes collaborationnistes. Ce catalogue de violentes imprécations antisémites ne sera jamais réédité pour cause de provocation à la haine raciale. L'écrivain germanophile et pro-fasciste Alphonse de Châteaubriant, fondateur de *La Gerbe*, joint aux doctrines nazies un mysticisme religieux (ci-dessus, à l'Institut allemand, à côté de Suzanne Abetz, en 1943).

Tout se vend, tout se lit

Les bibliothèques publiques sont dévalisées, jamais le négoce des livres ne s'est si bien porté, le couvre-feu et les coupures de courant découragent de sortir et servent au moins la lecture, cependant entravée par la pénurie de papier. On s'arrache les derniers exemplaires – avant interdiction en zone occupée – de *Moby Dick*, de *Sparkenbroke* de Charles Morgan et d'*Autant en emporte le vent*, *Corps et âmes*, la charge sanglante de Maxence Van der Meersch contre la caste médicale, la dizaine de romans de Georges Simenon, parmi lesquels *Le Voyageur de la Toussaint*, *La Veuve Couderc*, *La Vérité sur Bébé Donge* ou *Le Fils Cardinaud*, les innombrables livres de recettes liées aux restrictions alimentaires, les biographies des figures françaises du passé, Saint

Créée à l'initiative de l'Institut allemand et financée par le trust Hibbelen, la librairie Rive Gauche est « la librairie du livre allemand en France », gérée par Maurice Bardèche, beau-frère de Robert Brasillach et collaborationniste engagé. Son inauguration, le 21 avril 1941, marque une étape dans l'institutionnalisation de la collaboration littéraire (ci-dessus, l'intérieur de la librairie Rive Gauche, place de la Sorbonne).

Louis, Mermoz, Du Guesclin, Jacques Cartier, exutoires à la frustration ou exhortations subliminales. Et l'on assiste au développement d'un genre littéraire à lui seul, l'hagiographie du Maréchal, divinisé tel un messie thaumaturge et omniscient.

À Paris ou en zone libre

La réaction des écrivains à l'occupation est éminemment complexe, liée à tant de facteurs, souffrances et privations personnelles, mobilisation militaire, engagement politique, indifférence pacifiste ou résignée, tradition familiale. La majorité grommelle, sans bouger, en attendant des jours meilleurs. Paul Léautaud dans son *Journal* ne voit guère de différence avec le bon vieux temps. Saint-Germain-des-Prés préfigure ce qu'il sera à la Libération. « Nous n'avons jamais été aussi libres que sous l'Occupation », écrira imprudemment Jean-Paul Sartre, fort peu taraudé par l'idée d'un engagement effectif dans la Résistance.

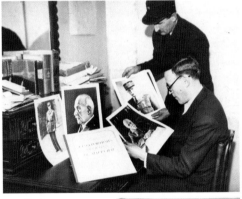

Le Maréchal dans tous ses états. C'est d'une véritable épiphanie à répétitions que l'on peut parler (ci-dessous). Plus prosaïquement, l'avènement d'une gastronomie de l'ersatz donne naissance à une abondante littérature. Les temps de privation ont aussi leurs livres de recettes (en bas).

En zone libre, certains se sont fixés pour un temps à Vichy, comme Rebatet, Berl ou Martin du Gard. D'autres se sont repliés à Lyon, suivant souvent le journal auquel ils collaborent, tels Camus, les jeunes Michel Déon et Kléber Haedens, ou encore l'universitaire et académicien Paul Hazard. Sur la Côte d'Azur se croisent le couple Louis Aragon-Elsa Triolet, Joseph Kessel et Francis Carco, André Gide et André Malraux. Des éditeurs y poursuivent leur activité car la censure ne sévit guère, du moins jusqu'en 1942 : Jean Vigneau à Marseille, Edmond Charlot, premier éditeur de Camus, à Alger, Édouard Aubanel à Avignon.

MARTINE

RECETTES
ALIMENTAIRES & MÉNAGÈRES
*pour le temps
des restrictions*

LIBRAIRIE HACHETTE

Zone Nord ou zone Sud : pendant les années 1940-1944, la vie littéraire continue, mais dans des décors différents.
À Paris, c'est dans les cafés que se retrouvent nombre d'écrivains, journalistes et artistes, – proches ou non de l'occupant. On voit ici Jean-Paul Sartre (en haut, à gauche) au café de Flore en mars 1943, assis derrière les comédiens Yves Deniaud, Raymond Bussières, Maurice Baquet et Annette Poivre. Autre ambiance, dans une autre brasserie où se réunissent en juillet 1943 (en bas, à gauche), les jurés du prix de la Nouvelle France, parmi lesquels Pierre Benoit (au centre) et Bernard Grasset (au fond, au centre). La même année, des habitués de la brasserie Lipp : debout, à gauche, le patron, Marcelin Cazes ; face à lui, Ramon Fernandez et Maurice Fombeure, qui allume sa pipe.

Zone Sud, la nature est présente. À Lourmarin, dans le Vaucluse, se réunit en septembre 1941 le groupe Jeune France, créé à l'origine sous le patronage de Vichy, mais qui s'en éloigne peu à peu. Il y a là des musiciens, des poètes, des universitaires comme Pierre Schæffer, Armand Guibert, Max-Pol Fouchet, Georges-Emmanuel Clancier... Page de gauche en haut, et de gauche à droite : Emmanuel Mounier (sa revue *Esprit* est interdite en août 1941), Yvonne Leenhardt, Max-Pol Fouchet et Loÿs Masson). Pierre Seghers, a transformé *Poètes casqués*, sa revue de « poètes soldats », en *Poésie (40, 41..)* et s'est installé à Villeneuve-lès-Avignon, dans le Gard (page de gauche, en bas, en veste blanche, avec Loÿs Masson). Marguerite Duras travaillait à la commission de contrôle du papier d'édition créée par Vichy. Elle s'engage en 1942, avec son mari Robert Antelme et Dionys Mascolo (ci-contre), dans un réseau de résistance dirigé par Morland, nom de code de François Mitterrand. En haut, François Mauriac dans sa propriété de Malagar en Gironde. L'écrivain a pris ses distances avec Vichy et écrit *Le Cahier noir*.

Exil, Résistance, insurrection

Victimes de lois antisémites, le philosophe Henri Bergson et le dramaturge Tristan Bernard trouvent des défenseurs courageux en Paul Valéry et Sacha Guitry, mais Max Jacob et Robert Desnos, déportés, perdront la vie. Tout comme Jean Prévost, abattu dans le Vercors en août 1944. Plusieurs écrivains refuseront de publier tant que durera l'occupation, comme Char ou Guéhenno. D'autres s'expatrient. L'exil, à New York en l'occurrence, contraint par la législation antisémite ou choisi par refus du régime en place, tel est le lot de Jules Romains, d'André Maurois, de Claude Lévi-Strauss, d'Henry Bernstein, d'André Breton, de Saint-John Perse.

D'autres encore, bien plus rares, s'insurgent. Les Amis d'Alain-Fournier – une société littéraire où se retrouvent entre autres Jean Cassou, Claude Aveline, Jean Paulhan, Christiane Desroches-Noblecourt, qui préfigure le Groupe du Musée de l'Homme, un des premiers réseaux – lance un mot d'ordre : « Résistez ! » Portées par l'esprit de résistance, en

François Lachenal crée les éditions clandestines À la Porte d'ivoire pour publier en Suisse *Le Silence de la mer* de Vercors (ci-dessus). Le livre sortira aussi au Canada, à New York, Londres...

REVUE MENSUELLE   NUMERO 12

CONFLUENCES

POÈMES

par ARAGON, MAX JACOB, GERTRUDE STEIN, ROBERT CABY, p. 3.

OLIVIER DE CARFORT	Deux exemples de la magie dans la poésie contemporaine.	16
ROBERT MOREL	En girouettant autour de la liberté sur le cheval de bois Poésie.	25
HENRI RODE	Battue (nouvelle).	29
RAYMONDE MICHAUD	Rémission.	49
P.-J. FELBER	Introduction à la poésie de Rainer Maria Rilke.	52
RENE TAVERNIER	Quatre aspects de la poésie (fin).	62

MÉLANGES

par Auguste ANGLES, J.-C. FILLOUX, p. 79.

LE MOIS

CHRONIQUE : Journal sans date, par F.-C. Bauer, p. 89.

LES LIVRES : Adam, par Pierre Darmangeat, p. 92. — Fièvre des souvenirs d'exil, par Émile Picq, p. 94. — Les marais, par Dominique Rolin, p. 96. — L'orage du matin, par Jean Blanzat, p. 97. — L'invitation à la vie, par Jacques Robert, p. 99. — Les Cahiers du Rhône, p. 101. — Comptes rendus, p. 104. — Les Revues, p. 109.

LES ARTS - LES SPECTACLES

zone libre ou dans les colonies, des revues de littérature et de poésie vont offrir des possibilités de publier en dehors des circuits légaux : *Poésie* de Pierre Seghers à Villeneuve-lès-Avignon, les *Cahiers du Sud* de Jean Ballard à Marseille, *Confluences* de René Tavernier à Lyon, *Fontaine* de Max-Pol Fouchet et *L'Arche* de Jean Amrouche à Alger.

La production livresque en langue française se poursuit également hors des frontières, portée par les idéaux gaullistes et anti-nazis, avec notamment les *Cahiers du Silence* à Londres, les Éditions de la Maison française à New York, les *Cahiers du Rhône* et *Le Milieu du Monde* en Suisse romande, *L'Arbre* à Montréal, et le périodique de Roger Caillois *Lettres françaises*, à Buenos Aires.

Mais c'est « publié à Paris aux dépens d'un patriote » que paraît, clandestinement au début de 1943, *Le Silence de la mer*, le premier ouvrage des Éditions de Minuit, celui,

Les revues *Poésie* et *Confluences* (en bas, à gauche) publient nombre d'écrivains et poètes résistants : Eluard, Aragon, Masson, Michaux, Ponge, Desnos, Max Jacob, Wahl, Paulhan, Guillevic...

Jean Paulhan, figure tutélaire de la Résistance intellectuelle (ici, de face, avec le romancier Jean Blanzat), est le fondateur, avec Jacques Decour, des *Lettres françaises*, clandestines et ronéotées. À la une du numéro d'avril 1943, un appel à la jeunesse pour qu'elle refuse le STO (Service du travail obligatoire) en Allemagne et la *Chanson du franc-tireur* d'Aragon (ci-contre).

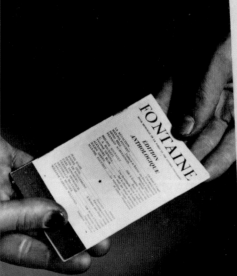

JULES ROMAINS

MESSAGES
AUX
FRANÇAIS

ÉDITIONS DE LA MAISON FRANÇAISE, Inc.
New York, N. Y.

ARAGON

LE
CRÈVE-CŒUR
et
LES YEUX
D'ELSA

ÉDITION
« LA FRANCE LIBRE »

Hors de France, la résistance littéraire se développe. À Alger, territoire de la France libre, Max-Pol Fouchet édite *Fontaine* sous format normal pour la France libérée et les pays alliés, en miniature pour la zone occupée (page de gauche en haut, le poète à son bureau; en bas, à gauche, le mini-format; à droite, numéro sur les écrivains des États-Unis). La solidarité internationale, aussi, est importante. La Suisse, l'Angleterre, le Canada, les États-Unis, le Brésil et l'Argentine sont les principaux pays à venir en aide aux artistes et intellectuels français en accueillant les réfugiés et en publiant les œuvres de résistants. Ci-contre, en haut et à gauche *Messages aux Français* de Jules Romains, Éditions de la Maison française, New York; ci-contre, en haut à droite, *Le Crève-cœur* et *Les Yeux d'Elsa* d'Aragon, édition « La France libre », Londres; au centre, *Traits*, revue créée par Lachenal, Genève (ci-contre, *Lettres françaises*, Buenos Aires).

1er. Juillet 1941

No 1

LETTRES FRANÇAISES

Cahiers trimestriels de littérature française, édités par les soins de la revue SUR avec la collaboration des écrivains français résidant en France et à l'Etranger.

SOMMAIRE

André Gide

Sur une définition de la poésie.
Poésies.
La fosse à tanks.
Racine et Mademoiselle.
Pour une esthétique sévère.

...xtes à relire:

... La barbarie en Europe

...ualité Littéraire.

...S: La Revue des Deux-Mondes, ...elle, Esprit, Les Cahiers du Sud, ...ance libre, Le Glaive de l'Esprit, etc.

Octobre 1940

ITS

...ocuments
mensuelle

l'abonnement :
— 6 mois : fr. 5o

Compte de chèques
II. 8894 Lausanne

...ENRI CRISINEL : *Alectone (fragments)* — EDMOND
ALFRED WILD : *Demain* — *Documents* — PIERRE
... — JEAN MOSER : *Journal (extraits)*.

...FACE

...résignés ou de confortables sceptiques
...et « objectifs » — qui jugeront notre
...ne : nous ne recherchons pas leurs
...que d'attendre. Persuadés de la néces-
...aussi croire et même prétendre à son

SUR
...N MARTIN 689

illustre, de leur fondateur le graveur Jean Bruller qui signe « Vercors ». Suivront une trentaine de livres souvent sous pseudonyme, pour beaucoup apportés par Paulhan, œuvres d'Aragon, Mauriac, Gide, Aveline, Elsa Triolet, Eluard, Chamson.

Une grande fécondité littéraire

Tout se passe comme si les circonstances de l'Occupation, loin d'affadir l'inspiration, l'avaient stimulée. Il n'est aucun genre qui ne se trouve brillamment sollicité. Sans trop de méthode, et parmi des

En mai 1942, Paul Eluard remet à Max-Pol Fouchet, un poème manuscrit alors intitulé « Une seule pensée » ainsi qu'un portrait dédicacé. Sous le titre « Liberté », il devient l'hymne de la Résistance intellectuelle (ci-dessous et à droite).

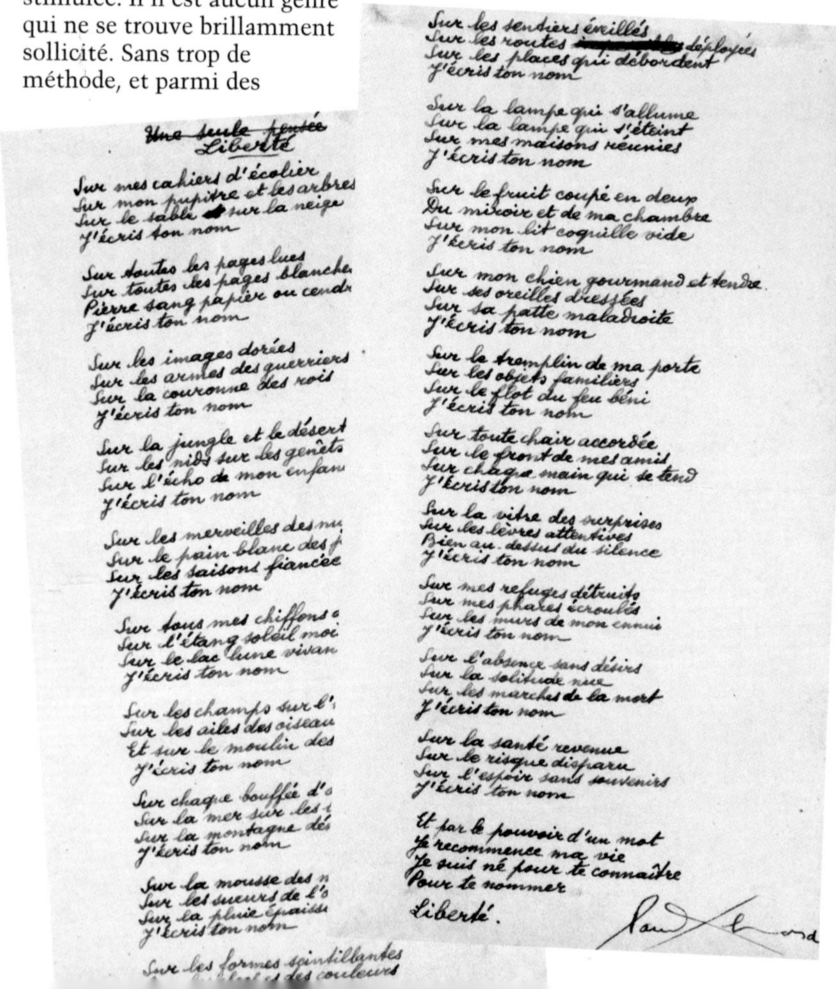

multitudes, on peut relever au nombre des romans *L'Homme pressé* de Morand, *L'Étranger* de Camus, *Pierrot mon ami* de Queneau, *Julie de Carneilhan* de Colette, *L'Invitée* de Simone de Beauvoir, *Le Passe-muraille* de Marcel Aymé, *L'Homme à cheval* de Drieu la Rochelle, *Les Voyageurs de l'impériale* d'Aragon, *Suzanne et les jeunes hommes* de Duhamel, *La Pharisienne* de Mauriac, *Le Solstice de juin* de Montherlant, *Thomas l'obscur* de Blanchot, *Ravage* de Barjavel, *L'Eau vive* de Giono, *Guignol's Band* de Céline, *Les Amitiés particulières* de Roger Peyrefitte. Simenon bien sûr, mais aussi les trop oubliés Pierre Véry et Jacques Decrest illustrent le genre policier, Sartre avec *L'Être et le Néant* et Lanza del Vasto avec *Le Pèlerinage aux sources*, la philosophie. Kléber Haedens donne une irrévérencieuse et tonique *Histoire de la littérature française*.

Mais c'est la poésie qui paraît le mieux correspondre aux interrogations de ce temps ô combien tourmenté. D'abord à travers les publications novatrices de Follain, de Guillevic, de Fombeure, de Genet, d'Alexandre Arnoux, de Michaux, d'Audiberti et des poètes de l'école de Rochefort, Cadou, Manoll, Béalu, Bérimont, Rousselot. Et simultanément par les recueils d'auteurs engagés en résistance, clandestins ou non, et dont la forme le plus souvent classique résonne comme une célébration, celle de la continuité du génie français : *État de veille* par Desnos, *Poésie et vérité* par Eluard, où figure le fameux « Liberté », *La Diane française* ou *Le Musée Grévin* par Aragon.

PAUL ELUARD

POÉSIE
ET
VÉRITÉ
1942

LES ÉDITIONS DE LA MAIN A PLUME
11, RUE DAUTANCOURT — PARIS (XVII°)

« Liberté » connaît de nombreuses réimpressions, dont celles des Éditions de Minuit clandestines et des éditions de La Baconnière en Suisse. En 1942, il paraît aussi en zone occupée dans *Poésie et Vérité*, revue semi-clandestine d'un groupe de jeunes surréalistes (ci-dessus).

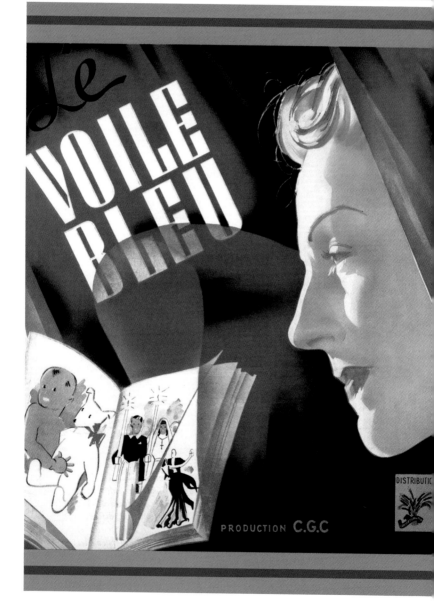

Paris et Vichy surent habilement se servir de la radio pour orienter l'opinion. Londres s'en mêlant, la guerre des ondes se propagea, toujours plus acerbe.

Le cinéma, opium du peuple, prit un essor inattendu pendant les années noires.

Malgré un double contrôle, profitant de son autarcie, il inspira ses réalisateurs, stimula ses acteurs, excita ses techniciens, résista aux tracasseries et aux bombardements et traversa son âge d'or.

CHAPITRE 4

IMAGES ET SONS

« J'ai donné des directives claires pour que les Français ne produisent que des films légers, vides, et si possible, stupides. » Les réalisateurs ne suivront heureusement pas la consigne de Goebbels (à droite, dernière scène de *La Fille du Puisatier* de Pagnol), même si certains films abondent en bons sentiments (à gauche, *Le Voile bleu* de Jean Stelli avec Gaby Morlay).

La radio, ce moyen de communication de masse, déjà populaire avant la guerre (5 millions de postes de radio déclarés en France en 1939), se révèle le premier antidote aux diverses censures en vigueur, qui décrédibilisent la presse écrite. La radio s'écoute en famille, et son pouvoir de suggestion comme de distraction la rend indispensable. Puissance excessive ? Certains, comme l'ultra Louis-Ferdinand Céline, l'affirment, et lui imputent les comportements erratiques des Français à l'endroit des nouvelles réalités politiques. Si bien que la vente des récepteurs est interdite en mars 1943 !

La Radiodiffusion nationale, symbole de la souveraineté de l'État français

Longtemps itinérante, la Radiodiffusion nationale finit par se replier à Vichy en juillet 1944. Elle épuise ses directeurs successifs et produit des journaux d'information conformes aux consignes du secrétariat d'État qui la coiffe. Mais ses programmes généraux mêlent le conformisme et l'audace, assez homologues en cela à la mentalité ambiante. Les émissions familiales de Jean Nohain cessent en 1942, usées et surtout compromises par l'exil en résistance du frère du producteur, l'acteur Claude Dauphin. Les concours de Robert Beauvais, le feuilleton policier de Georges Simenon et celui, bien

La Radiodiffusion nationale est le relais de la propagande allemande et vichyste. Elle retransmet les discours du Maréchal (ci-dessous, en 1943, Pétain prononçant son allocution radiodiffusée de Noël). Elle fait aussi la promotion de la Relève (échange des prisonniers contre des travailleurs volontaires), justifie les rafles et les déportations des juifs, vante la Milice et les Légions. Mais « Radio national » remplit également une mission éducative en valorisant notamment le patrimoine national : émissions littéraires, musicales, retransmission de pièces de théâtre (*Les Plaideurs* ou même *Le Soulier de satin*). Ci-contre, un programme de mai 1941.

mieux-pensant, de Louis Merlin, *L'Alphabet de la famille*, interprété par Larquey et Charpin, alternent avec les reportages sportifs de Georges Briquet et la chronique du jazz de Sylvaine Pécheral, qui survivra jusqu'à 1944 en dépit de l'énervement qu'elle provoque chez Philippe Henriot, le grand imprécateur de la Radio nationale aux éditoriaux enflammés à la gloire de l'Allemagne. Et c'est sur ces ondes que débutent alors de nouveaux producteurs appelés à faire aussi parler d'eux sous d'autres bannières, Pierre Schaeffer, Claude Roy, Albert Ollivier, Roger Leenhardt, Daniel Lesur.

Dans la salle des Fêtes du ministère des PTT transformée en studio d'enregistrement, Jules Gressier dirige pour la Radiodiffusion nationale, en mai 1943, *Hans le joueur de flûte.* Un conte lyrique en trois actes de Maurice Vaucaire et Georges Mitchell, sur une musique de Louis Ganne, inspiré par une légende rhénane...

**« Radio-Paris ment.
Radio-Paris est
allemand »**

À Paris, l'occupant
s'empare des studios
privés du Poste
parisien sur les
Champs-Élysées ainsi
que de sa fréquence
rebaptisée Radio-
Paris, station de
propagande au micro
de laquelle se
retrouvent des
zélateurs éprouvés de
la nouvelle Europe,

Un ouvrage de
propagande qui ne se
cache pas : le docteur
Friedrich, responsable
de Radio-Paris, publie
en 1943 l'ensemble de
ses éditoriaux voués
à la célébration de la
nouvelle Europe et de
la collaboration d'État
(ci-contre). Radio-Paris
est bien un poste
allemand, pour son
organisation et ses
missions de propagande
et de purification
culturelle ; c'est aussi
un poste français pour
ses professionnels
(beaucoup sont
français), son public
et ses programmes
culturels ou de
divertissement qui
évitent toute référence
à la situation politique
et lui donnent un
masque de normalité.

tels le Suisse Paul Ferdonnet, ancien de Radio-
Stuttgart avant guerre, ou l'éditorialiste fanatique
Jean Hérold-Paquis, qui clame régulièrement :
« Comme Carthage, l'Angleterre sera détruite. »

Mais leurs diatribes n'auraient pas suffi à réunir,
et donc à influencer, un auditoire significatif.
Aussi le docteur Friedrich, mandataire de Radio-
Paris, sollicite-t-il toutes sortes de personnalités
artistiques pour enrichir l'antenne à travers jeux,
feuilletons, enquêtes. Le poète Luc Bérimont,
Pierre Hiégel, le plus célèbre animateur de radio
du temps, les chefs d'orchestre Raymond Legrand
ou Richard Blareau, le chansonnier Jean Rigaux, le
chanteur de charme André Claveau, parmi tant
d'autres, s'aventurent sur les ondes de Radio-
Paris. La station diffuse aussi beaucoup de
programmes musicaux comportant du jazz et
des compositeurs français, qui aèrent son
orientation politique. La BBC anglaise ne
cesse de répéter sur l'air de *La Cucaracha*
son fameux slogan écrit par Pierre Dac :
« Radio-Paris ment, Radio-Paris est allemand. »

L'impact des « radios libres »

Cependant, ce sont évidemment les
émissions en français de la BBC, Radio-

Londres, qui retiennent l'attention d'auditeurs clandestins qu'il est difficile de chiffrer. Du moins est-il avéré que, dès le lendemain de l'appel du général de Gaulle, des programmes quotidiens y sont conçus par Michel Saint-Denis alias Jacques Duchesne, ancien bras droit de Jacques Copeau. Son émission « Une demi-heure après le dîner »

La radio s'écoute en famille (en bas). L'officielle comme la clandestine. Et tous les auditeurs savent que Radio Paris est diligentée par l'occupant (programme ci-dessous).

deviendra bientôt « Les Français parlent aux Français », pendant laquelle se succèdent des Français libres s'exprimant sous la forme de réflexions politiques (Maurice Schumann, Pierre Bourdan, Jean Marin) ou de chroniques plaisantes (Pierre

Au micro londonien de la BBC, Jacques Duchesne « parle aux Français », écouté par un nombre de fidèles dont le nombre croît avec les années, notamment après 1942, « l'année terrible ». Au début de chaque émission, Duchesne lance cette phrase « Aujourd'hui, (xième) jour de la résistance du peuple français à l'oppression » qui deviendra « Aujourd'hui (xième) jour de la lutte du peuple français pour sa libération » (ci-contre, Jacques Duchesne en pleine émission ; en bas, lettre de soutien de deux auditeurs de treize ans, envoyée

Dac, Jean Oberlé, Maurice Van Moppès) sans omettre les fameux messages codés, compris des résistants de l'intérieur et annonçant des décisions stratégiques, telle celle du débarquement du 6 juin 1944. L'occupant traque

Auditeur de la Radio Anglaise....
Considère ce papier comme un premier avertissement

Consciemment ou non, en écoutant et propageant cette propagande, fruit de l'alliance judéo-communiste, tu commets un crime envers ta Patrie.

Sans préjudice des sanctions judiciaires auxquelles tu t'exposes, saches qu'il est des Français décidés à tout pour que cesse ton action criminelle.

Essaie de comprendre où est ton devoir. . . .

Sinon, à notre grand regret, nous n'hésiterons pas à te l'imposer.

23-12-40-

Chaque soire nous écoutons vos émissions qui nous donnent tant de courrage.

Nous esperons et nous prions en la victoire alliée qui sauvera le monde du joug allemand. Pour tous les français le general De Gaulle, est un héros.

Vive la France ! Vive l'Angleterre !

Deux garçons de 13 ans

à la radio libre dès décembre 1940). L'efficacité de la radio clandestine préoccupe les autorités, d'autant que les mises en garde sont sans résultat (ci-dessous, un tract d'avertissement menaçant « l'auditeur de la Radio anglaise »).

évidemment les oreilles complaisantes à ces émissions interdites qu'il ne parvient pas à brouiller, et qui dénoncent avec constance et véhémence la collaboration et les exactions nazies, et qui exhortent à la résistance. Alors, on saisit des postes.

Balbutiements de la télévision

L'Allemagne a joué un rôle certain dans l'essor de la télévision en France, puisque c'est à destination de ses blessés soignés dans des hôpitaux parisiens que sont importés du Reich cinq cents récepteurs en 1943. On engage des techniciens, on aménage le studio de Magic City à proximité du site historique de Cognacq-Jay : au printemps 1944, on estime à un millier le nombre d'appareils pouvant recevoir le signal de Paris-Télévision, émis depuis la tour Eiffel.

Le nouveau média, déjà expérimenté pendant les années trente en Angleterre et aux États-Unis, en Allemagne et en France (par les ingénieurs René Barthélemy et Henri de France), n'apparaît nullement comme une priorité, ce qui explique la désinvolture d'une programmation fondée sur la rediffusion permanente. Les retransmissions de spectacles des salles subventionnées, théâtre, danse, opéra, alternent avec des numéros de cirque ou de chansonniers.

Comment empêcher concrètement les Français d'écouter Londres chez eux, après le couvre-feu ? De qui proviennent tous les « bobards » ? La contre-propagande la plus épaisse se donne libre cours

LES BOBARDS...
SORTENT TOUJOURS DU MÊME NID

par voie d'affiche, et concentre ses attaques sur l'ennemi qui répand des mensonges : de Gaulle, les alliés, les Juifs et les francs-maçons... (ci-dessus).

Le cinéma dans un double étau

Les décisions édictées par le COIC et contrôlées étroitement par la censure allemande paraissent dans *Le Film*, nouvelle revue corporative qui sévira du 12 octobre 1940 au 31 juillet 1944 et s'affiche comme le porte-parole de l'occupant (ci-dessous). Deux fois par mois, elle diffuse les nouveaux règlements de l'industrie et du commerce cinématographique, établis par Raoul Ploquin et contrôlés par le sourcilleux docteur Diedrich (ci-contre, à gauche et à droite). Les premiers numéros vantent la production allemande prête à envahir les écrans de la zone occupée et signalent les équipes de doublage qui travaillent à plein rendement.

Des deux côtés de la ligne de démarcation, le cinéma est bloqué par la censure. À Paris, la Propaganda Abteilung et son service cinéma sous l'autorité du Dr Diedrich surveillent attentivement les décisions prises à Vichy et applicables dans tout le pays. La production cinématographique est totalement réorganisée. Un Comité d'organisation de l'industrie cinématographique (COIC) est créé, dirigé par Raoul Ploquin. Le COIC regroupe les membres de la profession dans plusieurs branches du cinéma. Il instaure une carte d'identité professionnelle obligatoire, renouvelable tous les trois mois, accordée selon des

conditions très strictes, et bien sûr interdite aux Juifs. Quarante-sept cinéastes professionnels cessent leur activité, parmi lesquels Renoir, Duvivier, Clair, Feyder, Chenal. Le cinéma doit aussi raffermir la moralité défaillante. Le retour à la terre, la renaissance du travail artisanal, l'exaltation des vertus familiales et l'amour du drapeau sont au programme. Dès la fin de 1940, *La Fille du puisatier* de Marcel Pagnol puis *Vénus aveugle* d'Abel Gance, tous deux dédiés au sauveur du pays, témoignent d'un renouveau de la production française. Mais la popularité du Maréchal inquiète Otto Abetz.

Les films français antérieurs à 1937 sont interdits, comme le seront les films jugés tendancieux (*La Règle du jeu* et *La Bête humaine* de Renoir, *Le jour se lève* de Carné), les films de guerre ou ceux jugés immoraux. Les noms des acteurs juifs disparaissent des génériques et des affiches. Les films anglo-saxons

J'espère commencer à tourner vey le 15 août, et je n'ai pas encore ma pellicule !

Marcel Pagnol

Les services techniques de la Propaganda-Abteilung contrôlent la remise de pellicules aux réalisateurs, y compris en zone libre. Marcel Pagnol ne pourra finir *La Prière aux étoiles* faute de pellicule (ci-dessus, sa lettre à Ploquin). Ces services régissent aussi la fourniture des bobines aux salles (en haut, un centre technique du film chargé des cinémas de Bordeaux et sa région).

CONTINENTAL

sont interdits dès 1940 en zone occupée, en 1942 en zone libre. Tandis que l'ambassadeur convie le Tout-Paris artistique et mondain aux galas de lancement des films allemands.

Les occupants investissent dans de nombreuses sociétés à tous les niveaux de l'industrie cinématographique : distribution, production, exploitation. Les sociétés allemandes ACE (Alliance cinématographique européenne) et Tobis monopolisent la distribution. Et Alfred Greven, ami de Goering choisi par Goebbels, a tout pouvoir pour implanter en France la Continental, sa société de production, grâce aux capitaux de l'UFA, société de production allemande. La Continental annonce une liste de films dirigés et interprétés par des Français, qui toucheront de l'argent allemand. Aucun film ne peut être entrepris, sans accord signé. Les réalisateurs consultés finissent par se soumettre,

L'initiale de la Continental devient pour quatre ans la croix gammée du cinéma (ci-dessus). Alfred Greven, qui aime le cinéma français, admire Danielle Darrieux et honore Zarah Leander, est le moteur efficace de la puissante société (en haut, avec les deux artistes).

mais gardent le choix des scénarios (sauf allusion à la guerre ou aux restrictions) et se refusent à toute velléité de propagande. Continental Films « racole » des acteurs, tourne des films, les monte et les sort sans concurrence aucune.

Cependant en 1941, Pathé ressuscite et Charles Trenet entonne *La Romance de Paris* dans le film éponyme de Jean Boyer. *Nous les gosses* (Louis Daquin), apologie de la solidarité par des enfants en lutte contre l'apathie des adultes, est mieux accueilli. D'autres sociétés émergent, mais la Continental déferle. Danielle Darrieux atteint le zénith avec *Premier rendez-vous* (Henri Decoin) et *Caprices* (Léo

FILMS

Joannon). Harry Baur, Pierre Fresnay, Edwige Feuillère retrouvent leur public. Les vedettes allemandes multiplient leurs passages à Paris.

Les grands noms de la décennie précédente s'éclipsent. Renoir, Duvivier, Clair rallient Hollywood, Chenal fuit en Amérique du Sud, Feyder s'abrite en Suisse, Ophüls gagne les États-Unis où Michèle Morgan et Dalio retrouvent Charles Boyer. Jean Gabin, Jean-Pierre Aumont, Claude Dauphin combattront pour la France libre. L'acteur Robert Lynen, entré dans la Résistance, sera arrêté et exécuté.

La présence de la très populaire Danielle Darrieux (ci-dessous, l'actrice sur l'affiche de *Premier rendez-vous*) axe immédiatement la Continental vers le succès. *Premier rendez-vous, Caprices, La Fausse Maîtresse,* ces trois comédies légères et doucement musicales qu'elle anime de son charme et de

sa malice sont distribuées par l'ACE (Alliance cinématographique européenne ; ci-contre). Elles permettent au public de plonger dans l'oubli en voyant la vie en rose.

La principale occupation des Parisiens

Les chiffres de l'exploitation ne cessent de
progresser. En 1941, le cinéma enregistre
224,9 millions de spectateurs. En 1943, ils sont
304,5 millions. Les cinémas parisiens récoltent
416 millions de francs de recettes en 1941, 707
en 1942, 915 en 1943, avant de redescendre à 674
en 1944, à cause des bombardements sur la capitale.
À Lyon, *La Fille du puisatier* bat tous les records au
Pathé Palace avec 630 000 francs de recettes en trois
semaines.

La fréquentation des salles de cinéma est la
principale occupation des Parisiens. Le spectateur
s'y calfeutre en hiver. L'été, l'abondance des films
pallie l'absence des voyages. L'occupant l'a d'ailleurs
bien compris. Même si l'intérêt économique de la
production et de l'exploitation cinématographique
entre en jeu, le maintien des salles est d'abord jugé
nécessaire pour aider la population à surmonter son
désarroi et les difficultés du temps.

Et pourtant aller au cinéma n'est pas simple et les
soucis de l'exploitant et du spectateur se rejoignent
sur bien des points : évacuation des salles en cas
d'alerte, répression des manifestations hostiles au
passage des actualités vantant les victoires de l'Axe
Rome-Berlin, couvre-feu variable selon la
recrudescence ou l'importance des attentats,
absence de chauffage, coupures électriques et
restriction du nombre de séances.

L'écran, « une fenêtre, pas un miroir »

Les spectateurs veulent combler leur longue
patience. Les tentatives de cinéma à dessein
politique échouent. *Forces occultes*, qui entend
dévoiler les secrets de la franc-maçonnerie et se
présente comme un film de combat et de vérité,
n'attire pas les foules. Les sketches des *Corrupteurs*
dénonçant les Juifs, ceux de la série *Monsieur
Girouette* moquant les gaullistes passent inaperçus.
Le dessin animé de Raymond Jeannin qui tourne en
dérision l'approche du Débarquement n'amuse
personne.

En 1942, sur les grands
boulevards, la foule
se presse aux portes
de l'Olympia pour la
seconde époque du
*Comte de Monte-
Cristo* (ci-dessus).
Les salles de quartier
à Paris et celles des
grandes villes de la
zone libre connaissent
la même prospérité.

Les films allemands, peu adaptés au public français, ne réussissent pas à s'imposer, sauf quelques exceptions comme *Les Aventures du baron de Münchhausen* (Josef von Báky) ou *Le Juif Süss* (Veit Harlan). En zone libre, *Les Voyages du Maréchal* ou *Une journée de Pierre Laval* font bâiller le spectateur, qui subit sans broncher les actualités franco-allemandes et ricane aux actualités nazies.

Arborant le sigle du COIC, tickets de deux salles de quartier, La Scala et L'Eldorado.

PROJECTION   DES   ACTUALITES

    Le public est informé qu'aucune
manifestation ne sera tolérée pendant la
projection des actualités.

    Le moindre murmure ou rire, ainsi qu
les applaudissements peuvent entrainer des
<u>ARRESTATIONS</u> et la <u>FERMETURE IMMEDIATE</u> des
salles.

           LA   DIRECTION

Les vastes cinémas parisiens ou provinciaux qui, de l'orchestre au balcon, canalisaient la multitude, comme le Gaumont-Palace (ci-contre, la foule des spectateurs en 1943), devaient se méfier du moindre incident. Les actualités allemandes et leur triomphalisme provoquèrent très vite des mouvements divers. Des consignes sévères furent édictées (à gauche). Coups de sifflet, ricanements, toux prolongées, piétinements étaient passibles d'expulsion, de poursuites ou de séjours au commissariat. Des mouchards se dissimulaient dans la demi-obscurité de rigueur, prêts à intervenir. Des affichettes placardées, des disques diffusés obligèrent les directeurs de salle à se méfier des risques de fermeture. Ces avertissements n'empêchèrent pas les applaudissements vengeurs saluant une réplique bien sentie. Les salles de cinéma accueillirent aussi des rassemblements d'écoliers invités à célébrer les arbres de Noël et des enfants de prisonniers en Allemagne.

Le public souhaite que les films l'enlèvent sur les ailes du rêve (*La Nuit fantastique*, Marcel L'Herbier), le confrontent au surnaturel (*La Main du diable*, Maurice Tourneur), l'introduisent au cœur des légendes (*La Fiancée des ténèbres*, Serge de Poligny). Jean Cocteau, en ranimant le mythe de Tristan dans *L'Éternel Retour* (Jean Delannoy), bouleverse les foules. Il s'ébat dans le désuet et poudre de poésie lunaire *Le Baron fantôme*, puis, inspiré par Diderot, livre à Bresson un dialogue d'une parfaite densité : *Les Dames du bois de Boulogne*, triomphe de la passion sur la carapace glacée des sentiments mondains, ont suivi la fresque noire et blanche brossée par le metteur en scène en hommage aux sœurs de Béthanie (*Les Anges du péché*).

Le carnet tenu par un affamé de la pellicule, nommé Lachenay, le promène en zigzag dans l'Italie romantique à la rencontre du peintre Salvator Rosa puis à la recherche des *Faussaires* sortis des studios berlinois, ou dans l'épopée du misérabilisme adaptée de Victor Hugo. Guimauve et vitriol font bon ménage. Cette éphéméride, où Lachenay attribue des notes aux spectacles (huit sur dix pour *Le Corbeau* de Clouzot!) témoigne du plaisir que prennent les Français de 1944 à déguster des histoires hors du temps.

Le recours au patrimoine littéraire

Obligés de contourner l'actualité, les auteurs
empruntent au passé littéraire. L'adaptation par
Giraudoux de *La Duchesse de Langeais* (Baroncelli)
provoque un inventaire balzacien : *Le Colonel
Chabert* (Le Hénaff), *Le Père Goriot* (Billon), *Vautrin*,
La Grande Bretèche devenue *Un seul amour* se
succèdent. D'autres séries favorisent les récits
policiers de Simenon (*Les Inconnus dans la maison*
de Decoin, *Le Voyageur de la Toussaint* de Daquin,
Monsieur La Souris de Lacombe) et de nombreux
Maigret, de Pierre Véry (*L'Assassinat du père Noël*
de Christian-Jaque, *Madame et le mort* de Daquin,
Goupi Mains rouges de Becker), les récits policiers
de Stanislas-André Steeman (*Le Dernier des six* de
Lacombe), *L'assassin habite au 21* de Clouzot).

    Les Visiteurs du soir affichent leur ambition.
Fabliau médiéval où se devinent des allusions
politiques, ce film de prestige réunit Carné, Prévert,
Laroche, le musicien Maurice Thiriet, mais dissimule
le décorateur Trauner et le compositeur Kosma.

Gérard de Nerval
et *La Main du diable*,
Denis Diderot et *Les
Dames du Bois de
Boulogne*, le modeste
Albéric Cahuet avec
*Pontcarral, colonel
d'Empire*, et surtout
Honoré de Balzac et
son *Colonel Chabert* :
ces quelques affiches
proclament l'emprise
de la littérature sur la
production de l'époque,
qui plonge le
spectateur dans des
fastes surannés et
l'éloigne de la réalité
triviale. La qualité des
dialoguistes (Jean-Paul
Le Chanois, Cocteau,
Bernard Zimmer, Pierre
Benoit) contribue à ce
dépaysement mâtiné
de fantastique et
d'héroïques
réminiscences.

"LES VISITEURS DU SOIR"

Gilles (M. Alain Cuny) chante l'amour
devant les hôtes du baron Hugues (M. Ledoux).

Les deux ménestrels, Gilles (M. Alain Cuny)
et Dominique (Mme Arletty), au milieu des
baladins et des danseurs.

Pendant un arrêt du bal, Dominique va emmener Renaud
(M. Marcel Herrand) pour le séduire tandis qu'Anne
(Mlle Marie Déa) deviendra la proie de Gilles.

Le Diable (M. Jules Berry) promène ses

LES producteurs de films nous gâtent en cette fin d'année. Après *Pontcarral*, que nous avons applaudi au Marivaux la
semaine dernière, voici les *Visiteurs du soir*, que M. André Paulvé présente au Madeleine. Il s'agit cette fois d'un conte
fantastique de MM. Jacques Prévert et Pierre Laroche mis à l'écran par M. Marcel Carné.
L'action se passe au moyen âge. Le baron Hugues célèbre au château les fiançailles de sa fille Anne avec le chevalier Renaud. Deux ménestrels, Gilles et Dominique, viennent participer à l'éclat de la fête et chanter l'amour et ses joux
cruels et tendres. Tout de suite nous devinons qu'ils sont doués d'un pouvoir surnaturel extraordinaire. S'étant mal aimés
jadis, ils sont devenus les agents du diable et vont par le monde jeter la jalousie et le trouble dans le cœur de ceux qui s'aiment.
Leur tâche au château du baron Hugues ne paraît pas très compliquée tellement différente de son fiancé, Renaud,

Marcel Carné évite les pièges de la Continental, mais doit abandonner le filon du réalisme poétique. Il reste cependant fidèle aux collaborateurs de ses films précédents : Prévert à l'écriture, Roger Hubert à la photo, Trauner aux décors, Thiriet et Kosma à la musique, certains travaillant clandestinement pour raisons raciales (ci-contre, Carné sur le tournage). *Les Visiteurs du soir* sortent en décembre 1942. Ce fabliau médiéval est propice aux sous-entendus politiques. L'audace du propos, la maîtrise du réalisateur et des interprètes furent bien accueillies par le public et l'ensemble de la critique (en bas, à gauche, *L'Illustration*). Le tournage des *Enfants du Paradis* va s'étendre de 1943 à 1945, d'abord sur la Côte d'Azur, finalement à Paris. Les difficultés ne purent anéantir ce si beau projet. L'ampleur des décors, le foisonnement des costumes, le brio de l'interprétation exaltant les amours de Garance, chimère du Boulevard du Crime, trop aimée, mal aimée. Arletty, Jean-Louis Barrault, Maria Casarès, Louis Salou, Pierre Renoir et Marcel Herrand rendent ainsi hommage aux arts du spectacle et le chef-d'œuvre de Carné couronne le cinéma des années difficiles (en haut, à gauche).

Et Claude Autant-Lara, spécialiste des récits spirituellement enrubannés, grince avec *Douce*, histoire d'une jeune aristocrate du temps où s'édifiait la tour Eiffel qui, lasse des préjugés de sa caste, se révolte et en meurt.

France héroïque contre réalité sordide

Jean Grémillon et Henri-Georges Clouzot alimentent des querelles dont les braises restent brûlantes. *Le ciel est à vous* exalte l'acharnement d'une mère de famille subjuguée par l'aviation, prête à tout lui sacrifier. Revendiqué autant par les vichystes que par les résistants, le film de Grémillon s'oppose au *Corbeau* de Clouzot. Une petite ville gangrenée par une éruption de lettres anonymes découvre la corruption de ses habitants. Produit par la Continental, il déchaîne la colère des patriotes irrités par cet étalage de turpitudes. Quant à *Goupi Mains rouges* de Jacques Becker, il

Moment crucial du film d'Henri-Georges Clouzot : la dictée infligée aux notables suspectés d'écrire des lettres anonymes dévoilant les turpitudes de la cité, atteinte de maladie contagieuse (ci-dessous). Le film, produit par la Continental, est accusé de servir la propagande nazie en avilissant le peuple français et en calomniant les petites villes françaises. *Le Corbeau* devint, à la Libération, le symbole du règlement des comptes cinématographiques.

LE "CORBEAU" EST DÉPLUMÉ

Car aux estropiés, aux amoraux, aux corrompus qui déshonorent, dans _Le Corbeau_, une de nos villes de province, _Le Ciel est à vous_ oppose des personnages pleins de sève française, de courage authentique, de santé morale, où nous retrouvons une vérité nationale qui ne veut pas et ne peut pas mourir.

éclabousse l'imagerie traditionnelle du paysan. La figure du chef apparaît dans _Premier de cordée_, se fixe dans _Le Carrefour des enfants perdus_, se fige avec _Mermoz_.

Pierre de Hérain, beau-fils du Maréchal, se penche élégamment sur les préoccupations vichystes dans _Monsieur des Lourdines_, nouvelle variation sur le retour à la terre. L'émouvante composition de Gaby Morlay remporte un triomphe dans _Le Voile bleu_: veuve en 1914, elle accepte l'emploi de mère

LES LETTRES FRANÇAISES

La limpidité du _Ciel est à vous_ contre la noirceur du _Corbeau_. L'exploit d'une mère de famille passionnée d'aviation, aidée par son mari, qui bat, seule à bord, un record de distance, s'inspire comme le film de Clouzot de faits réels. Vichystes et résistants, se reconnurent dans ces humbles héros, tirant chacun à eux la symbolique du chef-d'œuvre de Grémillon. _Les Lettres françaises_ consacrèrent des textes enflammés à cette polémique (ci-contre).

occasionnelle pour enfants tenus à l'écart. Abnégation et dévouement : succès lacrymal assuré.

La production en zone libre

Les productions du midi de la France sont ignorées à Paris. Leur technique est médiocre, handicapée par la qualité douteuse de la pellicule très contingentée. Les équipes qui avaient cru à l'essor d'une production libre se découragent et, peu à peu, rejoignent Paris. La censure favorise la mise en images conventionnelle et ampoulée des romans d'Henri Bordeaux et d'Isabelle Sandy. Après Daudet et *L'Arlésienne*, Marc Allégret adapte brillamment Anatole France (*Félicie Nanteuil*), puis se contente d'enjoliver des anecdotes bulles de savon. Toutefois, Vichy protège le court-métrage et les Français vont s'intéresser aux documentaires. À partir de 1942 et l'invasion de la zone libre par les Allemands, la production et la censure seront totalement centralisées à Paris.

Le cinéma de ces années révèle aussi de grands acteurs, tels Madeleine Sologne et Jean Marais (ici dans *L'Éternel Retour*), François Périer, Micheline Presle, Maria Casares, Bernard Blier...

La richesse du cinéma des années noires

En 1943 débute le tournage des *Enfants du paradis*. Filmé par Carné, rêvé par Prévert, cet hommage aux arts du spectacle couronne le cinéma de cette période d'une créativité exceptionnelle. De 1940 à 1944, de *La Fille du puisatier* à *Mademoiselle X*, deux cent vingt longs métrages sont sortis, réalisés par quatre-vingt-deux metteurs en scène. Trente films sont des productions de la Continental. Les autres se répartissent entre une cinquantaine de studios français. Beaucoup d'entre eux appartiennent à la légende du cinéma.

Ces quatre années pendant lesquelles le cinéma s'est adapté à son autarcie, permettent à certains réalisateurs de s'imposer (Autant-Lara, Clouzot, Cayatte) ou de se révéler (Daquin, Bresson, Becker). À cette période, s'attachent aussi les noms de Spaak, scénariste, d'Aurenche, Aymé, Anouilh, de Bost, Chavance, Zimmer, dialoguistes, ceux de Giraudoux et de Prévert, sans oublier Henri Jeanson qui s'est faufilé masqué pour apporter son talent aux films qu'il ne pouvait signer.

La politique en faveur du court-métrage révèle Georges Rouquier, chantre des métiers oubliés (ci-dessus, accroupi, qui filme *Le Charron*). Avec *Falbalas*, Jacques Becker entraîne la fiction dans les coulisses de la haute couture (ci-dessous, Becker, assis près du projecteur, tournant les extérieurs du film en 1944).

Les grandes institutions artistiques, comme l'Opéra et la Comédie-Française, doivent composer avec la puissance occupante et sa volonté de mettre la main sur les scènes prestigieuses. L'ensemble des spectacles témoigne d'une belle tenue et impose de nouveaux auteurs. Le Boulevard continue sur sa lancée, le cirque garde ses fidèles et, en zone libre, les jeunes comédiens entretiennent la décentralisation.

CHAPITRE 5

LE SPECTACLE VIVANT

Dans la cour du Palais-Royal, le chef allemand Hans von Benda dirige le Berliner Kammer Orchestra, le 13 juillet 1941 : Mozart effacera-t-il le souvenir de *La Marseillaise* ? De son côté, à l'ombre de la croix gammée, la Comédie-Française réussit, au nom de la tradition et sans braver les interdits officiels, à maintenir une qualité et une dignité constantes dans son répertoire (ci-contre, en 1944, Raimu dans *Le Bourgeois gentilhomme*).

La musique rapproche les peuples

Lorsque, en juin 1940, les rares Parisiens demeurés dans leur ville voient défiler les troupes victorieuses au pas de parade, musique en tête, ils assistent au prélude d'une occupation en fanfare qui, très rapidement, va gagner les grandes places de la ville et rassembler bon nombre de badauds. Plus ou moins écoutés, ces concerts en plein air vont se poursuivre et se termineront quinze jours avant la Libération. Les dirigeants nazis, l'ambassadeur Otto Abetz sont persuadés que le rapprochement entre les deux peuples doit se resserrer grâce à la musique et à son enseignement.

La réouverture de l'Opéra a lieu le 24 août. Hitler, célébrant sa victoire, avait deux mois auparavant parcouru le palais Garnier sur lequel Jacques Rouché veille

La vogue des concerts militaires bat son plein : dans les jardins, sur les marches de l'Opéra, le parvis de Notre-Dame, la place de la Concorde... (ci-dessus, l'orchestre de l'armée de l'air allemande, rond-point des Champs-Élysées, le 1er août 1940).

depuis 1914. Ce dernier est un homme de goût, la somptuosité des représentations dans des décors signés Derain, Maurice Denis, Brianchon, De Chirico a toujours été reconnue.

Répertoire franco-allemand à l'Opéra

Rouché a l'oreille des Allemands. C'est aussi l'interlocuteur de Vichy dont il applique scrupuleusement les lois, même raciales. Il lutte pour conserver prioritairement le répertoire français, mais se voit contraint de programmer Wagner, Mozart, Richard Strauss avec les troupes du Staatsoper de Berlin ou de l'opéra de Mannheim. Lors d'une soirée strictement réservée, Karajan dirige Germaine Lubin chantant *Tristan et Isolde* ou *L'Enlèvement au sérail*, et, en 1941, Elisabeth Schwarzkopf enchante l'élite militaire allemande avec son interprétation de *La Chauve-Souris* de Johann Strauss. Plus tard, *Ariane à Naxos* de Richard Strauss sera créée.

Pour la danse, l'Opéra ouvre ses portes à Hans Pfitzner (*Palestrina*), à Werner Egk (*Peer Gynt*). Ce dernier remporte un vif succès en 1942 avec *Joan von Zarissa*, ballet choisi par Serge Lifar. Né à Kiev, entré à l'Opéra en 1929, à la mort de Diaghilev dont il fut l'élève, Serge Lifar, remarquable danseur étoile et maître de ballet prodigue, mène depuis l'entrée des Allemands une vie mondaine axée sur la collaboration. En 1942, trois voyages l'amènent à Berlin où on lui propose de diriger la danse. Il préfère Paris. Le succès l'impose comme l'interlocuteur de la puissance occupante. Le « manifeste du

L'Opéra à l'heure allemande : programme et affichage en allemand pour la *Walkyrie* de Wagner, en mars 1941 (ci-contre). En mai 1941, Germaine Lubin y interprète *L'Enlèvement au sérail* de Mozart sous la direction de Karajan, avec l'orchestre du Staatsoper de Berlin (ci-dessous). En 1942, après deux ballets de Werner Egk (*Peer Gynt* et *Joan von Zarissa*), la saison s'achève par un franc succès français, *Les Animaux modèles*, composition de Francis Poulenc et chorégraphie de Serge Lifar. À gauche, en bas, Jacques Rouché, le directeur de l'Opéra (assis), le corps de ballet de l'Opéra, Poulenc (en costume gris) et Lifar, à sa gauche.

chorégraphe » définit ses ambitions : anéantir toute convention et favoriser les danseurs.

La réunion des théâtres lyriques va permettre à l'Opéra-Comique d'enregistrer en 1941, sous la direction de Roger Desormière, la brillante réussite de Jacques Jansen et Irène Joachim : *Pelléas et Mélisande* tels que Debussy l'avait rêvé.

Opérette et concerts

Cependant, les salles parisiennes proposent d'agréables soirées, aimablement frivoles, grâce au renouveau de l'opérette. Si

Offenbach est proscrit en tant que compositeur juif, on retrouve très vite le *Phi-Phi* de Willemetz et Christiné créé le 11 novembre 1918 et qui revient en octobre 1940, sans amertume. Franz Lehar s'installe à deux reprises au pupitre pour diriger *Le Pays du sourire* et *La Veuve joyeuse*. Le Châtelet présente magnifiquement *Valses de Vienne*, puis *Valses de Paris*. Elvire Popesco s'essaie à chanter *Feux du ciel* aux côtés du compositeur Jean Tranchant. Le vieux répertoire tel que *Les Cent Vierges* ou *Les Cloches de Corneville* alterne avec les airs nouveaux d'*Une femme par jour* (dont Serge Veber n'a pas le droit de signer le livret), refrains qui permettent de retrouver la fantaisie du Paris d'avant-guerre. Curieusement, un festival swing se déchaîne à Pleyel en 1941.

Les mélomanes sont sollicités par les nombreuses salles de concerts : classiques, comme Pasdeloup affichant pour l'anniversaire de Honegger *Le Roi David* en 1942, comme Chaillot pour l'exécution la même année de *La Damnation de Faust* de Berlioz. Les grands chefs allemands se succèdent, de Jochum à Mengelberg, de Clemens Krauss à Knappertsbusch. Le pianiste français Alfred Cortot, acquis entièrement aux idées nouvelles, se prodigue dans des concerts outre-Rhin. Investi de hautes fonctions professionnelles, il aime, en tant que pianiste, se

Organisés par Denise Tual et André Schaeffner, approuvés par Gaston Gallimard, les concerts de la Pléiade sont lancés en février 1943. À partir de juin, ils auront lieu salle Gaveau (ci-dessous, affiche des premiers concerts donnés salle Gaveau). Ils font la part belle aux musiciens français oubliés, aux premières auditions et aux exilés. On y trouve les noms de Messiaen, Farfaix et Poulenc.

produire aux côtés de Wilhelm Kempff. Si l'orchestre de Radio-Stuttgart joue dans l'usine Gnome et Rhône, l'excellente formation de Radio-Paris, habituée à se produire en salle, affronte le Philharmonique de Berlin. Les concerts du Conservatoire, animés par Charles Münch, exaltent Beethoven, sans oublier Debussy, ni Ravel. En 1943, rendant hommage à Berlioz, Munch déchaîne six cents interprètes venus de différents horizons pour l'exécution du *Requiem*.

Vichy, la musique et la jeunesse

À Vichy, hormis les saisons de concerts toujours bien accueillies, les dirigeants se tournent du côté de la jeunesse avec l'espoir d'un renouveau patriotique. En novembre 1940, la création de Jeune France entend défendre toute tradition sans

Au palais de Chaillot : en janvier 1941, Franz Lehar dirige deux cents musiciens de la Wehrmacht (en haut, à gauche, signant des autographes). En juin, sous les acclamations d'un public vibrant, Charles Münch y dirige les quatre-vingt-dix musiciens de la Société des concerts du Conservatoire dans un programme Ravel, avec *La Rhapsodie espagnole* et *Daphnis et Chloé*. La musique française combat le répertoire allemand.

s'opposer aux influences modernes. Les airs populaires doivent retrouver leur vigueur perdue.

Le chant choral est à l'ordre du jour pour sa valeur morale. En 1942, le lancement des Jeunesses musicales de France est un succès. Elles ont mission de former des mélomanes, soit amateurs de concerts, soit simples auditeurs à l'écoute de la radio ou collectionneurs de disques. Elles contribuent à secouer le joug culturel que les Allemands font peser sur la vie musicale française et les Lyonnais accourent en foule salle Rameau lorsque les compositeurs français y sont honorés.

Les Juifs sont exclus du monde du théâtre : directeurs, auteurs et même techniciens et employés... Des questionnaires sont adressés à tous les théâtres (ci-dessus).

(Se trouve-t-il parmi vos collaborateurs
  (chefs techniques et employés) des Juifs
  c.a.d. des personnes, dont les parents o
  grand-parents étaient des Juifs ?

Réouverture des théâtres

Le 10 juin 1940, dans la capitale qui se vidait, le théâtre de l'Œuvre avait fermé ses portes en congédiant l'unique spectateur de *Juliette*, pièce de Jean Bassan. Un mois plus tard, le théâtre rouvre avec la même pièce. Sacha Guitry avec *Pasteur*, Michel Duran avec *Nous ne sommes pas mariés* participent à cette reprise théâtrale. Otto Abetz s'en félicite. Mais certains théâtres n'ont plus de directeurs : Les Ambassadeurs abandonnés par Henry Bernstein, l'Odéon retiré à Paul Abram. La censure est pointilleuse à Paris, tatillonne à Vichy. Elle conteste les origines de Sacha Guitry, reproche à Bourdet d'avoir administré la Comédie-Française au temps du Front populaire.

Si les occupants, avant d'interdire les théâtres aux

En septembre 1941, l'exposition « Le Juif et la France » dénonce leur « emprise nocive », responsable de la « perversion du goût et de l'esprit français ». Les visages et les noms juifs du milieu théâtral apparaissent sur les panneaux (en haut, en gros plan, Henry Bernstein, directeur des Ambassadeurs). Et la presse collaborationniste diffuse largement ces dénonciations.

Juifs, rejettent d'autorité les textes écrits par des auteurs, les autres pièces sont soumises à un double examen : à la lecture d'abord, à la répétition générale ensuite. L'Association des directeurs de théâtre de Paris, dirigée par Baty, Dullin et Pierre Renoir, est créée pour favoriser les échanges entre les autorités et les intéressés. Ceux-ci pratiquent avec succès une autocensure préalable susceptible d'économiser temps et argent. Dans ce domaine, il existe aussi un organisme corporatif, le Comité d'organisation des entreprises de spectacle (COES) qui gère scrupuleusement les bons-matière essentiels pour les décors et les attributions d'électricité.

Abel Bonnard, à la réouverture de la Comédie-Française (ci-dessus, à gauche, Bonnard ; à droite, Jacques Copeau, administrateur provisoire), proclame le devoir pour le théâtre de célébrer les valeurs politiques et culturelles de l'État français. Mais si Vichy tient à faire régner l'ordre moral, les autorités d'Occupation sont plus souples dans ce domaine et interviennent surtout en cas de trouble à l'ordre public.

La Comédie-Française entre humiliations et triomphes

La Comédie-Française fait sa rentrée le 7 septembre 1940, avec une conférence d'Abel Bonnard qui y exalte la grandeur de la France et affirme « la valeur de l'homme ordinaire », prélude mondain aux principes de la Révolution nationale. L'ambassade d'Allemagne veille sur la maison de Molière, figure de proue de la Ville lumière, qui se doit de rassembler son public. Jean-Louis Vaudoyer, écrivain sensible, remplace Jacques Copeau comme administrateur. Il doit se dépêtrer en décembre 1940 d'un imbroglio suscité par le retour des cendres du fils de Napoléon. Des rumeurs annoncent alors la mise au répertoire de L'Aiglon d'Edmond Rostand. La censure allemande se tait, mais compte les alexandrins qui énumèrent de cocardière façon les victoires impériales. À la veille de la première, le couperet tombe : interdiction définitive. Cuisante humiliation. Peu après, Vaudoyer se trouve contraint de recevoir la troupe du Schiller Theater, amenée par son directeur, Heinrich George, nazi militant. Le Français n'a jamais accueilli d'acteurs étrangers. Il se soumet et reçoit *Kabbale und Liebe*, encensée par la presse de l'époque. Les sociétaires sont tenus d'applaudir leurs confrères et de figurer aux réceptions. Le public, rebuté par la langue de Schiller, ne se presse pas aux guichets. Cependant, la collaboration artistique se profile et va s'affirmer en 1942. Différentes versions d'*Iphigénie* vont permettre aux interprètes munichois d'*Iphigénie en Tauride* de Hauptmann d'éclipser leurs homologues parisiens. L'interprétation française est ridiculisée par la critique, pourtant le public boude et Vaudoyer continue sa tâche en dépit de l'acharnement d'Alain Laubreaux qui rêve, dans *Je suis partout*, de devenir administrateur.

Pour la première fois des comédiens allemands ont joué chez Molière

En 1941, à l'initiative de Karl Epting, l'acteur allemand Heinrich George, l'un des protagonistes du *Juif Süss*, s'installe avec ses partenaires à la Comédie-Française (ci-contre) pour y interpréter *Kabale und Liebe* de Schiller. Mais, en dépit des festivités qui encadrent les deux jours de représentations, le public habituel demeure réticent. Pourtant, la Propaganda monte en épingle l'événement. La porte était ouverte à d'autres échanges culturels, car la carrure et la jovialité de Heinrich George avaient plu aux habitués de ces grandes réceptions mondaines où se pressait la nouvelle élite parisienne (ci-dessus, Heinrich George à l'ambassade d'Allemagne).

Persuadé que Montherlant doit retrouver au théâtre ses succès d'écrivain, Vaudoyer l'encourage à s'inspirer d'un vieil auteur ibérique pour écrire *La Reine morte*. Prévision exacte, succès considérable, qui permet à Jean Yonnel, l'acteur principal, de triompher des malveillances raciales dont on l'afflige. Le 27 octobre 1943, au terme d'un travail épuisant, Jean-Louis Barrault, sociétaire efficace, crée *Le Soulier de satin*. Spectacle foisonnant, d'une durée inusitée qui triomphe des réticences de Paul Claudel pour une adaptation élaguée. Prodige d'un spectacle d'une grande richesse au service d'une œuvre réputée injouable. Les occupants s'inclinent devant cette réussite qui consacre le travail acharné du metteur en scène, la performance dramatique de Marie Bell et le triomphe de l'auteur.

En finale, les débuts au Français de Raimu, comédien fétiche de Pagnol, puissante bête d'écran issue du music-hall marseillais, émoustillent les connaisseurs. Son entrée dans une troupe homogène, respectueuse de ses traditions, surprend. *Le Bourgeois gentilhomme* souffre du décalage entre le jeu du nouveau venu et les prestations de ses partenaires. Raimu le comprend. Il reparaît dans *Le Malade imaginaire* et, sans avoir démérité, démissionnera après la Libération.

En 1943, le café de la Régence reste fidèle à sa tradition d'accueillir en voisins les comédiens du Français au sortir des répétitions. Maurice Escande, grand sociétaire, vient saluer ses amis, dont Fanny Robiane, du théâtre de l'Odéon (assise, ci-dessous).

À la Comédie-Française, fin 1943, Jean-Louis Barrault crée *Le Soulier de satin*, dans des décors de Lucien Coutaud (page de gauche). Son énergie stupéfie Jean-Louis Vaudoyer et Paul Claudel (ci-contre, l'auteur avec Vaudoyer à sa droite et le doyen André Brunot derrière lui). La presse ne s'y trompe pas (ci-dessous).

Costumes « une vague ».

LE SOULIER DE SATIN
à la Comédie Française

Lorsque, en 1924, à Tokio, Paul Claudel eut achevé le *Soulier de satin* (ou le *Pire* n'est pas toujours sûr : action espagnole en quatre journées...) qu'il avait commencé à Paris en 1919, il écrivit en manière de préface : « Comme après tout il n'y a pas impossibilité complète que la pièce soit jouée un jour ou l'autre, d'ici dix ou vingt ans, totalement ou en partie... » Or, voici que la prophétie de l'auteur se réalise puisque, dix-neuf ans plus tard, le *Soulier de satin* est joué pour la première fois, sinon « totalement » du moins « en partie ». Dans cette préface, pétillante d'un espiègle humour qui continue tout au long de la pièce à coudoyer la mystique, Claudel donnait entre autres « directives scéniques » celle-ci : « Il faut que tout ait l'air provisoire, en marche, bâclé, incohérent, improvisé dans l'enthousiasme ! Avec des réussites, si possible, de temps en temps, car même dans le désordre il faut éviter la monotonie... » Et il poursuivait par cette savoureuse sentence que n'eût pas désavouée Léon-Paul Fargue — auteur d'un article publié naguère dans nos pages et intitulé *Éloge du désordre* : « L'ordre est le plaisir de la raison : mais le désordre est le délice de l'imagination... »

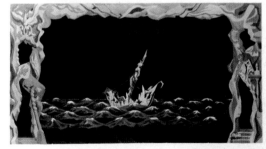

Le Père (situé 1ᵉ tableau) : sur la scène vingt élèves d'une école rythmique, portant chacune le costume « une vague », simulent les mouvements de la mer. Le décor est ici entouré du cadre fixe dans lequel apparaissent tous les tableaux. En textrine : Doña Prouhèze (Mᵐᵉ Marie Bell) à la cophinerie de Mogador.

La première de *La Reine morte* a lieu le 8 décembre 1942, à la Comédie-Française, dans une mise en scène de Pierre Dux, avec Jean Yonnel, Madeleine Renaud et Julien Bertheau (ci-contre). Montherlant note que « la générale fut pour le moins tiède ». La pièce rencontrera ensuite un succès considérable. Dans ce drame historique centré sur le conflit entre amour et raison d'État, Montherlant dont les sympathies collaborationnistes sont connues, se défend d'avoir glissé toute référence à l'actualité de la France occupée. Pourtant et inévitablement, les spectateurs de tous bords se montrent prompts à y déceler des allusions de résistance, en particulier dans la réplique : « En prison se trouve la fine fleur du royaume. »

Boulevard et grandes créations

Le Tout-Paris assiège les théâtres. Il applaudit
Anouilh avec l'escalade de ses pièces roses ou
noires. *Le Rendez-Vous de Senlis*, *Le Bal des
voleurs*, *Léocadia*, *Le Voyageur sans bagages*
mènent aux superbes représentations d'*Antigone*
qui mettent à vif certaines des blessures morales de
l'Occupation et imposent un style neuf à la tragédie
grecque. Le même que Sartre adopte pour *Les
Mouches* montées par Dullin et qualifiées par
Claude Jamet « d'essai où le prof de philo trop
souvent montre le nez ». En 1944, le désarroi
des occupants se précise, les restrictions
d'électricité augmentent, mais *Huis clos*, son
décor, ses interprètes remplissent le Vieux
Colombier. L'enfer selon Sartre éclipse
Le Malentendu exposé par Camus. L'année
précédente, Giraudoux, très attendu, avait
déçu l'auditoire par l'incontinence de son
verbe, mais Gérard Philipe, ange lumineux,
avait ravi le public de *Sodome et Gomorrhe*.

Aux Ambassadeurs, grâce à Salacrou, les
répliques d'*Histoire de rire* font mouche des
années durant. Dans la salle minuscule
des Noctambules, Jean Giono
additionne sans trêve les entrées du
Bout de la route. Marcelle Maurette
mobilise Cécile Sorel pour animer
ses images d'Épinal dans
Madame Capet et *La Reine
Christine*. À deux reprises,
Jean Sarment fait bavarder
plaisamment et joliment
Mamouret au théâtre de la
Cité. Sacha Guitry subjugue
les spectatrices de *N'écoutez
pas, Mesdames!* et Marcel
Achard, que les ultras de la
Collaboration n'aiment guère,
sourit avec *Colinette*, rêve avec
Mademoiselle de Panama, se
plante en compagnie d'Arletty à

Deux valeurs sûres : Guitry à la Madeleine avec 600 représentations de *N'écoutez pas, Mesdames!* (ci-dessous); Anouilh à l'Atelier avec *Antigone* (en bas), qui, à partir de Sophocle, alimente une controverse entre collabos et résistants.

la reprise de *Voulez-vous jouer avec moâ?*.
Gaston Baty, pour sa dernière mise en scène,
a la main heureuse. *Le Grand Poucet*, vu par
Claude-André Puget, paraphrase délicatement
le conte de Perrault. Alice Cocéa a maille à
partir avec la censure choquée par le
cynisme de Becque, qui exige de
rebaptiser *La Parisienne* et d'afficher
Clotilde du Mesnil. *Les J3*, bons enfants
de l'époque, vus par Roger Ferdinand,
vont triompher des aléas de la Libération.
Cocteau fait toujours parler de lui. Si
La Machine à écrire contrarie les abonnés
du Français, *Les Parents terribles* sont
interdits aux Ambassadeurs. Le poète
continue d'encourager Jean Marais qui
monte *Britannicus* en 1941 et déclenche un

Jean-Paul Sartre, pour
son premier essai au
théâtre, refaçonne lui
aussi la tragédie
grecque. Il utilise
le mythe d'Oreste
pour invoquer la
Liberté et stigmatiser
les louvoiements de
l'État français. En juin
1943, au théâtre de la
Cité, Charles Dullin
transforme le texte des
Mouches en spectacle
agressif en avance sur
l'époque (ci-dessus),
mal perçu par le public
dont les réactions
blessent profondément
le metteur en scène qui
n'admet pas cet échec.

scandale avec sa vision d'*Andromaque* trois ans plus tard : Laubreaux se déchaîne, Philippe Henriot s'égosille, la Milice intervient. Autant en emporte le vent de la Libération.

Tout ce bouillonnement se reflète dans les articles de *Comœdia* signés par Audiberti, Roger Régent, Émile Vuillermoz. L'obligation de plaire à Abetz avait conduit la direction du journal à insérer dans chaque numéro des « pages européennes », d'où ce qualificatif de Pascal Ory : « Français jusqu'au parisianisme, européen jusqu'au pangermanisme. »

Fourmillement des jeunes compagnies en zone libre

Les comédiens routiers sillonnent la campagne toulousaine. À Lyon, ce sont la troupe de l'Équipe et les Chantiers de Jean Vernier. Le réseau Jeune France de Pierre Schæffer patronne des essais littéraires et musicaux, rassemble les acteurs dispersés en zone libre et présente en 1941 l'exposition « Un an de théâtre ». Mais, soupçonné d'accointance avec les résistants, ce groupement sera interdit par ceux qui, à Vichy, l'avaient encouragé.

Fidèle à Marseille et au Rideau gris, André Roussin écrit et joue *Am stram gram* que les Parisiens découvriront beaucoup plus tard, mais c'est à Cannes qu'il triomphe avec *Une grande fille toute simple*. Les censeurs des deux zones croient flatter l'anglophobie latente en célébrant Jeanne d'Arc dans les textes de Shaw, Péguy et Vermorel. Frileuse, la censure d'État rechigne à autoriser *Tartuffe*. Même Sacha Guitry, réclamé par le Maréchal, franchit aussi difficilement la ligne de démarcation que les comédiens du Français.

Quant au cirque, une tradition populaire très respectée et admirée en Allemagne, il va

En zone libre, les tournées théâtrales sont particulièrement à l'honneur. Sourire aux lèvres et enthousiasme au cœur, les jeunes troupes parcourent la campagne comme Molière le fit en son temps. Ainsi le théâtre de la Saison nouvelle, sous la houlette de Jean Dasté ou les comédiens du Regain (clin d'œil à Giono) entraînés par Christian Casadesus (ci-dessous, la troupe de la Saison nouvelle et, en bas, l'emblème de la compagnie du Regain).

bénéficier de la bienveillance, et même de l'aide des occupants qui réglementent les allocations de nourriture aux bêtes. Rancy ou Bouglione élargissent leurs programmes : les numéros habituels continuent, mais l'opérette se faufile sur la piste. Le Cirque d'hiver, Medrano, administrés par la famille Busch (originaire de Berlin), propulsent les Chesterfollies dans des tableaux burlesques. En juin 1944, Jean Houcke s'empare du cirque du Grand Palais. Abetz et Brinon cautionnent l'événement que souligne une parade extérieure. Les flonflons de sa fanfare vont se noyer dans les remous de Paris libéré.

Autour de la piste du cirque Medrano, les militaires allemands, silencieux et impeccables, admirent le galop des coursiers de Micaëla Busch, prestigieuse écuyère qui a su se concilier les grâces du public parisien qu'on aperçoit groupé à l'écart de la puissance occupante.

Pas facile de clore le douloureux chapitre de l'Occupation. Le mot « épuration » à lui seul crée l'effroi. Certains voudraient passer l'éponge sur la collaboration, mais l'attente politique et populaire amène aux procès, avec leur incertitude. Coupables du même chef d'inculpation, Brasillach est fusillé, Rebatet épargné. La France essaie de se regarder à nouveau au fond des yeux. Les tensions s'apaisent à défaut de s'oublier. Il faut bien que la vie reprenne.

CHAPITRE 6

L'HEURE DES COMPTES

Ses voyages dans le Reich, ses violences anti-communistes, sa haine des juifs précipitèrent le rédacteur en chef de *Je suis partout*, Robert Brasillach, au peloton d'exécution le 6 février 1945 (ci-contre, lors de son procès). Ce verdict divisa les écrivains, y compris les résistants et ceux qui s'étaient exprimés dans des revues comme *Confluences* (ci-contre, bandeau accompagnant le premier numéro « libre » de cette revue).

Confluences qui... sous la domination de Vichy a toujours maintenu le point de vue Français.
ARAGON

Épuration sauvage, épuration légale

L'été 1944 voit les débarquements en Normandie et en Provence, puis la libération de Paris, qui acclame le général de Gaulle. Celle de toute la France sera longue et difficile. C'est l'heure des comptes. L'épuration en France est d'abord sauvage, durant la phase des combats de la libération, entre juin et novembre 1944. Enjeu des rivalités politiques issues de la Résistance, approuvée par de Gaulle dès 1943, elle vise les partisans de l'État français. Réclamée autant que redoutée, elle mûrit dans le climat pesant d'une occupation chancelante. Sur fond de bombardements et d'incendies s'inscrivent l'affrontement entre miliciens et maquisards, les représailles

allemandes au Vercors, les massacres d'Oradour-sur-Glane et de Tulle, l'assassinat de Philippe Henriot, les cercueils miniatures adressés en guise d'avertissement aux collabos. L'épuration culmine à l'automne 1944 et, plus tard, au retour des déportés. Des lois d'amnistie, en 1947 et 1951, y mettront fin. On a stigmatisé et exagéré les méfaits de l'épuration sauvage.

PARIS, 14, Faubourg-Montmartre (9°)
JOURNAL FONDÉ EN 1941
4° Année — N° 145

Vendredi 25 août 1944
330° Jour de Lutte, 6 Guerre : Sa Guerre

Directeur : Raoul FEIGNÉ
Publication Populaire de l'Association des Journalistes Français de la Libération

CONSEIL DE RÉDACTION
André MUTTER - Étienne NOUVEAU - Pierre RUHLMANN
Président et Membres du Comité Directeur de « Ceux de la Résistance »

Rédacteur en Chef : AYMÉ-GUERRIN
Secrétaire-Président du Mouvement de Résistance « Vengeance »

France libre

TOUJOURS À L'AVANT-GARDE DU PROGRÈS SOCIAL

Et maintenant, nach Berlin!
QUOTIDIEN DU MATIN
3 FRANCS

Les premiers éléments blindés de la division Leclerc sont entrés à Paris, cette nuit, au milieu d'un peuple enthousiaste

Paris dans la bataille

Les premiers soldats à l'Hôtel de Ville

Le général Leclerc

C'est oublier le climat passionnel dans lequel se débattaient les Français. Le trouble des derniers mois de l'Occupation, les crimes de la Milice, les massacres nazis, les bombardements meurtriers, la haine et la peur expliquent les exécutions et les incarcérations arbitraires.

La peur s'infiltre chez les tenants de l'ordre nouveau, plumitifs de toutes catégories ou personnalités notoires. Avant d'abandonner la Continental, Alfred Greven détruit ses archives. Certains essaient de franchir les frontières. La rédaction de *Je suis partout* s'entasse dans les fourgons de l'ennemi, passe la frontière et s'installe péniblement à Sigmaringen, une ville du sud de l'Allemagne sur le Danube, où se retrouvent le maréchal Pétain et la classe politique collaborationniste. Quelques-uns, comme Alain Laubreaux (*Le Cri du peuple*) ou Alphonse de Châteaubriant, s'exilent définitivement. Sacha Guitry, impavide, ne voit rien, n'écoute rien.

Appréhendé dès le 24 août 1944, il est libéré de prison deux mois plus tard.

À ses débuts, l'épuration légale condamne vite et fort. On fusille Georges Suarez, Paul Chack, Robert Brasillach. Henri Béraud et Charles Maurras échappent de justesse au poteau. À l'annonce des verdicts, les émigrés frémissent.

Listes noires dans l'édition et dans la presse

Le Comité national des écrivains (CNE), issu de la Résistance, veut faire respecter la mémoire des disparus et épurer le milieu des écrivains. Il établit des listes noires

Les collaborateurs « décampent » de Paris en août 1944 sans tambour ni trompette et, passant la frontière, s'entassent en Souabe dans le massif et rébarbatif château de Sigmaringen (en haut, à gauche). Les premières feuilles libres surgissent dans la capitale (page de gauche, en bas, la une du journal *France libre* du 25 août 1944 annonçant la libération de Paris ; au centre, Albert Camus, Jacques Baumel et André Malraux en uniforme, à la rédaction de *Combat*). Le climat de Paris s'alourdit, l'énervement gagne et les dénonciations alimentent toutes les formes d'épuration. Sacha Guitry, le bien-aimé maintenant honni, est particulièrement visé On le voit, ci-dessus, photographié par Cartier-Bresson, lors de son interrogatoire, dans les locaux de la police.

Devant la Cour de Justice

Paul CHACK

traître de plume
spécialiste antibolchevik
de la Gestapo

s'effondre
lamentablement
à l'audience

IL EST CONDAMNE A MORT

d'écrivains collaborateurs ou collaborationnistes. La première comprend 12 noms : Brasillach, Céline, A. de Châteaubriant, Chardonne, Jouhandeau, Drieu la Rochelle, Giono, Petitjean, Thérive, Montherlant, Maurras, Paul Morand. Ils connaîtront des sorts bien différents. Condamnation à mort et exécution pour Brasillach, suicide pour Drieu, réclusion perpétuelle et dégradation nationale pour Maurras, révocation pour Morand, suspension d'activité (un an) pour Montherlant, résidence surveillée puis non-lieu pour Chardonne, indignité nationale et confiscation de biens pour Céline...

Listes noires aussi pour les maisons d'édition. Si Gallimard est soutenu par ses auteurs, notamment Sartre et Camus, Robert Denoël est inculpé pour ses publications pro-allemandes. Il est assassiné avant son procès, dans des conditions obscures. Quant à Grasset, poursuivi pour ses relations avec l'occupant et la publication de Drieu et Chardonne, il est condamné à l'indignité nationale et à la confiscation de ses biens, avant d'être amnistié en 1953.

Les procès des journalistes et des grands patrons de presse commencent à l'automne 1945. Les plus importants sont condamnés à mort et exécutés tels Albert Lejeune, fidèle de la Propaganda et d'Abetz, Georges Suarez, journaliste de *Gringoire* et du *Temps* et rédacteur en chef d'*Aujourd'hui*, Paul Chack, journaliste à *Aujourd'hui* et membre du Cercle aryen, du Front révolutionnaire national et du Comité d'action anti-bolchevique, Jean Luchaire, véritable magnat de la presse en zone occupée, Jean-Hérold Paquis, chroniqueur de Radio-Paris. Les autres, c'est-à-dire la majorité, subiront des peines plus modérées :

Ouvrages à retirer de la vente (à droite, en haut, liste du Comité national des écrivains), suspensions, réclusions, exécutions : ci-dessus, le procès de Jean Luchaire, qui sera fusillé le 22 février 1946. En haut, à gauche, la condamnation à mort de Paul Chack annoncée dans *L'Humanité* du 19 décembre 1944. De Gaulle refuse la grâce de Chack, comme il la refusera à Brasillach, en dépit d'une pétition signée de 60 personnalités dont Valéry, Mauriac et Duhamel... (à droite).

Les soussignés, se rappelant que le Lieutenant
BRASILLACH, père de Robert BRASILLACH, est mort pour la
patrie le 13 Novembre 1914, demandent respectueusement su
Général de GAULLE, Chef du Gouvernement, de considérer
avec faveur le recours en grâce que lui a adressé Robert
BRASILLACH, condamné à mort, le 19 janvier 1945.

Paul Valéry

François Mauriac

Duhamel

Henry Bordeaux

Jérôme Tharaud

Louis Madelin

Latour

J. Cocteau

A. Chevrillon

Louis de Broglie

dégradation nationale, confiscation plus ou
moins longue des cartes de presse.

En France, l'opinion hésite. François Mauriac
et plusieurs écrivains présentent une pétition
en faveur de Brasillach, de Gaulle la repousse.
Aragon, Vercors, Seghers ne désarment pas.
Jean Paulhan et Albert Camus prêchent l'oubli.
Les hommes de lettres égarés au Congrès de
Weimar peuvent ainsi continuer à écrire et
publier. Les remous s'apaisent. Et quand Lucien
Rebatet, arrêté en 1945 et condamné à mort
en novembre 1946, échappe à la peine capitale,
on comprend que les temps ont changé.
L'épuration est une loterie : il ne faut pas
l'affronter trop vite.

En août 1944, au milieu des combats de la Libération de Paris, les services allemands font évacuer vers l'Allemagne 148 caisses des salles du Jeu de Paume. Le convoi de chemin de fer est arrêté par l'armée de Leclerc. Les Allemands avaient, depuis longtemps, dispersé sur tout le territoire du Reich une grande partie des œuvres d'art spoliées. Pour les retrouver, les alliés entreprennent des recherches difficiles. Des dépôts sont découverts en Autriche et en Tchécoslovaquie, en particulier dans les mines de sel d'Alt Ausser, près de Salzbourg, et dans le château de Neuschwanstein. La « collection » de Goering est retrouvée, éparpillée dans tout Berchtesgaden et dans sa résidence privée de Karinhall. Ci-contre, à Konigsee, le face à face des Américains avec les trésors pillés et tout particulièrement avec la statue de sainte Marie-Madeleine de Gregor Erhart (vers 1515-1520, chef-d'œuvre de la sculpture allemande qui sera restitué au Louvre). En France, une commission de récupération artistique est créée dès novembre 1944. Une ordonnance du 21 avril 1945 déclarera la nullité des actes de spoliation.

D'autres voyageurs imprudents sont suspendus : le peintre Dunoyer de Segonzac pendant trois mois, le sculpteur Despiau pendant deux ans. Le monde de la musique enregistre l'indignité nationale à vie de Germaine Lubin et Alfred Cortot perd de sa superbe. Serge Lifar et certaines étoiles de la danse ne scintillent plus

momentanément et Jacques Rouché doit surmonter bien des tracasseries.

Les vedettes qui s'embarquaient – allegretto – pour Berlin retrouvent vite le chemin des studios. Pourtant, Arletty voit sa carrière cinématographique compromise, mais son talent et sa vitalité lui permettront encore de belles créations théâtrales. En revanche, Mireille Balin, molestée, cassée, vieillie, paie cher son comportement et meurt à cinquante-neuf ans dans la pauvreté. Les metteurs en scène ne sont pas épargnés. Clouzot en est l'exemple. Suspendu à vie pour avoir occupé un poste éminent à la Continental et recherché l'opprobre avec *Le Corbeau*, il fait face mais se débat pendant trois ans avant d'entreprendre *Quai des Orfèvres*. Robert Le Vigan, bouc émissaire durement condamné, ne reparaîtra pas sur les écrans, ni Josseline Gaël que ses mauvaises fréquentations éloignent à jamais de la scène.

Dernier vestige : le Grand Rex réapparaît (ci-dessus). Et les victimes du nazisme sont honorées, comme ici, au Père-Lachaise, en octobre 1944, lors d'une manifestation du Front national du spectacle en leur mémoire (ci-dessous).

La Comédie-Française s'épure elle-même. Mary Marquet en est exclue : le Boulevard la console. André Claveau, Léo Marjane, Lys Gauty, Fréhel, Georgius, Suzy Solidor voient leurs noms, à peine ternis, briller de nouveau. Des livres plaidoyers *pro domo* paraissent peu à peu : Alice Cocéa, Sacha Guitry, Ginette Leclerc, Arletty, Antoine Balpêtré, Corinne Luchaire. Mais les dénonciations, les rafles, les tortures ne transparaissent pas dans ces écrits. Pas plus que les persécutions antisémites, les déportations, ou l'enfer concentrationnaire....

Ainsi se tourne la dernière page d'une époque ambiguë et angoissante.

Les qualités et les défauts s'y sont révélés en pleine lumière : héroïsme et lâcheté, loyauté et mensonge, générosité et entraide, cynisme et cupidité. Les reniements, la violence et les tortures ont suscité l'épuration, une remise en ordre, flamboyante au départ, flottante ensuite, traînée finalement comme un boulet.

Le malaise s'est installé et risque de durer.

Pourtant la France meurtrie et divisée a surmonté la pire de ses épreuves en protégeant sa culture et en sauvegardant ses richesses intellectuelles en dépit des tentations. La scène esthétique et artistique a échappé à un embrigadement complet. Malgré la propagande, la censure, l'exclusion des juifs, l'instrumentalisation et la dureté des temps, les quatre années d'occupation allemande et de régime vichyste n'ont pas abouti, comme le souhaitait Hitler, à l'anéantissement de la puissance culturelle française.

Dans les cinémas, les salles de spectacle, aux terrasses des cafés parisiens, les soldats alliés chassent les ombres de la Wehrmacht (ci-dessus).

Symbole d'une liberté retrouvée pour la France, la *Victoire de Samothrace* déploie à nouveau ses ailes dans le musée du Louvre (page suivante, sa réinstallation en 1945). Et à travers les archives – françaises et allemandes – disponibles aujourd'hui, les témoignages, les œuvres nombreuses laissées dans tous les domaines, la période de l'Occupation retrouve aussi sa juste place dans l'histoire culturelle de la France.

TÉMOIGNAGES
ET DOCUMENTS

La défaite

Juin 1940. Le pays envahi, l'armée battue, les Français pourchassés, l'armistice obtenu. Paris vidé de ses habitants, Vichy nouvelle capitale doivent s'adapter à l'Occupation et légiférer sur les ruines de la Troisième République. Réactions de certains témoins.

Paris déserté

Paul Léautaud rédigea durant soixante-trois ans son Journal littéraire, *témoignage biographique et panorama de son époque. Ici, dans Paris vide après la défaite:*

Je suis ensuite allé aux nouvelles chez mes voisins à T.S.F. Paris est déclaré ville ouverte. L'ordre et le ravitaillement seront assurés par la Préfecture de Police. Le ravitaillement assuré?... Le fort de Châtillon est évacué, de ses hommes et de ses engins. Les autres forts de l'enceinte de Paris également, très probablement.

Après déjeuner, je vais à Paris pour mes provisions. À la gare de Fontenay, encore des départs. À Paris, sur le boulevard Saint-Michel, toujours la file des partants. Au Mercure, aucun courrier. Rue Dauphine, mon tripier encore fermé. Mes bêtes vont commencer à pâtir un peu. Je vais à la poste de la rue du Louvre mettre ma lettre à M. D. Quand partira-t-elle? Quand lui arrivera-t-elle? Lui arrivera-t-elle jamais? Je voudrais bien qu'elle lui arrive. J'aurais l'air d'avoir été complètement indifférent et à son passage ce matin et à son mot. [...]

Sur tout mon parcours, aller et retour, Paris absolument désert. Le mot juste est: vide. Boutiques fermées. Un passant rare. La rue de Châteaudun un désert. Le quartier de l'Opéra, l'avenue de l'Opéra, les rues y donnant, de même. Tous les immeubles leurs portes fermées. Je me suis arrêté un instant, à mon retour, place de l'Opéra. Les grands boulevards dans la direction de la Madeleine, de l'autre côté jusqu'au tournant de la rue Drouot, jusqu'où s'étendait ma vue, absolument déserts, toutes les boutiques fermées. Et un silence! Un grand mail de province, sans un promeneur.

Une sorte de suie tombait du ciel, s'attachant au visage, aux mains. Les réservoirs à pétrole du Grand-Quevilly qui brûlent, paraît-il.

Je suis ravi d'avoir vu cela, que certainement peu de Parisiens ont vu.

Paul Léautaud, *Journal* XIII,
février 1940 à juin 1941
Mercure de France, Paris, 1986

Vichy 1940

Ami de Gide et pilier de la NRF, Roger Martin du Gard raconte le « grouillement » des débuts de l'État français à Vichy.

Je flotte comme un bouchon. (Et pour l'instant, c'est sur la vase la plus puante, la plus fermentée, que je flotte... Vichy est quelque chose qui dépasse toutes les images qu'on peut s'en faire.)

[...] Depuis le 14 juin nous errons à travers ce peuple de gens coupés de leurs racines, sans amarres, sans lits, sans ravitaillement. J'ai tout vu, tout regardé. Et avec un amusement et un désespoir mêlés – dosage pathétique. Les étapes de Royan et de Lyon ont été des repos très sombres. À Royan, j'ai vécu avec des officiers allemands ; vraiment envahi jusque dans les couloirs de la maison… De Lyon, je suis venu à Vichy. À temps pour tout voir, la chute du régime, les parlementaires affolés dans leur ruche détruite, la constitution, le défilé du 14 juillet. J'ai vécu dans les escaliers de l'hôtel du Parc, où l'on coudoyait les ministres, des actrices, des chiens, le maréchal, des garçons de café ; et la ruée inouïe de tous ceux qui voulaient quelque chose. J'ai approché de très près les pouvoirs. J'ai entendu et compris beaucoup de choses. J'ai vécu à la fois dans un rêve et dans la réalité, passivement, comme le bouchon ci-dessus, mais intensément aussi. Du matin au soir, passant de main en main, dans ce Pontigny pathétique. Me reposant par instants auprès des anciens amis, Martin-Chauffier, François Berge, Drieu, écoutant paradoxer le Berl. Quel grouillement. Quelles nausées. Pauvres nous. Je ne peux rien écrire de tout ça. (Pas pris une ligne de note.)

Roger Martin du Gard,
Journal III, 1937-1949, Gallimard, 1993

« Des balbutiements de rage »

Mauriac voit d'abord en Pétain un protecteur de la Nation. Dès août 1940, quand s'affirme le poids de l'Occupation et sa nature antisémite, il se dresse contre le régime de Vichy qui exploite les sentiments respectables d'un certain conservatisme français, pour camoufler l'humiliation et la collaboration. À l'automne 1940 – le temps du rendez-vous de Montoire entre Hitler et Pétain et du statut des juifs édicté par Vichy – l'écrivain devient un opposant sans réserve. Il se met à écrire le Cahier noir. *Signé « Forez », celui-ci paraît, en 1943 en pleine Occupation, aux éditions de Minuit clandestines.*

En Août 1943, dans cette aube, il est bon de relire les notes écrites, il y a trois ans, au, plus épais des ténèbres. Je rouvre le « Cahier Noir » : voici d'abord, en marge des premières homélies du Maréchal, des balbutiements de rage :

« Ce drame particulier à notre pays, cette fatalité qui lie le triomphe des principes traditionnels au désastre militaire et à la domination de l'ennemi…

Vous feignez de croire que le peuple exige la recherche et le châtiment des responsables, pour couvrir l'horrible nécessité de satisfaire la haine du vainqueur.

Et seriez-vous de bonne foi, l'Histoire vous accusera d'avoir servi la vengeance de vos maîtres. D'avoir cherché à les gagner par une hécatombe… Mais n'espérez pas que les juifs crucifiés par votre police vous dispensent de payer le vainqueur jusqu'à la dernière obole.

Calomniateurs de la France, vous qui n'avez jamais triomphé que grâce à son humiliation et à sa honte ! Médecins qui profitez de ce que le malade est ligoté et matraqué, pour lui ingurgiter vos remèdes !

Ces échos de presse, chaque jour, où un confrère masqué me dénonce, me désigne d'un doigt tremblant…

La haine qui monte du cœur transpercé de Paris est silencieuse, mais son cri couvre tout de même le chuchotement horrible des salles de rédaction…

Paris, qu'un rédacteur de la *Nouvelle Revue Française* nazifiée compare à "une pouffiasse qui s'étire péniblement, chaque matin, après une nuit obscène…" Paris dépossédé de lui-même, désert, noir et comme écartelé – plus sublime qu'il ne fut jamais ! – veillé par le chasseur Orion, durant les nuits de cet hiver féroce… »

François Mauriac, *Le Cahier noir*,
Desclée de Brouwer, Paris, 1996

Airs du temps

*De la musique avant toute chose : c'est aussi bien
les concerts militaires de la Wehrmacht que les extases
wagnériennes à l'Opéra. La jeunesse dorée fière
d'être zazoue irrite en dansant le swing au cabaret.
Et les Français reprennent, au refrain, les succès
des films et des idoles du moment.*

Festival de musique militaire à Chaillot

*Partout dans Paris, les orchestres de
l'armée allemande donnent des concerts.
Dans ses souvenirs des années noires,
l'écrivain collaborationniste André
Thérive décrit un festival de musique
militaire donné au Palais de Chaillot par
les troupes allemandes.*

L'immense salle du Palais de Chaillot
donne un festival de musique militaire
des troupes allemandes. Comme la
location est libre, je flaire que c'est là un
spectacle unique. Pour quarante francs,
j'ai vu en effet une chose inouïe : sur la
scène une colline humaine, où les divers
uniformes sont groupés avec un art
suprême de music-hall, les noirs, les gris,
les verts, trois cents exécutants rigides,
automatiques. Au premier plan, les
tambours, qu'on dirait des *robots* ; en
haut, un assemblage de chapeaux chinois
et d'enseignes à la romaine. Jamais le
Moulin-Rouge n'a rien réalisé de plus
parfait. Cette fanfare colossale joue des
marches militaires, du Wagner, du
Beethoven, et soudain le chef casqué se
retourne, salue la salle avec ostentation,
car l'air qu'attaquent ses trois cents
hommes, c'est *Sambre-et-Meuse*.

André Thérive,
L'Envers du décor, 1940-1944
éditions de la Clé d'or, 1948

Swing et zazou

Dans La Chasse à courre, *Maurice Sachs
raconte sa vie durant l'Occupation, faite
de trafics, d'aventures et de rencontres.
Ici, il analyse le phénomène swing et
zazou, à la fois musical et
comportemental :*

Ces jeunes étaient « swing » et « zazou »,
mots alors très répandus. Vogue qui
faisait le pendant à celle du jazz d'après
l'autre guerre. Mais *être* swing, ce n'était
plus aimer une forme d'art, c'était un
comportement, un rythme balancé du
pas de marche, une façon pour les
garçons de se coiffer en épaisseur qui les
faisait ressembler à des chiens pékinois,
ajustés de longues vestes, de pantalons
étroits et de cols fort hauts. Chez les
filles, ce n'était qu'accuser une certaine
négligence garçonnière avec un
enhardissement d'indépendance. Tout
cela, au demeurant, un peu sot, innocent,
et vain comme les modes de jeunesse.
Mais c'était dans les couloirs du théâtre
Édouard VII où se donnait le cours, à ne
pas savoir qui était fille ou garçon, et
sans que l'efféminement des mâles
prouvât le moindre penchant
homosexuel. Il est vrai que ce sont
toujours les maquereaux qui se poudrent
à blanc, et que la compagnie des femmes
dévirilise. Je me souvenais alors, non

sans un sourire intérieur, que les pédérastes anglais, anxieux de se dissimuler, portaient les tweeds les plus épais, affectaient de ne fumer que la pipe, se donnaient pour de terribles mâles.

Maurice Sachs, *La Chasse à courre*, Éditions Gallimard, 1948, réédition 1997

« La Romance de Paris »

Charles Trenet est auteur et interprète de « La Romance de Paris », chanson du film éponyme de Jean Boyer, dont il est aussi l'acteur principal.

Ils s'aimaient depuis deux jours à peine
Y a parfois du bonheur dans la peine
Mais depuis qu'ils étaient amoureux
Leur destin n'était plus malheureux,
Ils vivaient avec un rêve étrange
Et ce rêve était bleu comme les anges
Leur amour était un vrai printemps, oui
Aussi pur que leurs tendres vingt ans

(Refrain)
C'est la romance de Paris
Au coin des rues, elle fleurit
Ça met au cœur des amoureux
Un peu de rêve et de ciel bleu
Ce doux refrain de nos faubourgs
Parle si gentiment d'amour
Que tout le monde en est épris
C'est la romance de Paris

La banlieue était leur vrai domaine
Ils partaient à la fin de la semaine
Dans les bois pour cueillir le muguet
Ou sur un bateau pour naviguer
Ils buvaient aussi dans les guinguettes
Du vin blanc qui fait tourner la tête
Et quand ils se donnaient un baiser, oui
Tous les couples en dansant se disaient

C'est ici que s'arrête mon histoire
Aurez-vous de la peine à me croire ?

Si j'vous dis qu'ils s'aimèrent chaque jour
Qu'ils vieillirent avec leur tendre amour
Qu'ils fondèrent une famille admirable
Et qu'ils eurent des enfants adorables
Qu'ils moururent gentiment, inconnus, oui
En partant comme ils étaient venus

Charles Trenet, 1941

Le premier rendez-vous

La chanson du film Premier rendez-vous *d'Henri Decoin y est interprétée par sa principale actrice et héroïne, Danielle Darrieux :*

Quand monsieur le Temps
Un beau jour de printemps
Fait d'une simple enfant
Presque une femme,
Dans le songe bleu
D'un avenir joyeux
Fermant les yeux
Elle soupire au fond de l'âme

(Refrain)
Ah ! qu'il doit être doux et troublant
L'instant du premier rendez-vous
Où le cœur las de battre solitaire
S'envoie en frissonnant vers le mystère.
Vous l'inconnu d'un rêve un peu fou,
Faites qu'il apporte pour nous
Le bonheur d'aimer la vie entière
L'instant du premier rendez-vous.

Un amour naissant
C'est un premier roman
Dont on joue tendrement.
Le personnage
On ne sait jamais
S'il sera triste ou gai,
Mais on voudrait
Vite en ouvrir toutes les pages.

Paroles : Louis Poterat,
Musique : René Sylviano,
Éditions de La Continental, 1941

Patriotes !

Patriote pétainiste, patriote haineux, patriote « réversible » : le légionnaire à Vichy chante l'hymne de l'État français sous le regard bleu du Maréchal ; Brasillach, le romancier de Comme le temps passe, *est devenu un patriote collaborateur très actif et un redoutable anti-juif, anti-républicain ; et André Thérive, le journaliste tiède qui disperse ses chroniques au gré du vent collaborationniste, se dit aussi patriote, la main sur le cœur.*

« Maréchal, nous voilà ! »

Composée en novembre 1941 à la gloire du maréchal Pétain, cette chanson devient l'hymne officieux du régime de Vichy. Un hymne diffusé régulièrement sur les ondes, joué dans l'ensemble des territoires de la France et de l'Empire, en particulier dans les écoles. Durant l'Occupation, la chanson est interprétée, entre autres, par Andrex et André Dassary.

Une flamme sacrée
Monte du sol natal
Et la France enivrée
Te salue Maréchal !
Tous tes enfants qui t'aiment
Et vénèrent tes ans
À ton appel suprême
Ont répondu « Présent »

(Refrain)
Maréchal nous voilà !
Devant toi, le sauveur de la France
Nous jurons, nous, tes gars
De servir et de suivre tes pas
Maréchal nous voilà !
Tu nous as redonné l'espérance
La Patrie renaîtra !
Maréchal, Maréchal, nous voilà !

Tu as lutté sans cesse
Pour le salut commun
On parle avec tendresse
Du héros de Verdun
En nous donnant ta vie
Ton génie et ta foi
Tu sauves la Patrie
Une seconde fois

Quand ta voix nous répète
Afin de nous unir :
« Français levons la tête,
Regardons l'avenir ! »
Nous, brandissant la toile
Du drapeau immortel,
Dans l'or de tes étoiles,
Nous voyons luire un ciel !

La guerre est inhumaine
Quel triste épouvantail !
N'écoutons plus la haine
Exaltons le travail
Et gardons confiance
Dans un nouveau destin
Car Pétain, c'est la France,
La France, c'est Pétain !

Paroles : André Montagard,
musique : André Montagard
et Charles Courtioux

« La conjuration antifasciste au service du juif »

Le rédacteur en chef de l'hebdomadaire d'extrême droite Je suis partout *laisse transparaître dans ses articles son admiration pour le IIIe Reich, le fascisme et la collaboration, et sa haine des Juifs et de la République qui les protège.*

La Juiverie capitaliste et bolchevique a plus d'un tour dans son sac.

Certains lecteurs naïfs ont pu être étonnés de l'importance que lui accordait dans son dernier discours le chancelier Hitler : c'est que le problème est là et que le Juif sait très bien se souvenir de ses anciens alliés, serviteurs et amis, pour les faire agir comme il convient, et tirer les ficelles les plus surprenantes […]

En finira-t-on avec les relents de pourriture parfumée qu'exhale encore la vieille putain agonisante, la garce vérolée fleurant le patchouli et la perte blanche, la République toujours debout sur son trottoir ? Elle est toujours là, mal blanchie, elle est toujours là la craquelée, la lézardée, sur le pas de sa porte entourée de ses michés et de petits jeunots aussi acharnés que les vieux. Elle les a tant servis, elle leur a tant rapporté de billets dans ses jarretelles : comment auraient-ils le cœur de l'abandonner, malgré les blennorragies et les chancres ? […]

Disons les choses comme elles sont : tant que l'antifascisme restera la seule passion dont le politicien français soit capable, tant qu'il aura le loisir d'exprimer librement cette passion, tant qu'il servira le Juif par des moyens plus moins détournés, tant qu'on vénérera la démocratie qui protège le Juif, tant que le légalisme le plus absurde servira de paravent aux entreprises déterminées de corruption, il n'y aura rien à espérer…

Robert Brasillach
Je suis partout, 7 février 1942

Un virtuose du double jeu

Dans Les Lettres françaises, *journal clandestin du Front national des écrivains, Claude Morgan ironise sur le patriotisme d'André Thérive, écrivain et journaliste collaborationniste. Ce dernier, qui participa au voyage des intellectuels en Allemagne en 1942, figura aussi sur la liste noire des auteurs établie, à la Libération, par le Comité national des écrivains.*

M. André Thérive se livre actuellement à un petit jeu qu'il croit habile mais qui ne trompe personne, quand il rencontre un de ses anciens amis demeuré patriote, loin de s'enfuir et de cacher sa honte, il l'aborde et lui affirme qu'il est patriote lui aussi, malgré les apparences. Qui donc l'a obligé à revenir de la zone sud, où il se trouvait, pour se vendre à la propagande ennemie ? Qui donc l'oblige encore à écrire dans le *Parizer Zeitung*, *Je suis partout* et dans toute la presse nazie de langue française ? M. André Thérive a mis sa main dans la main des assassins de notre peuple. Comme eux, il se tient à présent sur la défensive. Regardez sa tête de valet obséquieux et perfide. Qui donc peut être dupe ?

Claude Morgan
« Je suis oiseau, voyez mes ailes ! »
Les Lettres françaises
n° 8, juillet 1943

Portraits en zones nord et sud

Le peintre apparaît en filigrane derrière le modèle. L'impeccable capitaine Jünger juge froidement les fureurs céliniennes. Le journaliste Roger Martin du Gard voit en Drieu l'ami d'avant. Léautaud jubile et épingle la vanité de Duhamel en butte à la censure allemande. Ramon Fernandez dévoile sa propre naïveté devant les journalistes repliés à Lyon.

Céline, « la monstrueuse puissance du nihilisme »

La partie centrale du Journal *d'Ernst Jünger, consacrée au Paris de l'Occupation, en décrit les milieux très fermés. Jünger fréquente l'état-major de Heinrich von Stülpnagel au Majestic, les lieux de plaisir parisiens, des boîtes de nuit aux premières de Cocteau ; et surtout les salons littéraires, esthètes et politiques des « collaborateurs de haute volée ». Rencontre avec Céline à l'Institut allemand de Karl Epting.*

L'après-midi à l'Institut allemand, rue Saint-Dominique. Là, entre autres personnes, Céline, grand, osseux, robuste, un peu lourdaud, mais alerte dans la discussion ou plutôt dans le monologue. Il y a, chez lui, ce regard des maniaques, tourné en dedans, qui brille comme au fond d'un trou. Pour ce regard, aussi, plus rien n'existe ni à droite ni à gauche ; on a l'impression que l'homme fonce vers un but inconnu. « J'ai constamment la mort à mes côtés » – et, disant cela, il semble montrer du doigt, à côté de son fauteuil, un petit chien qui serait couché là.

Il dit combien il est surpris, stupéfait, que nous, soldats, nous ne fusillons pas, ne pendons pas, n'exterminons pas les Juifs – il est stupéfait que quelqu'un disposant d'une baïonnette n'en fasse pas un usage illimité. « Si les Bolcheviks étaient à Paris, ils vous feraient voir comment on s'y prend ; ils vous montreraient comment on épure la population, quartier par quartier, maison par maison. Si je portais la baïonnette, je saurais ce que j'ai à faire ».

J'ai appris quelque chose, à l'écouter parler ainsi deux heures durant, car il exprimait de toute évidence la monstrueuse puissance du nihilisme. Ces hommes-là n'entendent qu'une mélodie, mais singulièrement insistante. Ils sont comme des machines de fer qui poursuivent leur chemin jusqu'à ce qu'on les brise.

Il est curieux d'entendre de tels esprits parler de la science, par exemple de la biologie. Ils utilisent tout cela comme auraient fait des hommes de l'âge de pierre ; c'est pour eux uniquement un moyen de tuer les autres.

La joie de ces gens-là, aujourd'hui, ne tient pas au fait qu'ils ont une idée. Des idées, ils en avaient déjà beaucoup ; ce qu'ils désirent ardemment, c'est occuper des bastions d'où pouvoir ouvrir le feu sur de grandes masses d'hommes, et répandre la terreur. Qu'ils y parviennent et ils suspendent tout travail cérébral, quelles qu'aient été leurs théories au cours de leur ascension. Ils s'abandonnent alors au plaisir de tuer; et c'était cela, cet instinct du massacre en masse qui, dès le début, les poussait en avant, de façon ténébreuse et confuse.

Aux époques où l'on pouvait encore soumettre à l'épreuve la croyance, de telles natures étaient plus vite identifiées. De nos jours, elles vont de l'avant sous le capuchon des idées. Quant à celles-ci, elles sont ce qu'on voudra; il suffit, pour s'en rendre compte, de voir comme on rejette ces guenilles, une fois le but atteint.

Ernst Jünger,
Premier Journal parisien, 1941-1943
Gallimard, La Pléiade, 2008

« Drieu dans notre zone »

Essayiste et journaliste français, cousin du romancier Roger Martin du Gard, directeur des Nouvelles littéraires *de 1923 à 1936, Maurice Martin du Gard côtoie les grandes figures intellectuelles et politiques qu'il décrit dans* La Chronique de Vichy *(1949). Ici, quelques pas avec Drieu la Rochelle en zone sud:*

L'autre soir, 11 février, à Clermont-Ferrand, autour du théâtre où allait se jouer sa *Charlotte Corday*, nous nous promenions du même pas allongé qu'il y avait vingt ans, quand nous découvrions le monde et l'Europe, dans Paris que nous pressions avec avidité, dans des villes étrangères, à Milan la veille de la marche sur Rome, dans la nuit au-dessus de Gênes, au long des quais qui nous appelaient à l'aventure. Depuis, Drieu avait voyagé à travers bien des livres et bien des pays, et je lui avais rapporté, de la profonde Afrique, des couleurs, des songeries, quelques raisons d'espérer. Dans Clermont noire et pluvieuse, nous

évoquions les amis divisés et le jour de notre rencontre quand nous n'avions devant nous que la victoire et que ces mêmes amis se croyaient seulement destinés au bonheur et au succès littéraire qu'ils affectaient de railler l'un et l'autre. Drieu pencha sa tête sur son épaule gauche et souffla sa fumée avec un ennui élégant. À Paris, sa solitude intellectuelle est presque totale. Interprété bassement, à contresens, goûtant un délice amer à contredire ses nouveaux admirateurs, finalement suspect à tout le monde à cause de cette lucidité et de cette noblesse, il ne se plaignait pas. Il ne s'était jamais plaint.
– L'absolu est une farce, lui dis-je. Le tragique finira bien par nous laisser quelque répit. Il y aura la paix. Il y a l'amour.

L'œil de Drieu s'adoucit.
– Ah, toi, fit-il, tu as l'optimisme du modéré !

La porte du théâtre était devant nous. Modeste, l'air lointain, comme s'il n'était pas l'auteur, il entra. On frappait les trois coups. Il jeta, par la porte entrebâillée d'une loge, un regard sur la salle qui était triste et clairsemée. Mais la rampe allumée donnait à son visage une animation enfantine, et il partit nonchalamment vers les coulisses pour s'entendre.

Maurice Martin du Gard,
La Chronique de Vichy, 1940-1944,
Flammarion, 1949

Duhamel censuré

L'œuvre de Georges Duhamel est interdite par les nazis. Nommé secrétaire perpétuel de l'Académie française (1942-1946), celui-ci tiendra courageusement tête à la frange collaborationniste des « Immortels ». Ici, l'œil acerbe de Léautaud sur les déboires de Duhamel avec la censure allemande:

Lundi 25 Novembre. – Le livre de Duhamel, *Le Lieu d'asile* [*sic*] ne sera pas mis en vente. D'ordre des autorités allemandes, deux officiers venus samedi au Mercure voir Bernard, tous les exemplaires du tirage sont mis sous scellés au dernier étage de la maison. Ils devaient revenir aujourd'hui à 5 heures vérifier l'inventaire de ce travail. On ne les a pas vus. Le compte exact des exemplaires doit leur être fourni et pas un exemplaire ne doit sortir.

Voici, d'après ce que m'en a dit Bernard, comment s'est passée la visite de Duhamel, samedi matin, au Docteur Kaiser. Quand il est arrivé, il a dû attendre. Au bout d'un moment, il s'est adressé à une sorte de dactylographe qui était dans la pièce d'attente : « Voulez-vous demander si on peut me recevoir ? Je suis un peu souffrant ce matin. » Cette dactylographe lui a répondu, fort poliment, en excellent français, qu'on attendait quelqu'un, dont la présence était nécessaire pour l'entretien. Ce quelqu'un était un M. Bremer, ancien lecteur d'allemand à l'École normale, avec qui Duhamel a eu quelques « piques ». Il paraît qu'ils ont encore eu tous les deux, dans le bureau du Docteur Kaiser, échange de propos peu sympathiques. Duhamel a fini par dire à tous les deux : « Je suis tout de même un grand écrivain français » (comme pour s'élever sur la façon dont on le traitait). Les deux Allemands se sont inclinés en signe d'assentiment. L'interdiction de la mise en vente du livre n'en a pas moins été décidée. Les deux Allemands auraient dit à Duhamel : « Vous êtes notre ennemi. Cela suffit pour nous dicter notre conduite. »

Mme Izambard dit que Duhamel avait le visage défait en assistant ce matin au rangement de tout le tirage de son livre, pour être ensuite mis sous scellés par les deux officiers allemands. Si vraiment Duhamel a eu cette mine effondrée, devant le sort donné à son livre, quel manque de ressort, d'esprit, de solidité. Il aurait pu rire, se moquer, même tirer avantage de compter à ce point pour les Allemands. Il est assez riche pour supporter cette perte momentanée de droits d'auteur et sa réputation n'en peut souffrir. Il est probable qu'il a offert le même spectacle samedi matin dans son entretien avec ce Docteur Kaiser et ce M. Bremer. Là encore, il aurait pu se moquer, leur dire : « Je vous fais vraiment compliment de vos procédés. Je n'en mourrai pas, ni mon livre. Il verra le jour un autre jour. Je suis vraiment flatté d'avoir autant d'importance pour vous. » On ne l'aurait pas fusillé pour cela. Il aurait même fait certainement une autre impression que celle qu'il a dû faire.

Paul Léautaud, *Journal XIII,*
février 1940 à juin 1941,
Mercure de France, Paris, 1986

Ramon Fernandez à Lyon

L'écrivain Dominique Fernandez a publié en 2009 Ramon, *une enquête biographique sur son père l'écrivain et critique littéraire Ramon Fernandez. Considéré comme un intellectuel parmi les plus brillants de son temps, celui-ci, dans un premier temps socialiste, suivit le Parti populaire de Jacques Doriot et la politique collaborationniste de Vichy. Rencontre à Lyon du journaliste parisien resté à Paris avec les journalistes parisiens repliés à Lyon :*

« Les Cercles populaires français, dont j'assume le secrétariat général, venaient d'accomplir un périple dans la zone libre avec M. Abel Bonnard qui, n'ayant pas encore pris le portefeuille de l'Éducation Nationale, les présidait alors. À Nice, à

Nîmes, à Béziers, à Toulouse, nous avions parlé, comme on dit, devant des salles combles, et ceux qui connaissent le théâtre du Capitole, à Toulouse, sauront ce que, dans ce vaste lieu, une salle comble veut dire. Nous terminions notre tournée à Lyon où près de cent personnes, faute de place, durent nous écouter debout dans les couloirs. La veille, jour de notre arrivée, nous allâmes, sur l'invitation de quelques camarades, rendre visite au Club de journalistes professionnels <u>parisiens</u>. Je souligne, car nous étions des journalistes professionnels parisiens et que c'est ici que commence l'aventure.

« Imaginez, au bout d'un de ces escaliers nus, vastes et contournés qu'on ne rencontre plus guère que dans *Myrelingue la brumeuse*, une grande salle qui faisait suite à une antichambre à peu près vide, et que suivait une salle plus petite. Dans la grande salle, un comptoir de bar, aussi anachronique qu'un sweater de Chanel sur une tournure, et quelques tables entourées de messieurs qui jouaient aux cartes. Nous avions poussé la porte tout rondement, en Parisiens qui s'attendaient à retrouver leurs concitoyens et confrères, à leur donner des tapes sur le dos et à vider quelques pots de compagnie.

« À notre entrée, un grand silence se fit, qui tout de suite nous parut insolite. Je ne saurais mieux rendre notre impression qu'en disant que nous nous serions crus au Musée Grévin, dans une cinquantaine d'années, dans la salle consacrée à la figuration céruléenne des journalistes parisiens retirés à Lyon pendant l'Occupation allemande de 1942. Les têtes nous étaient connues, les silhouettes familières. Mais un joueur tenait sa carte suspendue au-dessus du tapis vert ; un autre avait immobilisé une allumette enflammée à quelques centimètres de la cigarette qu'il venait de mettre dans sa bouche ; plus loin, contre une fenêtre, un

groupe avait changé un entretien animé en un dialogue de film muet. C'était bien, en effet, du musée de cire, du film muet, et aussi du film au ralenti que tenait la scène inattendue que nous avions sous les yeux.

« Nous nous approchâmes du bar, où le fils bien connu d'un polémiste célèbre se tenait accoudé. À ce moment, un vieux copain de Saint-Germain-des-Prés qui, devant une des tables, mimait une fausse partie de cartes, et qui m'avait tendu une main molle, et comme aveugle, et comme déclinant toute responsabilité dans la pression de sa main, se glissa près du comptoir et me demanda, d'une voix non moins molle et non moins irresponsable, des nouvelles de moi-même et des miens. Puis, brusquement, la vie surgit avec le mouvement, la cire redevint chair, une voix se fit entendre : Robert Brasillach s'étant approché du comptoir afin de commander un verre, le fils du polémiste célèbre s'en détacha, secoua sa chevelure d'encre et, scandant ses mots dans ce silence sous-marin, déclara : "Robert Brasillach, vous comprendrez que, devant votre présence, je me retire." »

« Les chiens étaient rompus, mais le silence, aussitôt, nous recouvrit. Nous serrâmes encore quelques mains fantômes, de ces mains qui claquaient sur les nôtres, à Paris, d'un mouvement rituel et machinal. À Paris, avant la guerre… Puis nous sortîmes, afin de retrouver nos voix, le son des choses, et de recommencer à vivre. »

« Conclusion : ces intellectuels, qui n'ont "rien appris" de la défaite, "rien oublié de leurs querelles d'avant-hier, ni de leurs petites espérances refoulées, ni de leurs manies et de leurs manilles", ressemblent, malgré l'apparence historique contraire, à des émigrés de Coblenz devant des patriotes de 1792. »

Dominique Fernandez,
Ramon, Grasset, Paris, 2009

L'Art n'a pas de patrie

Cocteau s'approprie la formule et, en flattant Breker, s'attire quelques ennuis. Pourtant lorsque Jünger rend plus discrètement visite à Picasso, le peintre et l'écrivain se laissent aller à une utopique rêverie.

L'ami Breker

Cocteau provoque l'indignation, en 1942, avec son « Salut à Breker », un éloge de l'artiste favori de Hitler lancé « au nom de la liberté et de la fraternité des artistes ». Cocteau ne « comprend rien à la politique » et le démontre de façon consternante en notant, avec une crédulité voisine de l'inconscience, les propos du sculpteur allemand. Son ami, le poète résistant Paul Éluard, le « rappelle à l'ordre ».

Breker est un artisan, un orfèvre, son goût du détail, du relief, s'oppose aux volumes ennuyeux de ses maîtres. Il choquera l'esthétisme. C'est pourquoi je l'aime. Il progresse beaucoup. Sa dernière statue (*Le Blessé*) m'étonne par ses veines, par ses muscles, par son réalisme, son plus vrai que le vrai. On devine que tout lui vient du *David* de Michel-Ange. Je ferai le « Salut à Breker ». Je lui explique pourquoi je me cabrais contre l'idée d'écrire ces lignes sur commande. Je voulais avoir envie de les écrire. Mon goût des mauvaises postures. Écrire avec tous et seul. Breker m'invite à Berlin pour faire mon buste. […]

Breker parlant de Hitler dit : « Qu'on lui laisse le temps de penser à autre chose qu'à la guerre. » Hélas, la malchance des dictateurs, c'est qu'on essaye de les abattre après la période destructive et qu'ils parviennent rarement à la période constructive. C'est le cas de Napoléon. La France doit beaucoup à Breker. C'est lui qui a montré Paris à Hitler, un jour, à

cinq heures du matin, comme un de nous aurait pu le lui montrer lui-même. Il était tellement ému qu'il bafouillait, prenait le Grand Palais pour un ministère. Hitler fut pris par cette émotion.

Breker a longtemps souffert en Allemagne. On le traitait de Français. Il vivait dans une Allemagne semblable à la France de 1942. Le dessous s'était mis dessus et le dessus se cachait dessous. Les médiocres triomphaient. Hitler l'a touché, comme un monarque. Sa gloire, sa fortune. Il reste très simple. (Il me dit qu'en Allemagne on essaye d'écraser Hitler sous les paperasses).

Jean Cocteau, *Journal,* 1942-1945

Mon cher Cocteau,
Freud, Kafka, Chaplin sont interdits, par les mêmes qui honorent Breker. On vous voyait parmi les interdits. Que vous avez eu tort de vous montrer soudain parmi les censeurs ! Les meilleurs de ceux qui vous admirent et qui vous aiment en ont été péniblement surpris.

Redonnez-nous confiance. Rien ne doit nous séparer.

Votre

Paul Éluard
in Jean Cocteau, *Journal,* 1942-1945
Gallimard, 1989

Un écrivain allemand chez Picasso

Picasso, résident espagnol, auteur de Guernica, peint et sculpte librement à Paris,

malgré la condamnation de son œuvre
par la censure nazie. L'écrivain allemand
et francophile E. Jünger, véritable amateur
de l'art pourtant décrété dégénéré par le
Reich (comme G. Heller, le responsable de
la littérature de la Propaganda Staffel),
visite l'atelier de Picasso :

Chez Picasso, cet après-midi. Il habite dans un vaste bâtiment dont certains étages ne servent plus, à présent, que de greniers et d'entrepôts. [...] Sur une étroite porte, une feuille de papier était fixée, où l'on avait écrit au crayon bleu le mot : « Ici ». Quand j'eus sonné, la porte me fut ouverte, par un petit homme en simple blouse de travail, Picasso lui-même. Je l'avais rencontré autrefois quelques instants, et j'ai eu de nouveau l'impression de voir un magicien [...].

Outre un logement exigu et des pièces de débarras, la demeure comprenait deux vastes greniers ; il utilisait, semblait-il, celui du dessous pour ses travaux de sculpture, et celui du haut pour peindre. Les planchers étaient carrelés de petites briques formant un dessin de nid-d'abeilles ; les murs, peints en jaune, étaient croisés de poutres de chêne sombre. Sous les plafonds également courait une noire ossature de chêne. L'endroit m'a semblé très propice au travail, à moi qui passe si volontiers des heures dans de vieux greniers, où le temps s'écoule bien plus insensiblement et fructueusement.

D'abord, nous avons regardé en bas de vieux papiers, puis nous sommes montés à l'étage supérieur. Parmi les tableaux qui s'y trouvaient, j'ai aimé deux simples portraits de femmes, et surtout un coin de rivage qui semblait, à mesure qu'on le contemplait, s'épanouir avec une vigueur croissante en tons rouges et jaunes. Nous avons parlé, tout en le regardant, des œuvres peintes et écrites d'après le souvenir. À ce propos, Picasso m'a

demandé quel était le paysage réel qu'il fallait chercher derrière les *Falaises de marbre*.

D'autres tableaux, comme une série de têtes asymétriques, m'ont fait une impression de monstruosité. Toutefois, à un talent aussi extraordinaire, quand on le voit se vouer à ces thèmes durant des années et des dizaines d'années, il faut reconnaître une valeur objective, alors même qu'elle échappe à notre propre compréhension. Il s'agit, au fond, de quelque chose que nul n'a eu encore, qui n'est pas né encore, et d'expériences de caractère alchimique ; plusieurs fois, d'ailleurs, le mot « cornues » est revenu dans notre conversation. Que l'Homunculus soit davantage qu'une futile invention, jamais encore je ne l'avais compris de façon si forte et inquiétante. L'image de l'homme peut être prévue magiquement, et bien peu soupçonnent la terrible gravité de la décision qui incombe au peintre.

J'ai tenté de l'entraîner sur ce terrain, mais il a éludé la question, peut-être à dessein :

– Il existe des chimistes qui passent toute leur vie à chercher les éléments cachés dans un morceau de sucre. Eh bien, moi, je voudrais savoir ce qu'est la couleur.

Au sujet de l'action exercée par les œuvres :

– Mes tableaux produiraient le même effet si, après les avoir terminés, je les enfermais dans une enveloppe scellée, sans les avoir montrés. Il s'agit là de manifestations de genre immédiat.

Puis, à propos de la guerre :

– À nous deux, tels que nous voilà assis ici, nous négocierions la paix cet après-midi même. Ce soir, les hommes pourraient illuminer.

Paris, 22 juillet 1942,
Ernst Jünger,
Premier Journal parisien, 1941-1943
Gallimard, La Pléiade, 2008

Cinéma en eaux troubles

Sous l'Occupation, le cinéma connaît un âge d'or en nombre de films et en créativité. Mais tout n'est pas bon à prendre ou à croire. Ici, le « rapt » d'un scénario par un réalisateur de la Continental, raconté par le scénariste Henri Jeanson ; l'imposture artistique des juifs dans le cinéma, proférée par l'écrivain pro-nazi Lucien Rebatet ; et les « petits films » de Vichy, à l'eau de rose ou à la « terreur blanche », dénoncés dans la presse clandestine.

« M. Léo Joannon fait un caprice, ou la mouche du Boche... »

M. Raymond Bernard, fils de Tristan et frère de Jean-Jacques, est revenu à Paris. Traqué pendant quatre ans, le metteur en scène des *Croix de bois* et des *Misérables* a retrouvé ses vieux amis, ses anciennes habitudes et sa sérénité avec une joie bien compréhensible.

Durant ces quatre années, Raymond Bernard avait perdu tout contact avec les gens de son métier. Un jour pourtant, il reçut en zone libre, *sic*, la visite inopinée de M. Léo Joannon, de la Continental. Et M. Léo Joannon de la Continental lui dit :
– Je sais que vous avez écrit un scénario intitulé *Caprices*.
– C'est vrai !
– Ce scénario me plaît beaucoup...
– Trop aimable.
– Vous allez me le remettre immédiatement et m'en abandonner tous les droits.
– Jamais de la vie ! Ce scénario m'appartient. Je le garde...
– Inutile de discuter. Il y a cinq ans que j'attendais l'arrivée des Allemands. Leur victoire me permet de réaliser tous mes rêves. Je suis un führer dans mon genre. Réfléchissez bien : si vous refusez de me donner *Caprices*, je ferai arrêter et déporter votre frère Jean-Jacques et ses deux enfants.

Raymond Bernard dut s'incliner et un mois plus tard M. Léo Joannon tournait *Caprices* pour la Continental.

Henri Jeanson,
Le Canard enchaîné, 4 octobre 1944,
Jeanson par Jeanson,
René Chateau éditions, 2000

« Leur Art »

Mais la condition première est d'éliminer inexorablement le Juif. À en croire certains gobe-mouches, cette élimination complète serait une catastrophe, car sans nier la piraterie évidente des Juifs, ils voudraient qu'elle fût compensée par leurs qualités artistiques, par les dons irremplaçables qu'ils apporteraient au cinéma, par leur rôle d'animateurs.

J'ai déjà fait rapidement justice de ces propos en parlant d'Hollywood et de l'Allemagne, d'après-guerre. Quand on est bien au fait du battage, des énormes hyperboles que les Juifs font colporter sur leur propre compte, leur part réelle de créateurs se réduit à des proportions très modestes.

[...] Pour les fameuses gloires du cinéma allemand, j'ai signalé le brusque dégonflement qu'elles subirent sitôt arrivées chez nous. Le cas le plus étonnant fut celui de Max Ophuls, qui débarquait de Vienne, précédé par la réputation de *Liebelei*, film d'une délicieuse sensibilité, et d'une facture de grand virtuose. M. Max Ophuls, une fois installé à Paris, commença à faire la petite bouche. Aucun des scénarios qu'on lui soumettait n'était digne de son génie. Il fallut mobiliser en son honneur Mme Colette, qui écrivit consciencieusement l'histoire et les dialogues de *Divine*. M. Ophuls dut se résigner enfin à tourner. Son produit fut une pauvre chose gauche et informe. Sur le plateau, M. Ophuls était apparu égaré, bafouillant, tâtonnant. Les langues se délièrent et on apprit que, selon toute vraisemblance, M. Ophuls avait à peine mis la main au *Liebelei* viennois.

À la lumière de ce fait, il faudrait réviser beaucoup d'illustrations du cinéma juif, rechercher les complicités tortueuses, les chantages, les pressions qui leur permirent de s'établir. On y verrait qu'après l'usurpation de la propriété matérielle, les Juifs pratiquent aussi froidement celle de la propriété spirituelle, et que parmi leurs plus fameux metteurs en scène, abondent les vulgaires négriers. Privés à Paris de leurs esclaves, ils ne pouvaient manquer de laisser transparaître leur imposture.

Lucien Rebatet,
« Tribus du cinéma et du théâtre »,
Nouvelles Éditions françaises, 1941

« Petits films »

Les trois couleurs de Vichy : marché noir, terreur blanche, bibliothèque rose.

La propagande de la vertu étant à l'ordre du jour, une censure composée d'amiraux en grande tenue, de policiers en petite tenue et de Paul Morand sans retenue se mit tristement à sévir.

Et l'on coupa… coupa… coupa…

Et l'on réalisa de grands films à l'eau de rose, des bonbons fondants désespérants, des retours à la terre, des mauvais garçons qui s'amendent et des histoires édifiantes, et tout et tout…

Et le public bouda… bouda… bouda…

Et pour le punir, comme il ne comprenait pas, on lui infligea des films de propagande : « La Force par la Joie » comme dit le Docteur Goebbels. Voyez plutôt quelle joie !

Le Péril Juif, M. *Girouette* (contre le Gaullisme), *Forces Occultes* (contre la Franc-Maçonnerie), *Français, vous avez la mémoire courte* (contre le Bolchevisme). Et le public bouda… bouda… bouda… […]

Ce n'est pas fini, il y en a d'autres : *Résistance*, une jolie histoire, où deux petits Français, au lieu d'aller se « dépayser » (comme dit le Maréchal) se laissent entraîner chez les vilains terroristes à grand renfort de mystères feuilletonesques. D'où il résulte que c'est très mal de désobéir au Maréchal et de résister à Hitler. Les Français qui ont payé leur place au cinéma résistent fortement, eux, devant ce film (dû à M. Evrard, journaliste – *sic*) et on est obligé d'allumer les salles pour éviter des résistances plus sensibles, et même, dans certains cas, il a fallu menacer de faire évacuer la salle pour ramener le calme.

Devant ces éminentes réussites, on pouvait penser que ces Messieurs s'en tiendraient là. Mais non… M. Griboff réalise un film sur *La Relève*, et M. Boisserand (qui, entre autres navets, fit autrefois *Après Mein Kampf, mes Crimes*, à l'époque où il était associé avec Jacques Haïk) prépare une nouvelle ordure : *Le crime ne paie pas*.

Peut-être… Mais les Allemands paient bien… eux.

Les Français paieront aussi, MM. Boisserand et consorts, et au centuple.

Georges Adam et Pierre Blanchar,
Les Lettres françaises, n° 14, mars 1944

Événements du monde théâtral

L'Enfer selon Sartre, la rhétorique d'Antigone revue par Anouilh, l'étonnant triomphe du Soulier de satin, *l'entrée en chattemitte de Raimu à la Comédie Française : l'Occupation touche à sa fin. Les dernières fusées du bouquet théâtral continuent d'illuminer les scènes françaises.*

Antigone, reflet des dilemmes de l'Occupation

L'Antigone d'Anouilh engendre la polémique dès sa création, en février 1944, par André Barsacq au théâtre de l'Atelier. Certains lui reprochent de défendre l'ordre établi avec un Créon très présent, expliquant ainsi que la pièce n'ait pas été censurée par les Allemands. D'autres, au contraire, soulignent l'insoumission d'Antigone qui devient l'allégorie de la Résistance aux lois iniques de l'État. Ici, le non d'Antigone à Créon :

CRÉON
Pourquoi as-tu tenté d'enterrer ton frère ?

ANTIGONE
Je le devais.

CRÉON
Je l'avais interdit.

ANTIGONE, *doucement.*
Je le devais tout de même. Ceux qu'on n'enterre pas errent éternellement sans jamais trouver de repos. Si mon frère vivant était rentré harassé d'une longue chasse, je lui aurais enlevé ses chaussures, je lui aurais fait à manger, je lui aurais préparé son lit… Polynice aujourd'hui a achevé sa chasse. Il rentre à la maison où mon père et ma mère, et Étéocle aussi l'attendent. Il a droit au repos.

CRÉON
C'était un révolté et un traître, tu le savais.

ANTIGONE
C'était mon frère.

CRÉON
Tu avais entendu proclamer l'édit aux carrefours, tu avais lu l'affiche sur tous les murs de la ville ?

ANTIGONE
Oui.

CRÉON
Tu savais le sort qui y était promis à celui, quel qu'il soit, qui oserait lui rendre les honneurs funèbres ?

ANTIGONE
Oui, je le savais.

CRÉON
Tu as cru peut-être que d'être la fille d'Œdipe, la fille de l'orgueil d'Œdipe, c'était assez pour être au-dessus de la loi.

ANTIGONE

Non. Je n'ai pas cru cela.

CRÉON

La loi est d'abord faite pour toi,
Antigone, la loi est d'abord faite pour les
filles des rois !

ANTIGONE

Si j'avais été une servante en train de
faire sa vaisselle, quand j'ai entendu lire
l'édit, j'aurais essuyé l'eau grasse de mes
bras et je serais sortie avec mon tablier
pour aller enterrer mon frère.

CRÉON

Ce n'est pas vrai. Si tu avais été une
servante, tu n'aurais pas douté que tu
allais mourir et tu serais restée à pleurer
ton frère chez toi. Seulement tu as pensé
que tu étais de race royale, ma nièce et
la fiancée de mon fils, et que, quoi qu'il
arrive, je n'oserais pas te faire mourir.

ANTIGONE

Vous vous trompez. J'étais certaine que
vous me feriez mourir au contraire.

CRÉON, *la regarde et murmure soudain*
L'orgueil d'Œdipe. Tu es l'orgueil
d'Œdipe.

Jean Anouilh,
Nouvelles pièces noires,
Éditions de La Table ronde, Paris, 1946

Le Soulier de satin : « Quelle entreprise »

*André Fraigneau, auteur d'une
« littérature dégagée de tout
engagement », publie ses critiques
théâtrales dans la presse parisienne
d'occupation, en particulier dans*
La Chronique de Paris. *Il est ébloui
par la richesse des décors que Lucien
Coutaud a réalisés pour* Le Soulier
de satin *de Paul Claudel, un spectacle
de cinq heures créé par Jean-Louis
Barrault à la Comédie-Française.*

Une autre exposition, mais mouvante,
ce sont les tableaux successifs de la pièce
de Paul Claudel, *Le Soulier de satin*, à la
Comédie-Française. Trente décors et
rideaux, des centaines de costumes, cinq
heures de spectacle. Quelle entreprise !

L'intrépidité de M. Vaudoyer qui
cherchait à dépasser ses propres records
me faisait frémir. J'avais tort. Le public
s'est amusé et moi aussi et personne n'a
trouvé longue cette revue à grand
spectacle, consacrée à l'Amour et à la
Foi. Si j'ose dire, paraphrasant sainte
Thérèse, qu'il s'agit là du *Châtelet de
l'âme,* j'espère que l'on prendra ce mot
avec le respect qu'il faut. Mais ici
Claudel, le premier, a fait appel avec une
adresse admirable à toutes les variétés
de distraction. On voit une négresse
danser la rumba, un poisson-robe
(comme les chevaux-robes), la lune qui
décroît ou s'arrondit, les machinistes en
plein travail et le régisseur de la scène
sur le dos de qui M. Dux dessine une
caricature à la craie. Il y eut même, à la
première représentation publique, un
signal d'alerte et M. Claudel, de son
fauteuil d'orchestre, fit signe
malicieusement à M. Valéry, son voisin :
« Ne bougez pas, c'est dans la pièce. »
Cependant il fallut sortir, mais nous
revînmes bien vite et bien décidés à
rester, puisque nous fîmes, après cinq
heures, relever quatorze fois le rideau,
acclamant l'auteur au milieu de ses
prodigieux interprètes.

J'étais reconnaissant à M. Jean-Louis
Barrault de son effort presque
surhumain et de son résultat, huilé, aisé,
libre, naturel. Je le remerciai aussi
d'avoir associé à cet effort et à cette
réussite le jeune peintre Lucien
Coutaud, que j'ai eu l'honneur de

découvrir et qui, il y a quinze ans, éblouit Paris par son premier décor pour les *Oiseaux* d'Aristophane, chez Dullin.

[...] Aujourd'hui, Lucien Coutaud a aggravé sa palette pour la mettre au diapason du drame catholique de Claudel. Ce sont des gris d'argent, des blancs mats, des verts sourds ; de temps à autre, un jaune un peu fiévreux rappelle l'or, que « Cipango mûrit dans ses mines lointaines ». Mais toute la splendeur se résume aux robes de Doña Prouhèze, incarnée par Marie Bell. Jamais l'épithète orgueilleuse qui sert de nom à cette artiste ne fut plus justifiée. Souple, tragique, hautaine ou capiteuse, Mlle Bell s'égalait à ces figures de l'Église triomphante dont M. Claudel s'est fait le chantre : celles du Bernin, de Tintoret, de Véronèse. Quand l'actrice étendue sur sa couche mauresque était tourmentée par l'ange gardien, je pensais à cette sainte Thérèse frappée de l'amour divin, à Rome, qui défaillante dans ses plis de marbre, propage un émoi si délicieux.
Et je rêvais qu'on écrivît sur un pan de la robe blanche de la tragédienne les vers charmants et reconnaissants qu'en bon disciple de Mallarmé, qui ne craignait pas de calligraphier sur des éventails, M. Claudel a composés pour son interprète et que je n'aurai pas, à mon grand regret, l'indiscrétion de vous révéler.

André Fraigneau,
La Chronique de Paris,
n° 2, décembre 1943

Sartre, « le plus grand "événement" du jeune théâtre français »

Claude Jamet, écrivain, journaliste et critique littéraire, favorable à la collaboration par pacifisme, reconnaît le talent d'auteur dramatique de Sartre,
après avoir assisté à Huis clos. *La pièce, écrite par Sartre en 1943, est créée le 27 mai 1944 au théâtre du Vieux-Colombier, à Paris.*

Ai-je besoin maintenant d'apprécier l'œuvre de Sartre ? Nous avions déjà vu, de lui, *Les Mouches*, à la Cité et certes, il y avait beaucoup mieux que des promesses dans cette tragédie de la putréfaction ; mais aussi, à mon goût, trop d'ondes Martenot (zzz ! zzz !) ; et trop de laïus, du reste fort remarquables, sur le problème de la liberté, où le prof' de philo montrait, sans discrétion, au moins le bout d'une oreille. Cette fois, au contraire, ce qui doit saisir quiconque n'est pas de parti pris, c'est le caractère intensément et immédiatement dramatique de ce *Huis clos*. À la réflexion on admire une si étrange réussite ; car il ne s'agit de rien moins, somme toute, que de la création d'un mythe de toutes pièces, en pleine pâte moderne, d'un enfer neuf, sans Erynnies, sans Styx, sans Eurydice, sans autre Charon (comme on l'a vu) que ce garçon d'étage sordide avec sa pipe entre les dents, et dont cependant la réalité – dès qu'on a compris – s'impose avec une sorte d'évidence indiscutable ; il y a là une puissance poétique, une virtuosité sans filet – mythologique ou théologique – devant laquelle on ne saurait s'incliner trop bas ! Mais le plus beau, j'y insiste, c'est qu'on n'a pas le temps de réfléchir, sur le moment ; c'est qu'on est pris, haletant, passionné de bout en bout ; et suant comme Garcin lui-même d'une angoisse que rien ne vient rafraîchir ou dénouer à la fin ; et pour cause ; c'est qu'on en sort comme d'un roman de Dostoïevski, ou d'un conte d'Edgar Poe, mais théâtral encore une fois. Car « c'est du théâtre », et du vrai !

Les pensées – s'il nous en vient, après – sont de surcroît ; la pièce n'en a pas besoin. Quant à ceux qui s'inquiètent de la moralité ou de la « morbidité » possible d'un tel spectacle, j'aurais honte de leur répondre. L'univers de J.-P. Sartre n'est évidemment pas celui de Claudel ou de Giraudoux. Mais tant mieux ! puisque c'est le sien. Allez-vous le refuser ? Je ne sais qu'une chose, en tout cas, c'est que Jean-Paul Sartre est certainement – depuis Anouilh – le plus grand « événement » du jeune théâtre français.

> Claude Jamet,
> *Images mêlées de la littérature*
> *et du théâtre,*
> L'Élan, Paris, 1947

M. Raimu dans *Le Bourgeois gentilhomme*

Cocteau reprend en 1947, dans Le Foyer des artistes, *l'ensemble de ses notes théâtrales parues sous l'Occupation. Il accorde toute son attention et prodigue son soutien aux débuts de Raimu à la Comédie Française. Le 22 mars 1944, celui-ci y joue* Le Bourgeois gentilhomme *de Molière. Le jeu de cette grande vedette de cinéma avait surpris les abonnés fidèles aux traditions, esquivées par le nouveau pensionnaire.*

Le Bourgeois gentilhomme est une des seules grosses farces de Molière qui se hausse jusqu'au type, où la victime, à distance, échappe au rire cruel de la cour et nous montre un brave homme, soucieux de quitter l'ombre dédaignée par le soleil de Versailles.

Le snobisme de ce bourgeois prouve un besoin confus de s'élever, d'apprendre et, s'il se trompe, n'en reste pas moins l'exemple d'une audacieuse tentative de participer à des mystères.

M. Raimu humanise tellement ce fantoche, il le charge de tant de grâce enfantine, de bonne volonté naïve, de confiance charmante dans les prestiges de la noblesse, que tous les personnages qui le bernent se trouvent en mauvaise posture et nous semblent inhumains [...].

La leçon de danse de M. Raimu est un chef-d'œuvre. Elle est au bord de nous émouvoir. De quel œil il observe son professeur ! Il ne songe pas une minute à être drôle. Il compte, il s'applique, il se balance, il glisse, il plonge, il déplonge, il écarte ses bras et lance ses jambes roses avec la gravité des phoques ou des éléphants d'une piste lorsqu'ils exécutent leur numéro.

Il est admirable de voir M. Raimu éviter les effets conventionnels et trouver le style dans la simplicité. Cette simplicité risquait de perdre le relief par contraste avec le cérémonial de la Maison. Mais il arrive qu'un tel contraste souligne la différence des classes et oppose au délicieux ridicule de M. Jourdain les ridicules féroces du grand monde.

Mme Marie Bell et M. Escande expriment à merveille cette férocité de l'élégance sûre d'elle-même. Rien n'est plus adorable que la minute où M. Raimu, empêtré dans son rêve, demande à la marquise de prendre le recul nécessaire à l'exécution de sa troisième révérence. Il le lui demande tout bas, comme s'il la prenait en faute et que sa délicatesse hésitait à le lui faire remarquer.

> Jean Cocteau.
> *Le Foyer des artistes,*
> Plon. 1947

Poésie, Résistance et liberté

Poèmes écrits de loin, ici par Supervielle en Uruguay, publiés dans les revues clandestines comme Marche française *d'Aragon, devenus symboles de la Résistance comme le* Chant des partisans *de Kessel et Druon, ou* Liberté *de Paul Éluard.*

La France au loin

Je cherche au loin la France
Avec des mains avides,
Je cherche dans le vide
À de grandes distances.
[...]
Faites que je retrouve
Et qu'on me les redonne,
Les Français tous en groupe,
Le ciel qui les couronne.

Qu'est-elle devenue
Qu'elle ne répond plus
À mes gestes perdus
Dans le fond de la nue.

Son grand miroir poli
En forme d'hexagone
Où passaient les profils
De si grandes personnes,

Ah ! comment se fait-il
Qu'il ait cédé la place
À l'immobile face
D'un soldat ennemi.

Jules Supervielle, *Poèmes 1939-1945*,
Gallimard, La Pléiade, 1996

Le Chant des Partisans

Ami, entends-tu le vol noir des corbeaux sur nos plaines ?
Ami, entends-tu les cris sourds du pays qu'on enchaîne ?
Ohé, partisans, ouvriers et paysans, c'est l'alarme.

Ce soir l'ennemi connaîtra le prix du sang et les larmes.

Montez de la mine, descendez des collines, camarades !
Sortez de la paille les fusils, la mitraille, les grenades.
Ohé, les tueurs à la balle et au couteau, tuez vite !
Ohé, saboteur, attention à ton fardeau : dynamite...

C'est nous qui brisons les barreaux des prisons pour nos frères.
La haine à nos trousses et la faim qui nous pousse, la misère.
Il y a des pays où les gens au creux des lits font des rêves.
Ici, nous, vois-tu, nous on marche et nous on tue, nous on crève...

Ici chacun sait ce qu'il veut, ce qu'il fait quand il passe.
Ami, si tu tombes un ami sort de l'ombre à ta place.
Demain du sang noir séchera au grand soleil sur les routes.
Chantez, compagnons, dans la nuit la Liberté nous écoute...

Ami, entends-tu ces cris sourds du pays qu'on enchaîne ?
Ami, entends-tu le vol noir des corbeaux sur nos plaines ?
Oh oh oh oh oh oh oh oh oh oh oh oh
Joseph Kessel et Maurice Druon, 1943

Marche française

Quand il arriva la saison
Des trahisons et des prisons,

Quand les fontaines se troublèrent.
Les larmes seules furent claires.

On entendait des cris déments,
Des boniments, des reniements.

Des hommes verts et des vautours
Vinrent obscurcir notre jour.

Ils nous dirent : « Vous aurez faim ! »
Dans la main, nous prirent le pain.

Ils nous dirent : « Jetez vos livres !
Un chien n'a que son maître à suivre. »

Ils nous dirent : « Vous aurez froid ! »
Et mirent le pays en croix.

Ils nous dirent : « Les yeux à terre !
Il faut obéir et se taire. »
Ils nous dirent : « Tous à genoux !
Les plus forts s'en iront chez nous. »

Ils ont jeté les uns aux bagnes.
Pris les autres en Allemagne…

Mais ils comptaient sans Pierre et Jean.
La colère et les jeunes gens.
Mais ils comptaient sans ceux qui prirent
Le parti de vivre ou mourir.

Comme le vent dans les cheveux,
Comme la flamme dans le feu !

Croisés non pour une aventure,
Une lointaine sépulture,

Mais pour le pays envahi
Contre l'envahisseur haï !

Chassons, chassons nos nouveaux maîtres.

Les pillards, les tueurs, les traîtres !

Le bon grain du mauvais se trie :
Il faut mériter sa patrie.

Chaque jardin, chaque ruelle
Arrachés à des mains cruelles.

Chaque silo, chaque verger,
Repris aux mains des étrangers.

Chaque colline et chaque combe,
Chaque demeure et chaque tombe.

Chaque mare et ses alevins,
Chaque noisette d'un ravin.

Chaque mont, chaque promontoire,
Les prés sanglants de notre histoire.

Et le ciel immense et clément,
Sans nuage et sans Allemands…

Il faut libérer ce qu'on aime
Soi-même, soi-même. soi-même !

Aragon,
Les Lettres françaises, n° 14, mars 1944
Œuvres poétiques complètes,
Gallimard, La Pléiade, 2007

Liberté

Sur mes cahiers d'écolier
Sur mon pupitre et les arbres
Sur le sable sur la neige
J'écris ton nom

Sur toutes les pages lues
Sur toutes les pages blanches
Pierre sang papier ou cendre
J'écris ton nom

Sur les images dorées
Sur les armes des guerriers
Sur la couronne des rois
J'écris ton nom

Sur la jungle et le désert
Sur les nids sur les genêts
Sur l'écho de mon enfance
J'écris ton nom

Sur les merveilles des nuits
Sur le pain blanc des journées
Sur les saisons fiancées
J'écris ton nom

Sur tous mes chiffons d'azur
Sur l'étang soleil moisi
Sur le lac lune vivante
J'écris ton nom

Sur les champs sur l'horizon
Sur les ailes des oiseaux
Et sur le moulin des ombres
J'écris ton nom

Sur chaque bouffée d'aurore
Sur la mer sur les bateaux
Sur la montagne démente
J'écris ton nom

Sur la mousse des nuages
Sur les sueurs de l'orage
Sur la pluie épaisse et fade
J'écris ton nom

Sur les formes scintillantes
Sur les cloches des couleurs
Sur la vérité physique
J'écris ton nom

Sur les sentiers éveillés
Sur les routes déployées
Sur les places qui débordent
J'écris ton nom

Sur la lampe qui s'allume
Sur la lampe qui s'éteint
Sur mes maisons réunies
J'écris ton nom

Sur le fruit coupé en deux
Du miroir et de ma chambre
Sur mon lit coquille vide

J'écris ton nom

Sur mon chien gourmand et tendre
Sur ses oreilles dressées
Sur sa patte maladroite
J'écris ton nom

Sur le tremplin de ma porte
Sur les objets familiers
Sur le flot du feu béni
J'écris ton nom

Sur toute chair accordée
Sur le front de mes amis
Sur chaque main qui se tend
J'écris ton nom

Sur la vitre des surprises
Sur les lèvres attentives
Bien au-dessus du silence
J'écris ton nom

Sur mes refuges détruits
Sur mes phares écroulés
Sur les murs de mon ennui
J'écris ton nom

Sur l'absence sans désir
Sur la solitude nue
Sur les marches de la mort
J'écris ton nom

Sur la santé revenue
Sur le risque disparu
Sur l'espoir sans souvenir
J'écris ton nom

Et par le pouvoir d'un mot
Je recommence ma vie
Je suis né pour te connaître
Pour te nommer

Liberté.

Paul Éluard, *Poésie et Vérité 42*, 1942,
Œuvres complètes,
Gallimard, La Pléiade, 1968

BIBLIOGRAPHIE

Ouvrages généraux
- Serge Addad, *Le Théâtre dans les années Vichy*, Ramsay, 1992.
- Henri Amouroux, *La Vie des Français sous l'Occupation*, 5 vol., Bouquins/Laffont, 1997-1999.
- Laurence Bertrand-Dorleac, *L'Art de la défaite*, Le Seuil, 1993.
- Charles Braibant, *La Guerre à Paris*, Corréa, 1945.
- Patrick Buisson, *1940-1945, années érotiques*, 2 vol., Albin Michel, 2008-2009.
- Philippe Burrin, *La France à l'heure allemande*, Le Seuil, 1995.
- René Chateau, *Le Cinéma français sous l'Occupation*, Mémoire du cinéma, Éditions René Chateau, 1995.
- Myriam Chimènes (dir.), *La Vie musicale sous Vichy*, Complexe, 2001.
- Raymond Chirat, *Le Cinéma français des années de guerre*, Hatier, 1983.
- Stéphanie Corcy, *La Vie culturelle sous l'Occupation*, Perrin, 2005.
- François Dufay, *Le Voyage d'automne*, Plon, 2000.
- Hélène Eck (dir.), *La Guerre des ondes*, Armand Colin, 1985
- François Eychard et Georges Aillaud (dir.), *Les Lettres françaises et les Étoiles dans la clandestinité, 1942-1944,* Le Cherche-Midi, 2008.
- Pascal Fouché *L'Édition française sous l'Occupation*, 2 vol., Université de Paris 7, 1987.
- Pierre Giolitto, *Histoire de la jeunesse sous Vichy*, Perrin, 1991.
- Pierre Hebey, *La NRF des années sombres*, Gallimard, 1992.
- Gerhard Heller, *Un Allemand à Paris*, Le Seuil, 1981.
- Marie-Agnès Joubert, *La Comédie-Française sous l'Occupation*, Tallandier, 1998.
- Thierry Kubler, Emmanuel Lemieux, *Cognacq-Jay, 1940*, Calmann-Lévy, 1990.
- M. Laclotte, A. Larquié, A. Pierret (dir.), *Le Pillage de l'art en France pendant l'Occupation et la Situation des 200 œuvres confiées aux musées nationaux*, Paris, La Documentation française, 2000.
- Hervé Le Boterf, *La Vie parisienne sous l'Occupation*, France-Empire, 1997.
- Bernard Loiseaux, *La Littérature de la défaite et de la collaboration*, Fayard, 1995.
- Herbert Lottman, *L'Épuration*, Fayard, 1986.
- Corinne Luchaire, *Ma drôle de vie*, Déterna, 2000.
- Aurélie Luneau, *Radio-Londres 1940-1944, les voix de la liberté*, Perrin, 2005.
- Roger Maudhuy, *Les Grands Procès de la collaboration*, Lucien Souny, 2009.
- Henri du Moulin de Larbathète, *Le Temps des illusions*, Le Cheval ailé, 1946.
- Pascal Ory, *Les Collaborateurs*, Le Seuil, 1976.
- *Les Parisiens sous l'Occupation*, Jean Baronnet, photographies d'André Zucca, Gallimard-Paris Bibliothèques, 2008.
- Claire Paulhan et Olivier Corpet, *Archives des années noires, artistes, écrivains et éditeurs,* Institut Mémoires de l'édition contemporaine (IMEC), 2004.
- Robert O. Paxton, Olivier Corpet, Claire Paulhan, *Collaboration and Resistance, French Literary Life under the Nazi Occupation*, catalogue de l'exposition de New York, Tallandier/IMEC, 2009.
- Gilles Perrault, *Paris sous l'Occupation*, Belfond, 1987.
- Martine Poulain, *Livres pillés, lectures surveillées*, Gallimard, 2008.
- Jean Quéval, *Première page, Cinquième colonne*, Fayard, 1945.
- Gilles et Jean-Robert Ragache, *La Vie quotidienne des écrivains et des artistes sous l'Occupation*, Hachette, 1988.
- Roger Régent, *Cinéma de France*, Bellefaye, 1948.
- Henry Rousso, *Les Années noires, Vivre sous l'Occupation*, Découvertes-Gallimard, 1992.
- Maurice Sachs, *La Chasse à courre*, Gallimard, 1948, réédition 1997.
- Gisèle Sapiro, *La Guerre des écrivains*, Fayard, 1999.
- Jacques Siclier, *La France de Pétain et son cinéma*, Veyrier, 1981.
- Claude Singer, *Vichy, l'Université et les Juifs*, Les Belles-Lettres, 1992.
- André Thérive, *L'Envers du décor 1940-1944,* La Clef d'or, 1946.
- Dominique Veillon, *La Mode sous l'Occupation,* Payot, 2001.

Mémoires d'écrivains
- Jean Cocteau, *Journal 1942-1945*, Gallimard, 1989.
- Pierre Drieu La Rochelle, *Journal 1931-1945,* Gallimard, 1992.
- Jean Galtier-Boissière, *Mémoires d'un Parisien*, La Jeune Parque, 1944.
- Jean Guéhenno, *Journal des années noires*, Gallimard, 1947.
- Sacha Guitry, *Quatre ans d'occupation*, L'Élan, 1947.
- Marcel Jouhandeau, *Journal sous l'Occupation*, Gallimard, 1980.
- Ernst Jünger, *Journal de guerre et d'Occupation*, Julliard, Paris, 1965.
- Paul Léautaud, *Journal littéraire,* tomes 12 à 16, Mercure de France, 1962-1964.
- Maurice Martin du Gard, *La Chronique de Vichy, 1940-1944*, Flammarion, 1948.
- Roger Martin du Gard, *Journal*, Gallimard, 1993.
- Léon Werth, *Déposition*, Viviane Hamy, 1992.

de la Nouvelle France : Pierre Benoit de face au centre et à sa droite Bernard Grasset, Paris, juillet 1944.

67 Brasserie Lipp, 1943, debout MM Cazes, père et fils, ; assis de dos Maurice Fombeure ; en face de lui Ramon Fernandez, photographie Seeberger.

68h Emmanuel Mounier, Yvonne Leenhardt, Max-Pol Fouchet, Loÿs Masson à Lourmarin, 1941. Fonds Max Pol Fouchet/IMEC.

68b Pierre Seghers et Loÿs Masson, Villeneuve-lès-Avignon. Fonds Éditions des Trois Collines/IMEC

69b Dyonis Mascolo, Marguerite Duras et Robert Antelme en 1942. Fonds Marguerite Duras/IMEC.

69h François Mauriac dans sa propriété à Malagar en Gironde, vers 1942.

70h *Le Silence de la mer* de Vercors, éditions de la Porte d'ivoire, Fonds Les Trois Collines/IMEC.

70bg *Poésie 41*, revue fondée par Pierre Seghers. Fonds Jean-José Marchand/IMEC.

70bd *Confluences*, n° 9, revue fondée par René Tavernier, mars-avril 1942. Fonds Éditions des Trois Collines/IMEC.

71d Jean Paulhan et Jean Blanzat en Normandie en 1942, photographie de Daniel Wallard. Fonds Jean Paulhan/IMEC.

71b *Les Lettres françaises* n° 6, avril 1943. Fonds Jean Tardieu/IMEC.

72h Max-Pol Fouchet dans les bureaux de *Fontaine* à Alger. Fonds Max-Pol Fouchet/IMEC.

72m *Fontaine*, n° 27-28, juin-juillet 1943. *Idem.*

72b *Fontaine,* format miniature. *Idem.*

73hg *Messages aux Français* de Jules Romains, Éditions de la Maison française, New York, 1941. Fonds J.-J. Marchand/IMEC.

72-73b *Traits*, n° 10, octobre 1940. Fonds Éditions des Trois Collines/IMEC.

73hd Aragon, *Le Crève-cœur* et *Les Yeux d'Elsa*. Fonds IMEC.

74 Manuscrit de « Liberté » de Paul Éluard. Fonds Max-Pol Fouchet/IMEC.

75h Photographie de Paul Éluard dédicacée à Max-Pol Fouchet, photographie d'André Rogi. *Idem.*

75b *Poésie et Vérité 42*. Fonds J. J. Marchand/IMEC.

CHAPITRE 4

76 Affiche du film *Le Voile bleu* de Jean Stelli, 1942.

77 *La Fille du puisatier* de Marcel Pagnol (1940) : le discours du Maréchal.

78 Programme de Radio nationale, mai 1941.

78b Message radiodiffusé du maréchal, Noël 1943.

79 Jules Gressier enregistrant *Hans le joueur de flûte* pour Radio nationale en mai 1943.

80h *Causeries du Dr Friedrich* à Radio-Paris, éditions du Pont, avril 1943.

80-81b Famille écoutant la radio en 1942.

81d Radio-Paris, programme des émissions et propagande, 1942.

82h Jacques Duchesne à la BBC de Londres.

82m Tract menaçant les auditeurs de la radio anglaise.

82b Lettre de deux enfants à la BBC, décembre 1940.

83 Affiche de propagande anti-alliés et anti-de Gaulle, 1941.

84h Raoul Ploquin, président du COIC (à gauche) et le Dr Diedrich de la Propaganda Staffel.

84b *Le Film*, unes du journal du COIC.

85 Un centre technique du film (670e compagnie de propagande alimentant en pellicules les cinémas de Bordeaux et sa région), photographie de Reitzner, octobre 1941.

85b Lettre de Marcel Pagnol à Raoul Ploquin président du COIC en 1941, extrait. Arch. Nat. (AN F 142/114), Paris.

86 Alfred Greven directeur de la Continental (à sa droite, Danièlle Darrieux).

86-87 sigle de la Continental Films.

87h Danièle Darrieux, affiche de *Premier rendez-vous* d'H. Decoin, 1941.

87b ACE, Alliance cinématographique européenne (sigle).

88-89 Queue devant le cinéma Olympia, 1943.

89 Tickets d'entrée pour le cinéma La Scala avec le sigle du COIC, Archives de la Cinémathèque, Paris.

90-91 fond Salle du Gaumont Palace, Archives Gaumont.

90h Avis d'interdiction de parler ou de manifester durant les Actualités, 1943.

92h *La Main du diable* (M. Tourneur) avec Pierre Fresnay et Josseline Gael, 1942.

92d *Les Dames du Bois de Boulogne* (R. Bresson) avec Maria Casarès.

92b Carnet illustré de Robert Lachenay.

93g *Le Colonel Chabert* (R. le Hénaff) avec Raimu, 1943.

93d *Pontcarral, colonel d'Empire* (J. Delannoy), 1942.

94h Scène des *Enfants du paradis* de Carné : Jean-Louis Barrault et Arletty.

94b *L'Illustration* du 23 décembre 1942 pour la sortie des *Visiteurs du Soir*.

95 Marcel Carné sur le tournage des *Visiteurs du soir* en 1942.

96 Scène de la dictée, dans *Le Corbeau* d'Henri-Georges Clouzot, 1944.

97 *Le Ciel est à vous* (J Gremillon) avec Madeleine Renaud et Charles Vanel.

97b *Le « Corbeau » est déplumé* in *Les Lettres françaises*, mars 1944.

98 Madeleine Sologne et Jean Marais dans *L'Éternel Retour* (J. Delannoy), 1943.

98-99b Jacques Becker (assis) sur le tournage de *Falbalas*, mai 1944.

99h Georges Rouquier tournant *Le Charron*, 1943.

CHAPITRE 5

100 Concert Mozart par le Berliner Kammer Orchestra, sous la direction de Hans von Benda, dans la cour du Palais-Royal à Paris, 1941. Archives Karl Epting, Hänner (Courtesy of Wilhelm Epting).

101 Raimu dans *Le Bourgeois gentilhomme,* Comédie-Française, avril 1944.

102h Orchestre de l'armée de l'air allemande, Champs Élysées, 1er août 1940.

102b Jacques Rouché, directeur de l'Opéra de Paris, avec M. Poulenc et la troupe interprétant *Les Animaux modèles*, 1942.

103h Livret en allemand pour la *Walküre* de Wagner à l'Opéra de Paris, mars 1941. Archives Karl Epting, Hänner (Courtesy of Wilhelm Epting).

CHAPITRE 6

INDEX

A

CRÉDITS PHOTOGRAPHIQUES

AKG/Denise Bellon 50h, 51h, 51b. BPK, Berlin Dist RMN/DR 104h. Coll Christophe L 92d, 96b. Coll. DB 77. Coll part. 19h, 52h, 60b, 84b, 111b, 114,120bg, 122g. Archives Karl Epting (Courtesy of Wilhem Epting) 63h, 100, 103m. Archives Gallimard 57h, 59h, 59b, 60h, 61m, 61h, 61b, 104b. BNF 65m, 107d, 115, 116m. CGC/DR 76. CIRIP 36b, 38h, 43h, 49h, 90m. Coblenz Bundersarchiv 33. Corbis/Hulton Deutsch Collection 124-125. DR 16h, 24b, 27, 28b, 29h, 46-47b, 52m, 58, 62h, 82m, 84h, 86h, 87b, 99h, 117b, 106m. ECPAD 85h. Musée Gaumont 90-91. GETTY images 15b. IMEC 73hd. IMEC/Fonds Cercle de la Librairie 57b, 122d. IMEC/Fonds Confluences/René Tavernier 119. IMEC/Fonds Denoël 62md. IMEC/Fonds Max-Pol Fouchet 68h, 72h, 72m, 72b, 74, 75h. IMEC/Fonds Hachette 13, 54-55b, 56h, 65b. IMEC/Fonds Jean-José Marchand 70bg, 73hg, 75b. IMEC/Fonds Jean Paulhan 71d. IMEC/Fonds Jean Tardieu 71b. IMEC/Fonds Les Trois Collines 68b, 70h, 70bd, 72-73b. INA 111h. Keystone 35m, 40h, 127. Kharbine-Tapabor/Collection IM dos, 35hetb, 36mg, 39d, 41h, 52b, 83b. Kharbine-Tapabor/Jean Vigne 18b, 19b, 21b, 47h, 108h. Robert lachenay 92b. Leemage 21h, 23m, 92g. Leemage /Gusman 87d. Jean Mascolo 69b. Magnum Photos/Henri Cartier-Bresson, 121. Ministère des Affaires étrangères/Direction des Archives/Fonds Récupération Artistique 32h. Pixplanete/L'Illustration 36-37h, 94b. Roger Viollet 22, 45, 48m, 53h, 53m, 78h, 80, 81h, 112-113, 114b, 122-123h, 128. Roger Viollet/Jacques Boyer 53b. Roger Viollet/E. Emo et St Piera/Galliera 40b. Roger Viollet/Albert Harlingue 62b, 101, 120h. Roger Viollet/Pierre Jahan/41b. Roger Viollet/LAPI 17h, 18h, 20h, 20b, 24hg, 24hd, 25hg, 25hd, 30h, 98-99b, 30b, 31b, 42h, 43b, 48h, 49b, 55hd, 66b, 78b, 80-81b, 88-89h, 103b, 106h, 126b. Roger Viollet/André Zucca/BHVP 1er plat, 1, 2-3, 4, 5, 6-7, 8-9, 15h, 44, 64, 105, 110-111, 129. Rue des Archives 14, 16-17b. Rue des Archives/BCA 98h. Rue des Archives/PVDE 82h, 102b. Rue des Archives/RDA 93g, 93d, 97h.. Rue des Archives/René Saint Paul 120-121b. Rue des Archives/Seeberger frères 66h, 67, 79, 109. Rue des Archives/Suddeutsche Zeitung 28h, 94h. Rue des Archives/Tal 31, 34h, 46h, 69h, 82b, 95, 102h, 118, 123b, 126h. Roger Schall 12, 26, 117. SIPA/Collection Ribiere 23h. SIPA Press /AP 37b. SIPA/LIDO 38-39b, 39h.

REMERCIEMENTS

Les Éditions Gallimard remercient Mélina Raynaud de l'Institut Mémoires de l'édition contemporaine (IMEC), Claire Paulhan, Wilhem Epting des Archives Karl Epting, Carole Gascard, conservateur à la BHVP, Noëlle Giret, conservateur à la BNF, Laurence Duhamel, aux éditions Tallandier, et Laurent Lemire.

ÉDITION ET FABRICATION

DÉCOUVERTES GALLIMARD
COLLECTION CONÇUE PAR Pierre Marchand.
DIRECTION Elisabeth de Farcy.
COORDINATION ÉDITORIALE Anne Lemaire.
GRAPHISME Alain Gouessant.
COORDINATION ICONOGRAPHIQUE Isabelle de Latour.
SUIVI DE PRODUCTION Géraldine Blanc.
SUIVI DE PARTENARIAT Madeleine Giai-Levra.
RESPONSABLE COMMUNICATION ET PRESSE Valérie Tolstoï.
PRESSE David Ducreux.
LA VIE CULTURELLE DANS LA FRANCE OCCUPÉE
ÉDITION Michèle Decré-Cyssau.
MAQUETTE Vincent Lever.
ICONOGRAPHIE Anne Soto.
LECTURE-CORRECTION Pierre Granet et Marie-Paule Rochelois.
PHOTOGRAVURE Station Graphique.

Oliver Barrot, journaliste, produit et présente *Un livre un jour* (France 3, TV5 MONDE) depuis 1991. Chargé d'enseignement à l'Institut d'études politiques de Paris, à l'École nationale du théâtre de Montréal et à New York University, il a publié des ouvrages sur le voyage, les spectacles, la littérature. Et notamment, avec Raymond Chirat, dans la collection Découvertes *Gueules d'atmosphère* (1994), *Le Théâtre de boulevard* (1998), *Sacha Guitry, l'homme orchestre* (2207).

Depuis sa naissance en 1922, Raymond Chirat n'a jamais quitté Lyon.
Il y a puisé le goût du spectacle, du cinéma et particulièrement des films français.
Il en a conçu la série de catalogues couvrant la production nationale de 1908 à 1970.
Grâce à la collaboration amicale d'Olivier Barrot, il a ressuscité dans divers ouvrages
les acteurs oubliés et les réalisateurs dédaignés, mais aussi les époques fastueuses
du théâtre de boulevard et les portraits de ses auteurs et interprètes.
Pendant quatorze ans, Raymond Chirat a dirigé la bibliothèque
de l'Institut Lumière dont il avait assuré la création.

*Dépôt légal : août 2009
Numéro d'édition : 159607
ISBN : 978-2-07-035821-2
Imprimé en Espagne par Grafos*